Corporate Affairs:
Codes of Misconduct

Corporate Affairs: Codes of Misconduct

Reece

Reece Ardor

This book is a work of fiction. Names, characters, places and incidents are products of the author's imagination or are used fictitiously. Any resemblance to actual events or locales or persons, living or dead, is entirely coincidental.

ISBN 978-0-557-50178-6

Dedication

This book is dedicated to my family and friends for their unrelenting support of my writing, my ideas and my dreams. Without your feedback and encouragement to stay the course, this book would have not been possible. I also give thanks to my supporters that have passed on, starting with my father, E. Jacob Johnson for always reminding and pushing me to value education and "to get my lesson." I got it dad. To my grandmother, Vastie K. Ellerbee for providing her knowledge and wisdom talks that have provided the foundation for my character and thought process over the years. I miss you Grandma. To Bertha Bruce, Lincoln Ellerbee, Aldorithy Ellerbee, Daniel Ellerbee, Curtis Ellerbee, Islee Johnson, Faye Exnicious and Willie Woods and the multitude of supporters to innumerable to count. Thank you very much.

"Some things in life require you to devise new ways to cope in order to be happy."
-Reece

Foreword

One of the first questions I get when talking about my book with others is "Where did you get the material from to write the book?" Quickly followed by, "Are the stories all experiences you had?" Despite knowing that the book is a work of fiction, these questions used to surprise me when I first began writing, but after pointing things out about the very nature of working in a corporate environment the answers become very clear and quite enlightening.

Beginning with the material for the book, my experiences as a natural observer and great listener to couples in various relationship situations from girlfriend-boyfriend couples, to engaged couples and marriages both newlywed and experienced are where the bulk of the content is rooted. Through high school, I was branded from the ninth grade through graduation as an ad-hoc counselor to many of my female classmates. I counseled them through their relationships as well as a variety of home situations. My counseling career continued through my enlistment in the U.S. Army for fellow soldiers in which a variety of domestic situations were tackled due to my close connections while working in close support of the Military Police. In my undergraduate and graduate studies, I incorporated aspects of my dating experience as well as fine tuning advice and coaching sessions to my classmates and fellow students. Lastly, the bulk of my knowledge comes out of my experiences and current observations in corporate America. This fact alone was the primary motivation for writing this book.

The most intriguing fact about relationships in corporate America is the clash of traditional relationships versus company policy, i.e. Codes of Conduct. Most companies have Codes of Conduct to govern employee behavior and interactions among associates, despite this fact, more than 35% of companies have enacted special provisions to these codes of conduct to specifically deal with workplace relationships. With high stakes that can lead to termination, divorce or even death, affairs in corporate America are on the rise.

When one sits back and observes the corporate workplace environment, the components that fuel affairs are rampant. First, employees spend more time at work with their co-workers versus time at home with their spouses or partners. This creates a relatively close bond due to the investment in one another from project work in some cases, through company outings and company travel. Secondly, the corporate work environment is not unique, by its very nature it is a placed filled with flirtation and overt sexual advances that are the result of placing men and women in close proximity. These two facts constitute the fuel for corporate affairs and indiscretions. The then needed spark to light the fire, actually comes from outside the walls of the workplace. It is primarily the condition the employee comes into the workplace as a result of strained relationships and ailing marriages placing the employee in a vulnerable position. The workplace provides the gap filler or fix the employee has yearned for, promoting the onset of an affair.

In closing, <u>Corporate Affairs: Codes of Misconduct</u> brings to light several situations that are inherent in the daily culture of corporate America. In some instances, it unlocks the seldom discussed "secret world" of corporate relationships and affairs for some and for others it takes a creative and safe portrayal of employee interactions to fill employee fantasies and desires without crossing over into reality.

Table of contents

Chapter 1

The Enterview

"Hello? Sparks residence."

"Hi, my name is Karen Gilbert and I am calling from E. Jacob Wineries. Could I please speak with Mr. Gene Sparks?"

"Speaking."

"How are you doing Mr. Sparks?"

"Oh, I am doing pretty good. No complaints."

"That is very good to hear. Well, the reason I am calling today is to gage your interest in an open position at our company as plant engineer in our west coast winery. We pulled your resume off Engineers.com and think that you will be a great fit in our organization with your extensive experience in the wine industry and in engineering. I would like to say we have a very competitive salary and benefits package along with full relocation, which includes the purchase of your house in the event you are unable to sell it before relocating. So, having said all that, Mr. Sparks, are you at the least bit interested?"

"Oh most definitely, Ms. Gilbert!"

"Oh, Gene, call me Karen."

"Ok. But I would like to find out a little more about what the job entails as well as the career path and opportunities for advancement."

"Well, Gene, let me tell you now from seeing your photo—I mean your resume on Engineers.com, you will have no problem with opportunities for advancement." (Whew! I hope he didn't notice that.)

"That sounds really attractive, Karen."

(Not as half as attractive as you are.)

"So then, what are the next steps in the process?"

"Well, first off, I would like to schedule a phone interview with you to get more information about your background and skills. How does a week from now sound?"

"That would be excellent!"

"Ok then, let's say next Tuesday at 7:00 PM."

"That works well for me."

"Ok, I'll plan on calling you at this number next Tuesday. Thank you for your time, Gene, and I look forward to talking with you next Tuesday."

"Likewise, Karen."

"Believe me, Gene, the pleasure was all mine. Have a great evening!"

"Same to you...And thanks for offering up this opportunity."

"You're quite welcome! Good night, Gene."

"Good night, Karen."

(The garage door opens.)

"That must be Gwen. Oh she will be so excited about the opportunity at E. Jacob Wineries and for relocating to the west coast.

(Gwen shuts the door to the garage as she enters the house)

"Hey baby! Got some real exciting news! Before that, how was your day?"

(Frowning) "Fine...What is it this time!"

(What's with the attitude? I want to share some good news... Anyway) "Oh! I got a call from E. Jacob Wineries today and I have a phone interview next Tuesday at 7:00 PM!"

(Sarcastically) "Oh, that's great. Well, I got to go start dinner."

"Uh, honey, I wasn't finished."

"Oh (rrggh!), please continue!"

"I just wanted to tell you that the position is located on the west coast and...Never mind..."

"Oh that's good" (I really could care less).

"Well, I thought you would be really excited about that since you've always wanted to move out there ever since we got married."

"Well, things change and I'm just beat from today. Can we talk about this later? Is that fine?"

"Yeah, babe, no problem." (I'm not sure what's eating her...well...Mmm...Nothing new. I guess I'll go prepare for this interview next week.) "I'll be in the office if you need me."

"Good morning, Gwen!"

"Morning, Gene."

"How's it going this morning?"

(Sarcastically) "Oh, just dandy, just dandy. What are you all excited about?"

"Well, you know I have the phone interview today with E. Jacob Wineries!"

"Oh yeah, that."

"What do you mean, 'oh yeah, that'?"

"It's just another interview that will probably end up like the others—going nowhere!"

"Honey, I think this one is a little different. This company has really sought me out, so I feel real good about it."

"Well...we'll see."

(I just don't get Gwen, I don't know what I can do to make her happy.) "Ok baby, you just have a great day at work and I'll see you later on. Don't forget, the phone interview is scheduled for 7:00 PM."

"Yeah, yeah, I got it."

"I'm out of here. Aren't you going to wish me luck?"

"Good luck, Gene."

"Talk to you later. Bye, honey." (What is up with her? One minute she wants me to get a new job and at other times she doesn't even care. Hmm...Forget it!)

(Gwen waves off Gene as he leaves for work)

(After a long day)

"Hi, baby, how was your day?"

"Same old shit, day after day."

"Well, hopefully it wasn't that bad."

"Yeah, yeah."

"Well, hopefully this job comes through and you'll have a reason to cheer up." (With a big grin) "I'm really excited about this interview! This job would represent a two-level promotion and of course a bigger salary. The kids would love sunny California more than this cold Midwest town."

"Yeah, Whoop-dee-do. That all sounds good. I hope you get it honey." (Blowing out) "Pluugh! He, he, he." (Even though I know you won't.)

"Thank you, Gwen, I really appreciate it." (Wow, that's a switch. It's not perfect, but I'll take it).

(Gene goes to the family office to put in more study for the interview. He takes a seat at the desk).

(Exhaling) "Well...I think I'm ready. I still have to review..."

"Ring" "Ring"

"Hmm, I wonder who that is. Oh, it's mother. Let me talk to her before the interview starts." (He picks up the phone). "Hello, mom, how you doing?"

"I'm doing just fine."

"Hold on, mom." (Covering the phone microphone with his hand) "Gwen?...Honey?"

"Yes!"

"Don't forget that the interview is scheduled for 7:00 p.m.; could you let the boys know I'll need the phones clear and for them not to disturb me in the office?"

"Ok, no problem." (I wish he would leave alone about that damn interview).

"Thanks, baby. I really appreciate it."

"Mom?"

"I don't know what Lula is going to do..."

"Mom?"

"Yes?"

"Ok, I'm back. Just getting ready for an interview this evening with a big company in California."

"What's the name of the company?"

"E. Jacob Wineries."

"Oh, that's real nice. So that means I'll get free wine?"

"Ha, ha, ha! Well, perhaps mom, perhaps."

"So, how are my grandboys doing?"

"Well, you know Mark just started playing the Oboe and David is playing with the Junior Varisity soccer team."

"Oh my goodness! I love the way you keep them involved in a variety of activities."

"Yeah, we try. We certainly try."

"Well, good. The reason I called is to let you know that I ran into one of your high school classmates at the grocery store yesterday."

"Oh really, who was it?"

"I think he said is name was Albert."

"Oh yeah, Albert and I were best friends in school."

"Well, he said you guys are having your 20th reunion this summer."

"Oh that's exciting. I was wondering about it! Thanks mom, I really appreciate it."

"Here is his number. You ready?"

"Yes...(864) 132-1234."

"Ok, let me read it back to you. (864) 224-1900."

"Yes, that's it."

"Thanks again, I'll give him a call tomorrow. Ok mom, I'm going to have to jump off. It's 6:30 PM and the interview is at 7:00 PM. I have to go and make my last minute preparations."

"Ok, son, good luck!"

"Thanks mom! I'll talk to you later. Goodbye."

"Bye, son."

"Ok, it's 6:50 PM, let me make sure I got everything together. Hmmm...Ok, resume, check! Ok, company study guide, check! List of questions about E. Jacob, check! Well, looks like we are a go." (Wow, I'm so excited!)

"Gene!"

(I think I have a good chance.)

"Gene!...Gene!"

"Oh, yes, dear?"

"I've been calling you for the last few minutes."

"Oh sorry, dear, I was getting prepared for the interview."

"Oh, yeah, yeah, whatever!"

"How can I help you, baby?"

"I was wondering if you have all the trash taken out for tomorrow."

"No, I haven't, babe. I have the interview in about 2 minutes. Could you get one of the boys to do it?"

"Hmmm...Never mind! I'll do it myself! Every time I ask you to do something, there's some..."

"Hold on, baby, this interview is very important to me—actually it is very important to us." (Why am I explaining this?)

"Well...I...go ahead and do your interview. I got the trash!"

"Thanks, baby. I'll see you soon after the interview ok?"

"Yeah, yeah..."

"Thanks, could you close the door behind you? Let the boys know I'll be busy for the next hour. Thanks so much." (Ok, focus, focus. Well, its 7:05 PM and the phone hasn't rung yet. Hmmm... I wonder if she forgot. Nah...She probably got real busy. Be patient, be patient.)

Ring!!!! Ring!!!! (Phone display reads, E. Jacob Wineries)

(All right, all right...Ok, let's do it.)

(Picks up phone). "Hello?"

"Hi! May, I speak to Gene Sparks?"

"Speaking!"

"Hi, Gene, this is Karen from E. Jacob Wineries."

"Hi, Karen, so nice to hear from you again."

"Same to you, Gene! First let me apologize for my tardinesss. I got called in to an emergency meeting at the last minute that I couldn't avoid."

"Not a problem at all. I'm just excited about exploring opportunities at your company."

"Well great! Well, let's get started. So, Gene, let me tell you in general how this interview will go. First off, it will be very informal so I would appreciate you just relaxing and being yourself."

"Ok, Karen, no problem with that."

"So tell me a little bit about your background and then we will move on to more specifics about your experience."

"Well, I was born in Dillon, South Carolina..."

"Oh, excuse me. What month where you born?"

"Excuse me?" (What does that have to do with anything?)

"I'm just curious about your birthday. I believe people's work performance is tied to their birth date..."

"Well...Ok...January 29, 1969."

"Hmmmm...How nice, you have a birthday coming up next month! And you will only be 21!"

"Ha,ha, ha! Oh, very funny, Karen!"

"Oh no, I am very serious. Hopefully you will be with us for your birthday?"

"I hope so."

"Yeah, maybe we can go celebrate it together." (Oh, you will be with us no doubt. I'm going to make sure you get up in here in more ways than one.)

"Oh wow, is that one of your standard practices?"

"Yes, but of course. It's just another way to keep our employees' work life balance."

"Oh, ok then, that sounds like a real nice program."

(Whew! I gotta be a bit more careful with this one.) "Yes, so go ahead and proceed, Gene. I apologize for interrupting you."

"Oh, no problem at all. Ok, well after high school, I served three years in the U.S. Army as a bomb disposal technician. After completing my enlistment, I..."

"Whoa! Whoa! You did what?"

"I was on the bomb squad."

"My goodness! I thought that's what you said. Whew!"

"Ha, yeah, I get that reaction a lot."

"Ok, please continue. I won't interrupt again."

"Ok, so after my enlistment, I went on to get my bachelors and masters in chemical engineering. I've spent the last few years developing new products from concept to market as well as creating engineering work processes and platforms."

"Very impressive, Gene, very impressive. Thanks for the info on your background."

"Your welcome, Karen."

"Well, let me tell you more about the position. The position you are applying for is our Director of Engineering. Your responsibility would be to lead our process and packaging engineering departments. Those departments in total have about 20 associates."

"That sounds great, Karen! I would love to have the opportunity to manage the engineering departments for you."

"Oh baby, you will..." (I hope he missed that!) "Excuse me, I mean you have a great chance at getting this position based on your credentials, but I will hold off until we have the onsite interview." (Karen asks more questions about Gene's background and wraps up the interview) "Ok, Gene, I think I have all of what I need. Do you have any questions for me?"

"Just one."

"Ok, shoot!"

"When can I expect to hear back from you concerning an onsite interview?"

"Well, actually, let's go ahead and set that up now as far as scheduling and my assistant can confirm your travel arrangements. I would like to get you in as soon as possible so a good time is two weeks from today. How does that sound?"

"Hmmm...the 18 of December works great! I will be there."

"Great! I look forward to seeing you then, Gene."

"Same to you, Karen."

"Oh thanks, Gene, the pleasure is all mine. One last thing: I will be your host and will pick you up for dinner. Let's say I pick you up around 7:00 p.m.?"

"I'll be ready!"

"Great! I'll make sure my assistant gives you plenty of time to get settled in."

"Thank you very much, Karen!"

"No problem, Gene, I'll see you soon. Have a great night!"

"You too, Karen. Goodbye."

"Bye now."

(Gene hangs up the phone and runs upstairs to tell his wife about the interview) "Gwen! Gwen! Where are you?"

"What do you want? I'm up here! I'm trying to go to sleep!"

"Oh, I'm sorry. I just wanted to tell you about the interview. I thought you would be happy."

"Yeah, whatever...Ok, how did it go!"

"Well, Karen seems like she'll be a great boss to work for. The position is Director of Engineering in which I manage both the process and packaging engineering departments. Also..."

"Well...It's about freakin' time! I've been telling you to get a job better than the one you got. Shit, Terry and your friend Milo both have been directors for a while."

"But, darling..."

"No excuses, Gene!"

"I was just going to say..."

"I don't want to hear it!"

"Ok, ok, good night, baby. I'll let you know how it goes." (Gene is puzzled why Gwen is so angry.)

"Good! 'Bout damn time!"

(Why am I still here? I treat her good. I'm only trying to make things better for our family. Arrgggh! I run in to women daily that would gladly trade places with her. But I...I don't know! Maybe I should...Nah...Forget it.)

"What did you say, Gene?"

"Oh nothing, I was just thinking about the onsite interview. Its two weeks from today. Get some rest, baby. I'm going to watch the rest of the football game downstairs. See you in the morning." (Gene walks down stairs to the family room to watch the football game)

(Two weeks later, Gene arrives at the host hotel for his onsite interview. Gene approaches the hotel front desk) "Hello, sir! Welcome to the Drakeford Hotel!"

"Thank you!"

"How can I help you, sir?"

"Yes, reservation for Sparks?"

" Ah yes, Gene Sparks?"

"Uh...Yes, how did you know that?"

"Sir, you are a very special guest. You will be staying in our executive penthouse suite. We only have two in the hotel so that's why it's easy to locate you."

"Oh my, I'm just here for an interview. I wasn't expecting that."

"Well, sir, E. Jacob is a great company and they have a lot of pull in this town."

"Wow! I guess so. That must be terribly expensive!"

"Well, just be glad that you have no expenses whatsoever beyond any incidentals."

"Wow, thank you!"

"Oh, don't thank me; you can thank E. Jacob. Hmmmm... A Mrs. K. Gilbert in particular." (He must be a hell of an employee or something else must be up. Most candidates for E. Jacob stay in our Delux rooms).

"Oh yes, Karen is my host for my on site interview. I can't wait to thank her."

(I bet you can't. Oh now I got it! Karen Gilbert is President of the Technology Division at E. Jacob. She must be up to her old tricks) "Oh, you definitely will once you see the room."

"I can only imagine."

"Well, just sign here and I will escort you up to your room. Place your bag over here and the bellboy will bring it up for you."

"First class treatment!"

"Yes, sir, we pride ourselves on excellent customer service at the Drakeford Hotel."

"Oh...oh! What time is it!"

"It's 5:30 PM sir."

"Oh ok, I have to be ready by 7:00 PM. Mrs. Gilbert is coming to pick me up for dinner."

"No problem, let's go to your room."

"Ok, here is your special key and code for opening the door."

"Wow! That is really hi-tech!"

"Yeah, we want to assure the utmost privacy for our guests that reserve these executive suites."

"Ok then."

(Gene and the desk attendant arrive at the penthouse suite) "So, welcome to your room. Here is the—"

"Are you kidding me!"

"He, he, he."

"This is a house inside a hotel room!"

"Well, let me show you around first, Mr. Sparks."

"Oh my goodness! I have never imagined a room..." (Oh, I got to take pictures and call Gwen to...No...no, bad idea.) "Wow, this I know is very expensive."

"Ha, ha, ha. Oh no worries, Mr. Sparks. Just enjoy it and do well on your interview."

"Thank you so much, thank you!"

"Well, let me show you the bedroom and kitchen area and let you get ready for dinner. I'm sure you can figure out the rest."

"What? I'm not sure about that. I'm overwhelmed right now!"

"Ha, ha, ha. So, here is the bedroom. It has a large master bathroom with a Jacuzzi tub. You have a wide assortment of toiletries and bathrobes in the bathroom."

"This is incredible! Too bad I'm here for only one night."

"Well, enjoy your stay all the better. Ok, Mr. Sparks, I am going to leave you now. I think you can figure out the kitchen. I want you to get prepared for your dinner and interview tomorrow. Your bags will be up within the next few minutes."

"Thank you!"

"If you need anything at all, please dial '0' for the front desk. We are at your service."

"Thank you again."

"Have a great evening!" (The door closes. Gene runs and jumps on the bed like a kid looking up at the ceiling). "This is really incredible. I can't believe how nice this room is. I really hope I get this job. I can appreciate a company that goes all out for their employees. Yeah I said it—their employees. I can feel it!" (Sitting back up) "Ok, let me get up from here and get ready for dinner. Hmm...6:15, damn I better hurry up and get a shower." (Gene takes off his robe and grabs the robe hanging next to his bathroom door) "Mmm...nice feel to it. Only the best. Ha, ha, ha."

(Turning on the radio) *"Nothing but slow jams, 24 hours a day."*

(Gene removes his clothes and tries to figure out how to turn on the shower)

"Ok."

(Reading) "'Set water to desired temperature. Select shower spray pattern via the diagram above. Pull inside handle for 2 seconds for gentle shower and longer for progressively harder shower.'"

"Oh wow, am I glad that I'm an engineer, otherwise I might be out of luck! Ha, ha, ha. Ok, that feels about right." (Gene steps into the shower) "Ahhhhhhhh! That feels just like heaven! I need to get one of these at home! Hmmm...'I'll fly away ole glory, I'll fly away... Hallelujah by and by...'" (Looking at the soap in his hand) "What kind of soap is this? Hmm... Smells ok. Guess it can't hurt. I'll fly away... Wait a minute, let me get ready for this dinner. Ok, should I bring my resume or...nah, just go and relax. You know what you need to know at this point. Right, right...Ok, I won't bring it. But then if she asks..."

"Ding, dong!"

That's a real doorbell. Am I really at a hotel?

"Ding, dong!"

"I'm coming, just finishing my shower."

"Ding, dong!"

"Ok, ok, I am coming!" (Gene shuts off the water and grabs a towel to begin drying off. (Rushing to the door) "I'm coming! That must be my luggage." (Gene grabs the robe and puts it on as he continues running toward the door). "It's only 6:40; that must be my luggage. Perfect timing."

"Ding..."

(Gene swings the door open) "Hello."

"Hi, Gene! It's Karen."

"Karen!!!" (Gene fumbles with his robe straps, trying to tighten them). "Oh...Um...My...I..."

"It's ok, Gene. It really is. I know I'm early." Karen is wearing a black fitted body dress with high heels.

"Yeah, I'll hurry up. I thought it was the bellboy bringing my luggage. I apologize for not being dressed."

"Gene, Gene...really, it's fine. I know I surprised you. Well...you are half way right; I do have your luggage."

(Whoa! This is incredibly weird and uncomfortable).

"Nice robe, by the way!"

"Oh, ok...I...umm...thank you. It's nice to meet you by the way, and you look very nice this evening as well." (Damn! Karen is fine! Look at that phat ass and the small waist! Unh!)

"Well, don't you want your luggage?"

"Yes, yes." (Breathing hard) "Come in! Let me grab those."

"Oh no, Gene, I can handle them. I'll take them to your bedroom."

(Oh my!) "Thank you, Karen. Just give me 5 minutes and I'll be ready to go."

(Karen places the luggage in the corner) (Perfect timing. He looks even better in person!) "Again, Gene, there's no rush."

(Gene starts to go open the luggage and Karen jumps in front of him.) "Oh sorry, Karen, I didn't mean to bump into you."

(In a soft seductive voice) "Oh, Gene, as an employee, you are going to have to learn to listen better." (Karen is now standing directly in front of Gene with her body lightly pressed against him while looking up at him). "I said, there's no rush, baby."

(Nervously stuttering) "Oh...uh...ok..."

"Your job interview starts right now."

(Damn! What the fuck is happening! I'm about to pass out. I do want this job! I don't know what to...)

"Are you ok, Gene?"

"Uh...uh...yes!" (Gene swallows hard.)

"Well, let's just start off by saying you all ready have the job."

"I do?"

"Yes—that's if you want it." (Karen tip toes and gives Gene a peck on the mouth.)

"But how can I get the job..."

"Did you forget that I'm the President?"

"Oh, um...yes." (Oh my God! I shouldn't be doing this, but my body won't let me stop. What about Gwen?...Fuck Gwen!...Oh shit! Please don't get hard, please don't get...Damn too late.)

"Oh my, Gene! That's nice and hard. I wish my husband could get it up like that—or was even interested."

"Oh yeah," (Nervously) "I...I...I...know what you mean. I face similar issues with my wife."

"Hmmm...I'm sorry to hear that, Gene. But ever since I saw your profile coupled with your phone interview, I've wanted to meet you!"

"Wow, me...What was it about me?"

"Well, I could tell you're a good man." (Karen begins to untie Gene's robe).

(Gene looks up briefly) "Oh really?"

"Yes, and now, I can see why." (Gene's dick is sticking straight out. Karen leans in and begins to suck on his chest).

"Ohhhh Shit! Damn, I forgot how good that feels! Shit...that feels so good Karen!"

(While sucking Gene's chest) "You don't...Ssss...have to...sssss! Call me Karen. Call me 'baby.'"

"Yes, baby, suck that chest. (Gene grabs the sides of Karen's head and kisses her passionately on the mouth).

"Oh, Gene! I was wondering when you were going to wake up."

(Gene reaches down underneath Karen's dress). "Oh God! You don't have any underwear on!"

(Karen forces Gene's hand onto her pussy.) "Ohhh, it's been throbbing waiting on you to touch it." (Gene slides his finger slowly in and out of Karen's pussy while continuing to kiss her) "Unnh! Unnh! Unnh! Oh Gene! Damn you feel so good!"

"Oh this pussy is so damn hot and wet inside!"

"You liking that baby!"

"Ohhh yess, rrgghhhh! Oh damn...I'm about to cum all ready..."

"Do it baby! Go ahead—cum for daddy!"

"Unnhh! Unnhhh! Oh shit! Oh! Oh! Ohhhhhhhhhh!" (Breathing hard).

"That's it baby! That's how you let that shit go!"

"Damn, Gene! I'm so embarrassed. I can't believe I came that fast! That shit felt so good! Did you feel that?"

"Oh, hell yeah. It's all over my hands. (Gene licks his finger and then places it in Karen's mouth.) "Doesn't that taste good baby?"

"Oh yes, but it can't replace how good you're going to taste!" (Karen begins to kiss Gene again while stroking his dick lightly) "Oh yes! Mmmm!" (Karen sucks on his chest and moves down his body.)

"Oh baby, that feels so good." (Karen squats all the way down while continuing to hold and stroke Gene's dick.) "Oh baby! Don't tease me. I need you to suck it!"

"You sure about that!" (Karen kisses the tip and licks up some pre-cum.) "Mmmmm! Mmmmm!" Slurp! "Oh, Gene, your pre-cum taste so damn good. I can't wait for the rest!"

(Oh my God! She swallows too! I can't even get Gwen near my dick!) "Baby, it's all yours." (Karen slides Gene's dick all the way to the back of her throat.)

"Oh, God! Damn!...Damn! Damn!" Slurp! "Unnnh!" Slurp!! "Unnh! Suck it baby! Unnhh! Oh shit!"

"Oh this dick tastes so good!" Slurp! "When..." Slurp! "Are..." Slurp! "You..." Slurp! Slurp! "Going to cum..." Slurp! "In my mouth!"

"Unnnh!!! Shit..." (Breathing hard) "Anytime baby, any time!"

"Mmm...mmm...mmm...oh yes, more cum. Taste so fucking good!" Slurp! Slurp! Slurp! "So tasty!"

(Karen pulls Gene's dick out of her mouth for a moment) "Baby, baby?"

"What happened!"

"Nothing, sweety." Slurp! "I'm just at a crossroad. I can't decide if I want you all in my mouth or backing this ass up to that dick!"

"Ummm...that is hard. Fuck it! Stand up." (Gene picks Karen up and carries her over to the large desk in the bedroom, sitting her down on the edge).

"Lay back, baby." (Gene pushes the items on the desk behind Karen onto the floor. Karen is turned on by his aggression. Gene flips her dress back onto her breasts) "Have mercy! That is one beautiful pussy! Oh, I got to taste that!" (Gene bends over and lightly sucks her clit.)

"Ohhhh shit! Damn, Gene! What are you trying to do? Turn my ass out!

"Oh no baby, I always do my best to please the pussy!"

"Oh my God! Baby, let me feel that dick." (Gene takes his dick and beats on Karen's pussy while alternating between sticking his dick's head in.) "Unnh!" Plap! "Ummm!" Plap! "Oh, baby don't tease me! Don't teaaassssssssssssse me!"

(Gene pushes his dick all the way inside Karen.) "Unnh!"

"Oh shit! Unnhhh! Unnh! Oh, Gene! Unnh! Oh, Gene! Yeah, baby! Oh I love that shit. I love watching a dick go in and out of that sweet pussy! Unnhhh!"

"You wanted to be fucked right?"

"Oh yes, daddy!"

"You don't want no other dick, do you!"

"Oh no, daddy! Unnh! Unnh! Get this pussy, Gene! It's your pussy, baby! It's all yours! Unhh!"

"Oh you feel so good, Karen! Damn, I better slow down before I explode!"

"Oh no, baby! Keep going! Pull out and give me that shit when you're ready."

"Oh shit! I'm ready baby! Oh, God! Oh, God! Oh, God!" (Gene pulls out and Karen quickly sits up and pushes his dick in her mouth.) "Unnnnnnnnnnnh! Shittttt!"

(Karen in a muffled voice.) "Mmmmmmm! Mmmmm! Yummmy!"

(Breathing hard) "Oh my God, baby! I haven't cum like that in a long time."

"Mmmmm..." Slurp!

"Thank you so much!"

"You're welcome, baby. Unnh! Your cum is so sweet! Fuck that shit turns me on! The way your cum hit the back of my throat with so much force!"

(Breathing hard) "Oh yeah..."

"Damn, that is some good shit!"

"Whew! Oh, God! I got to sit the fuck down". (Gene walks slowly over to the bed and plops down) "My legs are like rubber!"

"He, he, he." (Karen sits up and hops down from the desk to go join Gene on the bed) "Let me join you."

(Karen lies down beside Gene on the bed. Gene slides over slightly as she lays her head onto his chest) (Exhaling) "Woooo. Baby, I can't tell you how good that felt."

"Go ahead, tell me. He, he, he."

"Whew! I haven't felt like that in years."

"Believe me, I know exactly what you mean. Well, you know we at E. Jacob want to make you feel right at home."

"Ha, ha, ha! I think your company far exceeds my expectations."

"I know; that's an understatement."

"You got that right. The most important question is did I get the job? "

"Hmmmm...let's see. With an interview like that, do you really need to ask?"

"Ha, ha, ha. I guess you're right."

(Karen raises her head up and kisses Gene in the mouth) "Muah! Welcome to E. Jacob!"

(Gene and Karen both laugh).

Chapter 2

A Mute Point

"Hey, Carla, will you be here tomorrow for the global technology conference call?"

(Carla stops a few front her office door and turns around) "What's that, Amber?"

"The global technology call?"

"Oh damn!! I almost forgot. I definitely can't afford to miss..."

(Looking through Carla's calendar) "Uh huh...well, I see you have a doctor's appointment prior to the meeting."

"That's it! I knew for some reason it was slipping my mind. He, he, he...I know it has to be in my phone."

"It is, Carla. That's the main reason I asked you. I just thought it was strange that you had the appointment and would be able to make the call from where you live."

"You are always on top of things, Amber. I'm so glad you keep me straight. I must have just seen the appointment in my phone and didn't think to read further. Hmmm...I got to work on that."

"It's no big deal, Carla. That's part of my job. You would have eventually seen it, but I just wanted to make sure because of how important it is."

"Right. But again, I really appreciate it Amber."

"You're welcome."

"So I will come in after...wait!" (I can't come in here. Derek is coming over after my appointment. Shit! That's the reason I forgot about that meeting) "Umm. I'll have to take the call from home." (Carla starts to stare off into space thinking about Derek).

"Ok, Carla, I'll double check that you have all teleconference numbers and pass codes. Do you want me to call and remind you?"

(Damn! It's been a minute since I've seen Derek. I haven't felt that big chocolate dick up in me in almost 2 weeks. Fuck! I'm so glad his ass is back from Europe! He needs to get up in this...) (Carla is unnoticeably licks her licks as she daydreams about Derek).

(Amber stands up from her desk waving her arms to get Carla's attention) "Carla?...earth to Carla?...Carla!"

(Shaking out her trance) "Oh! Oh, sorry! Um...what did you say?"

(Responding in a matter-of-fact tone). "Uh, the call to remind you?"

"Oh, no." (Waving her hands signifying she has control of things) "I got it now, Amber. Thanks though. I'll put in on my reminder board at home since I had planned to stay home anyway after the appointment. Because by the time I drive in the call will be over already. And you know how much I hate conference calls using my cell phone."

"Yep. I know. But you do live out in the counnnnnnnn-treeee! Ha, ha, ha."

"He, he. Whatever, Amber. Nothing wrong with country living."

"No it isn't. But seriously, you know you live out there!"

(Rolling her eyes and waving Amber off). "Whatever!"

"Anyway, I'll double check your calendar and make sure you have all the information you need."

"Thank you so much..." (Carla thinks about her preparation for the meeting). "Oh! By the way, the main part of the call is about the site study for the new technical center, right?"

"Yes, that's it exactly. I organized all the documents you need so you'll be ready to go."

"Wow! Again, thanks for reminding me. This call is so critical to how our budget gets spent next year."

"No problem, Carla, I got you covered."

"You always do! Couldn't make it without you." (Carla begins to turn toward her office).

"Oh wait! One last thing."

(Carla stops and turns back toward Amber) "Yes, Amber?"

"Well, what will you do after the conference call? The rest of your schedule is empty."

"Hmm..." (Getting my ass fucked!) "Take a guess..."

"Um...probably working?"

"Ha, ha, ha! You know me so well. Work, work, work...yes, I don't have a life. I thought about taking the rest of the day off, but..."

"You thought work would be much more relaxing?"

"He, he, he. I know, I know. I'm pathetic."

(So, so sad. I hope I never enjoy work that much.) "Nah. Nothing wrong with that, Carla, if that drives you and makes you happy by all means have at it."

"Well...I wouldn't say all that, but I really don't mind it." (And the Academy Award goes to...yeah, work, work, work, Carla. When Derek gets up in this pussy! Unh!... Fuck! I can't wait!)

(Looking at Carla strangely). "Well, umm...have a good rest of the day and a great weekend after the call."

"Thank you, Amber, I appreciate that. I will catch you later." (Carla goes back into her office and shuts the door so she can call Derek about tomorrow's plans)

(Phone ringing) "Hello? Derek Grayson's office."

"Hi Patty! It's Carla. Is Derek around?"

"Oh, hi, Carla. I think he's about to go to his 4 o'clock meeting, but let me check if he has a second? Hold on..."

(Getting moderate performance from your portfolio? Contact your McKeague representative today. We offer an extensive line of...) "Carla?"

"Yes?"

"Connecting you now. Have a great day."

(Derek gathers papers while holding the phone between his shoulder and chin) "Hey baby, how is it going?"

"Very good, sweet D!"

"Ha, ha, ha. Don't you go starting that. You know I'm about to go to a meeting."

"Starting what?"

"Yeah, real cool showing up with a hard on!"

"He, he, he. Ok baby, I just wanted to hear your voice. Plus, I'm really looking forward to seeing you tomorrow."

"Uh huh. So am I baby, so am I."

"Look, I'm not going to hold you up. I'll see you after my appointment and conference call tomorrow."

"Thank you, baby. I can't wait to see you. I love you."

"Love you too, Derek. Later."

"Bye now."

(Carla sends out a couple of emails, reviews her information for tomorrow's meeting and decides to leave for the day).

"Hey Amber, where's Carla?" (Josie asks as she walks up to Carla's desk).

(Carla motions to Josie to hold on for one second while she finishes a phone call). "Ok, Mr. Holt. I will send out the agreement as soon as we hang up...That's right...Yeah, no problem...You're welcome...Ok, talk to you later...Goodbye." (Carla hangs up the phone and looks up at Josie standing in front of her desk). "Hey, girl?"

"Sorry about that, Carla, I didn't see..."

"Girl please! No harm done. Mr. Holt is always flirting anyway. You gave me a good reason to get off the phone."

"Ha, ha, ha. Well, I was just asking where Carla was."

"Oh, can you believe she's gone for the day."

"What? Not Ms. Workaholic!"

"Yep! Ha, ha, ha!" (Amber covers her mouth to muffle her laugh).

"Oh my goodness! That prudish ass finally left the office before all the lights get turned off. Ha, ha, ha."

"Yeah, I guess she went to work extra at home tonight to make up for her appointment in the morning. She's going to work the rest of the day from home tomorrow."

"What! You got to be kidding me."

"Nope! Nothing new! And here's the kicker—it's actually her day off!"

"Wow...wow..."

"I guess it's her form of relaxation.

"I suppose."

"Oh my, she really needs to get a life."

"You could say that again!"

"Does she even have a man?"

"Please! Do you think she would be working like that!"

"He, he, he. Good point."

"Even before a man, she needs to get her recommended daily allowance of..."

(In unison) "Vitamin D!"

"Ha, ha, ha! Ha, ha, ha! Oh shit, girl." Cough! Cough! "I'm about to choke!"

"He, he, he. Amber, you are too crazy!"

(Amber notices someone peeping from two offices down from Carla's because of all the noise. Amber regains her composure and motions Josie to bring the noise down). "Shhh...Shh...we got to keep it down."

"Ok, ok." (Muffling her mouth to contain her laugh). "Ok...I'm good now. Whew!"

"So..." (Struggling to keep from laughing out loud), "did you need me to leave her a message?"

"Oh, no, no, no. It's not that important. I can catch her on Monday. I just wanted to talk about any future opportunities in her department."

"Girl, you should have come to me first. You know I know everything that goes on in this department."

"You're right, you're right. It really slipped my..."

"Well, there are some openings. I can set you up to meet with her early Monday for you to at least see if there's something you're interested in. Will that work for you?"

"Yes, that'll work. That'd be great."

"Ok, I will send you a meeting invitation."

"Thanks, Amber."

"No problem, Josie." (Amber starts to gather her things and shutdown her computer).

"Uh, where do you think you're going?"

"I don't know about you, but I'm about to head the hell out."

"He, he, he. I'm just kidding. I'm one step behind you."

"Ok, Josie, I'll see you tomorrow. Have a good one."

"Goodnight, Amber." (Josie heads back to her department to grab her things and leave for the day. Amber picks up her keys and purse and head for the elevator).

(Carla is just finishing up her doctor's appointment when she notices that she needs to be on the conference call in 30 minutes) "Ha, ha, ha! Dr. Davis you are so funny. Girl, you always make me laugh about the simplest things. I actually try to make up appointments just to..." (Carla looks over the Dr.'s shoulder at the clock on the wall while hopping up from the exam table). "Oh shit!"

(Slightly startled) "What? What is it? Do you feel ok?"

(Grabbing her purse and suit jacket) "Yes, yes. I'm fine doc. I didn't mean to scare you like that. I just have a conference call in about 30 minutes and I need at least 20 minutes to get home."

"Oh, ok." (The doctor grabs Carla's chart and hurries her to the front to check out at billing) "Come on then! Let's get you out of here." (Giving consult as she walks Carla hastily to the front) "Ok, Carla. Remember, eat more fruit and extend your exercise from 3 to 5 days a week. So far, I like everything I see. I don't expect any problems from your blood work, but if I see something you know I will be giving you a call..." (Standing by the front office checkout, Dr. Davis waves Carla on through towards the parking garage). "Donna, go ahead and set Carla up..."

(Waving as she exits the double doors from her Dr.'s office). "Thank you so much, girl."

(Motioning Carla to keep going). "It's fine. Now go. Go!"

(Carla hits the remote lock on her Lexus as she approaches her car).

(Breathing hard from a light trot). "Whew! Man, wish this car had automatic start. He, he. Or even remote pick-up! Damn, I better really start doing more exercise!" (Big sigh as she plops down in the driver's seat). "Whewwwww! Ok. Let's hit it." (Looking at the clock on the dash as she turns to back out of the parking space). "Twenty-five minutes. Yeah, it'll be close..." (Let's just hope traffic treats me right.)

(Carla sees a fire truck and a police car with lights flashing as she enters her neighborhood. The cop waves her to stop as she approaches them. Carla rolls down her window as she comes to a stop) "Good morning, officer. Is there a problem?"

"Hello ma'am! There's no problem at all. We are just out in the neighborhood collect donations for the kid safety program."

(Placing one hand on her chest in relief). "Ok then. I thought something was really wrong." (Looking down and reaching into her purse for a donation) "Here you go, officer. I hope this helps."

"Thank you so much ma'am. Every amount helps. Have a great day."

(Carla continues down her street glancing back in the mirror at the flashing lights) (He, he. That's one time I don't mind seeing flashing lights in my rearview mirror.)

(Carla presses the remote for her garage door and pulls in. She looks at the clock on the dash before turning off the engine). "Hmmm...five minutes to spare! All right, let's get ready." (Carla turns off the car and heads into the house pressing the button to let the garage down. She set's her purse and keys on the kitchen table. She starts removing her jacket as she walks through the house to her home office).

Click.

(As she turns on the desk lamp and places the jacket over the back of her office chair). (Ok, here is the call in number and notes I need...hmmm...laptop. We're all set.)

(Carla hurries to her bedroom to set up for the call) "Might as well be comfortable, girl. No conference room for you!" (Carla strips down to her royal blue thong with no bra. She looks in the mirror and stares at her perky breasts). "Uh huh...look at you girls. Are you expecting someone? He, he. Oh, I know. I am expecting..."

"Ding Dong!" "Ding Dong!"

(Carla dons her sheer negligee and hurries toward the front door) "That can't be Derek. It's too early." (Shoot! I got to hurry and get on this call).

"Ding Dong!" "Ding Dong!"

"Hold your horses! I'm coming!"

"Ding Dong!" "Ding Dong!"

(Carla looks through the peephole at the front door and can't make out the person standing off to the side) "Who is it?"

"Supah-Bisuh!" (He, he)

"Say again please!"

"Supah-Bisuh!" (He, he)

(Carla finally picks up that its Derek's voice. As she unlocks the door, Derek rushes in and grabs her) "Woo hoo! Boy! You were about to be left standing out there! With your crazy..."

"Ha, ha, ha! You weren't going to let your man in?" (Derek quickly notices that Carla has on just a thong and negligee).

"I don't know no supah-bisuh. I was about to..."

(Derek grabs Carla by the shoulders pushing her back to admire how sexy she's) "Mmmm...unh! Damn!" (Derek pulls Carla close so that he can kiss her).

"Ummm!" (Breathing hard). "Whew! Shit! You about to get things...I mean, I have the call...I wasn't expecting you this early."

"Oops, I'm sorry. I can go and come back if you want?" (Releasing Carla and pretending to walk towards the door).

"Oh hells no!" (Grabbing Derek by his jacket) "Yo ass ain't going nowhere!"

"Ha, ha, ha. Well you said..."

"You know what the hell I meant!"

"I know baby, I know. Go ahead and take your call. I'll see you when you finish."

"Thank you, baby. Thank you." (Placing her hands under her breasts and pushing them up at Derek) "Once I'm done. I am all yours."

"Go on with that, baby! Don't be starting no shit!"

"He, he, he. What? What did I do?"

"Oh you know!...I'm not going to even touch that. Anyway, I'll be out here waiting so that you have some privacy while you're on the call."

"You can come back to the bedroom if you like; it's not like I can't put the phone on mute when the call is not referring to me."

"Well..." (Looking at Carla's ass as she walks toward the bedroom). "Hmmm... No, I'm good. I'll be fine. I just don't like to interfere with your work, baby."

"Ok, suit yourself. You know I don't mind. I always got time for my baby."

"I know baby, I know. Surprisingly, I can never complain about that given the fact you're a workaholic."

"He, he, he. Ok then. Well make yourself at home, baby. I would fix you something to eat but I got to jump on the call shortly."

"No problem, darling, you go get ready for the call. I assure you, I'll be fine."

"You sure?"

"Yes, I'm sure."

(Carla's voice fades back into her bedroom as Derek heads for the kitchen). "Ok, I'll be back as soon as possible."

(Derek opens the refrigerator door to get the strawberry jelly and cream cheese).

(Yes indeed. My baby looking good. Walking round the house with all that ass just jiggling. Unh, unh, unh).

(Derek grabs a bagel out of the bag near the toaster).

(She knows that she's...ok, wrong is too strong...fuck it. I can't wait to put my face dead in those ass cheeks.)

Cha-Clunk!

(Derek grabs his toasted bagel from the toaster. He spreads cream cheese on his bagel followed by strawberry jelly) "Yessur. That looks like some good eatin there." (Derek puts the cream cheese and jelly back in the refrigerator while grabbing a small carton of orange juice).

(Let's go see what's on the tube).

"Beep!"

"Please enter the conference pass code followed by the pound sign." (Sound of phone pulse tone as Carla enters the conference pass code).

"8, 6, 7, 5, 3, 0, 9".

"Your code has been accepted."

"Please state your name after the tone"

"Beep!"

"Carla."

"Beep!"

"So, if we... hello, hello... Hey, who just joined?"

"Good morning everyone, this is Carla."

"Good morning, Carla. I didn't think you would be calling in this morning. I thought for sure this was a day off for you."

"Yeah, it is, but you know me. Work, work, work."

(Laughter in the conference room).

(Tristan looks around the conference room as he introduces everyone). "Well, in the room we have Elliot, Amber, James, Skip, Kwame, Percy and Liza. On the phone is Brendan from the UK, Wei-Mei from China, and Hector from Brazil."

"Hi, guys! Good morning to you all. Thanks Tristan for the introduction. Sounds like we got everybody we need."

"Let's get started then. Ok, we have several topics to cover with the primary discussion centering around the site study for the new technical center. So let's begin there and follow the agenda as I have outlined. Everybody on board with that?"

"Sounds good to me, Tristan."

"How about you Carla?"

"Sounds good to me."

"All right then."

"So we are looking at pretty good sized technical center. I believe it will be around 400,000 square feet and sit on about 31 acres."

"Oh my! That is very near the size of some of our smaller producing plants!"

"Yeah, this is a very big investment for the company. I think it will be the biggest Wear Wise Guys® technical facility ever built. This way we will be able to not only research and develop products, but have small producing lines to handle consumers and test market studies. And we would..."

"Tristan? This is Carla."

"Yes, Carla?"

"What is our projected opening date and will it coincide with our R&D planning cycle for next year?"

"Thanks, Carla, two excellent questions. Well, we are planning to have the center go live in the middle of the 4th quarter of 2010. So we should catch the tail end of the planning cycle. Does that sound about right, Percy?"

"Yes, Tristan. That falls in line with the latest schedule I sent out. So we should be in good shape."

"Oh, that's good. I'll make sure to inform the strategy team about the scheduled opening so they can adjust accordingly."

"But bare in mind, Carla, this schedule is only tentative."

"Oh yeah. I assumed that. I know changes come up, so I will account for that. Thanks for the heads up though."

"Great, great. Well, next on the agenda is..."

"Excuse me, Tristan. That was my main concern for now. I'm going to remain on the call but will be on mute as you move down the rest of the agenda."

"Ok, Carla, sounds good." (Carla places her phone on mute and looks through her notes to see if there is anything else she needs to discuss with the group).

(Tristan continues with the conference call)

"Now the other big item concerning the site study is the number of employees to hire..." (Derek overheard Carla telling Tristan she was going on mute. As Tristan continues with the agenda, Derek comes into the bedroom where Carla sits on the edge of the bed near the phone listening in).

(Derek sneaks in behind her and whispers in her ear before she turns to see him).

"Oh hi, big D! How are things going?"

"Well, I..."

(Looking back over her shoulder).

"And how did you know I was on mute, mister?"

"He, he, he. I overheard you from the kitchen, baby. So, I thought I would come in and see if my baby needed anything."

"Yeah, yeah. Right, right. You must think..."

"No seriously." (With a smirk on his face). "I have to make sure my honey..."

"Um hum. Awe... you are so sweet." (Grabbing Derek's cheeks and lightly pinching them). "My baby is so damn sweet!" (Letting his cheeks go and briefly turning to the phone to check if she was needed). "Speaking of sweet, how about you come around and give me a lick of that tootsie roll!"

(Backing off the bed on his knees, Derek comes around in front of Carla) "Wow baby! I did ask what you wanted." (Derek begins to pull his shirt out of his sweat pants).

(Carla looks up a Derek as he holds his shirt up looking down at her. She slowly pushes his sweat pants and boxer briefs down causing his hard dick to spring out of his pants) "Mmm...damn that dick looks tasty!"

(Derek whispers). "Are you sure the phone is on mute?"

"Yes, I'm sure silly!" Slurp! "Ummm...that's so yummy." Slurp! (Taking Derek's dick out of her mouth) "Look down at the phone. You see the button flashing, 'phone muted.'"

"Ok, baby, just...unh! Oh, Carla. Unh... just check...ummm..." Slurp! (Derek moves in closer between Carla's leg's as she spreads them wider while sliding her hand into her thong massaging her clit).

"Unh!" Slurp! "Unh!" (Briefly taking Derek dick's out of her mouth). "Look at that nice piece of chocolate!" (She kisses his dick lightly and looks up at him). "You ready to feed mommy!

"Oh yeah, baby! Take your candy. Take it all. Ummh!" Slurp! "Unnh!" Slurp! "Oh baby, suck that dick. Suck it!"

"Unnh!" Slurp! (Carla begins to finger fuck herself while sucking Derek's dick). "Oh shit, niggah! Ummm!" Slurp! "Oh fuck! I love the way that dick hits the back of my throat! Unh..." Slurp! "This shit makes me so wet! Umm..."

(Tristan has a question for Carla). "Sorry Carla, we have a question for you...Carla?"

(Derek and Carla both stop and turn to the phone. Carla pulls Derek's dick out of her mouth while continuing to hold it in one hand while gently stroking it to keep it hard. She rushes to un-mute the phone). "Uh, um...yes, Tristan. Sorry about that. I stepped away a second."

"No problem. We were wondering if you were able to identify a lead engineer for the equipment install and line start up?"

"Yes, we looked at three candidates and settled on Case Montgomery. He has an extensive background in plant start-ups. He will be transitioning from a project in our Latin American division and should be getting up to speed by the end of the month. So he will be here well in advance of the install." (Carla quietly and discretely sucks on Derek's dick and smiles up at him as she listens to Tristan) Slurp! "umm!" (Derek can hardly stand it).

"That's excellent, Carla. I look forward to meeting him when he arrives on site. Thanks again for that. We shouldn't have to bother you for the rest of the call."

"No problem, Tristan. Just let me know what you need."

"Thanks, Carla." (Tristan returns to the conference call).

(Carla returns the phone to mute). "So where was I? Oh yeah, sucking on this fat juicy chocolate dick! Ummm!" Slurp! "Umm! Damn, this dick is so good." Slurp! "Umm...shit! I can't wait until you explode in my mouth!"

"Oh fuck yeah! I know you need your early morning protein! Umm..."

Slurp! Slurp! "Damn straight! Mmmm...oh the pre-cum is like fucking honey!" Slurp! "Umm! You know I love swallowing your cum!" Slurp! (Muffled while talking with Derek's dick in her mouth). "Let-umm-it go-in-umm-my-mout-uh!" Slurp! "Baby, let that shit go!"

"Whoa! Whoa! I'm not ready to do that yet baby! I got to get some of that juicy pussy first!

"Fuck! Take it then! You ain't said nothing but a word baby! Takes this pussy. Beat this pussy from the front or rip it from behind!" (Carla stands up and faces Derek).

"Damn, girl. You got me hard as hell!"

"That's how I like..."

"Well fuck me then!" (Carla reaches down and starts massaging Derek's dick and begins to suck on his chest).

"Umm...girl, you know that is my spot. I want..." Kiss! "To hit..." Kiss! "That..."

"Well hit it then!"

(Breathing hard) "Don't you think..."

"Think what?"

"Umm...that we should wait until..." Kiss! "Umm...after the conference call."

"Oh no, niggah! I want some dick now! Stop teasing me!"

"Ok, baby, fuck it!" (Derek pushes Carla back on to the bed. He picks up her legs by both ankles and stands in between then). "Oh yeah. Look at that juicy mutha fucka!" (Derek spreads Carla's legs as far apart as they can go).

"Oh shit, baby! Get up in that shit!"

"Oh yeah, I'm about to get all up in you. Mmmm...that's what I need: Sweet pussy all on my breath."

"Ooooooohh, shit! Do your thang, baby, do your thang! Ummm!" (Derek places one leg on each shoulder and begins to lick and kiss Carla's inner thighs lightly while gently stroking Carla's clit).

"Ummmmmmmm!" (In a soft voice) "Ooh, that feels good, baby! Damn! Your breath is tingling my clit! What are you waiting on! Please suck my pussy!"

"Relax, baby, relax. I got this! You just lay back and enjoy. Let your man do his thang."

"Ummm! Ok, baby, ok. It just feels so good!" (Derek begins to lightly lick Carla's clit).

"Whew! Oh, God...Goddamn! Ummm! Damn, that's what I been waiting for!"

"Carla?...Carla?"

"Ummm...Ummm!"

"Carla?" (Derek stops as he hears Tristan ask for Carla on the phone).

"What the fuck! Why did you stop?" (Carla remains on her back with legs up looking up at Derek puzzled).

"Baby! Baby! They need you on the conference call." (Derek quickly moves the phone near Carla's head. She takes it off mute).

"Um, uh...hi, this is Carla." (Catching her breath) "I'm sorry, I was across the room."

"No problem."

"Sorry, one last thing for you."

"Shoot."

"We wanted to make sure we budgeted enough funds for install and start-up."

(Continuing to catch her breath). "Hmm...well, barring any major delays in acquiring the long lead equipment, the budget was set with a 10% overage for minor adjustments. So we shoullddddddddddddd (As Derek licks her clit) be in great shape."

"Thanks again, Carla. I promise...what's that Kwame?"

"No problem, Tristan. I'll be right here." (Carla places the phone back on mute).

"Ha, ha, ha! Is there a problem honey?"

(Carla lightly kicks Derek in his side). "Ha, ha! You know yo ass ain't right."

"Well, baby, you said..."

"Said what! Lick my clit while I'm on the phone? He, he!"

"You said we didn't have to wait."

"Yes, I did. Oh my God it was feeling so damn..." (Carla un-mutes the phone as Tristan finishes tell her thanks).

"Again, thank you, Carla. I promise that's it for today. We know that you are always on top of it."

"No problem at all."

"Thanks again."

"You're welcome."

(Tristan resumes the conference call). "So team, I think we have what we need. Let's recap the notes."

(Carla quickly presses the mute button and tells Derek to finish what he started. Derek immediately goes to sucking her clit and stick his tongue deep in her pussy).

"Damn it, baby! Ummmmh! You didn't...Oooohhh! Waste any time!...Damn! Unnnnh! Oh suck it, D, suck it baby! Wait! Wait! Make sure the phone is on mute."

Slurp!

"Unnh!" (Breathing hard) "Ok, baby, ok." (Derek looks at the phone and is not sure which button to press). "Which button, baby, which button?"

"Just press the mute button, baby! The...unh! The red one!"

(Derek quickly glances at the phone and unknowingly presses the red button taking the phone off mute.) "Ok, baby! I pressed it baby!"

(Tristan is setting up the next team meeting). "So our next mee—"

"Suck it again, baby!" (Tristan stops mid sentence).

"So our next meeeee... (The conference room goes silent. Carla and Derek are unaware the phone is not muted).

Slurp!

"Oooh, baby! That's it! Unnnh! Unnh!"

Slurp!

"Unhh! Oh yeah, pull on my clit just like that!"

Slurp!

"Unnh!"

Slurp!

"Unnh! I'm about to cum baby! Oh, I don't want to cum yet!"

"Let it go, baby! Let that shit out!"

"Unnnhh! Ohhhhhhhhhhh! Godddddddddddddd! OOOOOOhhhhhhh shit! Damn, that shit felt good!"

(Derek pulls out and motions for Carla to turn around). "Turn that ass over!"

(Breathing hard as she gets up with her ass sticking up in the air with her knees at the edge of the bed. Derek bends over to quickly suck her pussy from behind) "Oooooooooh, damn, baby! What are you..."

(Derek stands up and slaps Carla on the ass).

Slap!

"Ooooh!" (Breathing hard). "Damn baby! You bout to get up in this ass!" (Carla's team members in the conference room continue to look around at each other in shock).

"Ha, ha, ha! You know that's right." (Derek dips his fingers in to Carla's pussy and rubs the pussy juice on his dick. He then spreads Carla's ass cheeks apart).

"Oh damn! My pussy is so sensitive!" (Gasping for air) "Whew!...Baby!...I don't knowwwwwwwwwwww!" (Derek rams his dick in hard and fast)

"Unh!"

Slap!

"Unh!"

Slap!

"Unh!"

Slap!

"Unh!"

Slap!

"Unh!"

Slap!

"Unh!"

Slap!

"Take that dick baby! Take it! This my ass! Who's ass is it! (Tristan's face is beet-red as he stands motionless at the end of the conference room table).

(In between strokes) "Your...Unh!"

Slap!

"Yours...unh!"

Slap!

"Baaa...Unh!"

Slap!

"Baby! Unh!"

Slap!

"That's right! Umm! Give it to me! Umm!! Yeah baby, come on now! Umm!! Paint that white cum all over my dick! Umm! Oh yeah baby! Ummm! Oh shit! Ummmmm! Oh, baby! Umm! Oh shit! I'm about to cum! Umm! Oh shit!"

"Pull it out, baby! Give me my protein shot!"

"Ok, baby, I'm cumming! Oohh shit! Turn around!" (Carla swings around quickly holding her mouth open). "Bring your head closer!" (Derek grabs a hand full of Carla's hair and pulls her mouth on to his dick).

"Oh shit, baby! Ohhhhhhhhhhhhhhhhhhh!" (Derek explodes in Carla's mouth.) "Unhhhh! (Holding his breath and placing one hand on the bed to keep his balance). "Oh shit!" (Breathing hard). "Suck it all baby! Oh my God! Whew!"

"Mmmmmm...oooohh...ummmm...hell yes! I love the way the hot cum warms my throat as I swallow it down. Shit, it tastes so damn sweet!"

(Derek gasps for air while moving to the side of the bed to sit down before he collapses). "Damn, baby! My legs feel like fuckin' rubber. Shit! You sucked out every drop. He, he."

(Percy hits the hang up button on the conference phone disconnecting the call. Carla's teammates in the conference room look around at each other speechless).

(Percy takes a deep breath). "Wow. I guess this meeting is adjourned."

"Um...yes...I'll send out notes. Hmm..." (Tristan is dumbfounded). "Well, I gotta go." (Folks leave the meeting room stunned by what they just heard).

(Carla and Derek are lying in bed next to each other talking about how wonderful their lovemaking was).

"Baby, I am so glad you came over today. I really needed to see you." (Carla perks up). "I got my protein shot and a serious ass waxing! Damn! What more could a girl ask for?"

"Ha, ha, ha. Any time, baby. You know I only want to please you."

"And that you do really well. He, he, he." (Carla notices that there is no one speaking on the phone). "Hey, why is the call playing the wait music until the conference host comes on? Interesting. Well I guess they just ended the meeting and didn't let me know."

(Derek and Carla laugh).

"That's a strong possibility, baby."

(Carla presses speaker button to hang up the phone without realizing the phone was off mute). "Well, that's the only call I had today. Let's get cleaned up and go take in a movie."

"Sounds good to me."

(Carla and Derek spend all weekend together. Carla feels really refreshed as she goes to work Monday morning. Carla greets Amber on the way to her office). "Good morning Amber!"

(Amber stares at Carla without responding as she passes by. Carla stops before reaching her office door to figure out why Amber didn't respond to her). "I said, Good morning, Amber!"

"Oh... oh, I'm sorry, Carla. I must have been daydreaming."

"Oh, ok. No problem. I just felt like some folks were staring at me in a strange way as I walked in. Almost like I had the plague! And then you were looking the same way. I'm calling out your name and nothing. I mean, what is it?"

(Amber with a big smirk on her face). "Well, you sure you want to know?"

"Want to know what?"

"About the looks?"

"Yes, I am absolutely sure!"

"Well, you remember the conference call yesterday?"

"Uh huh."

"Well, apparently, you took your phone off mute after Tristan asked..."

"What! Are you saying I wasn't on mute for..." (Carla face is flustered). "You mean you could hear..."

"Yes! Everything!"

"Oh my God! Oh my God!" (Carla's heart starts pumping rapidly). "What did Tristan...what did the team say?"

"Actually, nobody said anything. They were all speechless. I was too. I'm sorry, Carla, but that was some hot shit!"

"Oh shit! Oh damn! I...I gotta leave. Please forward all my calls. I'm taking the rest of the day off! Fuck! I could get...I gotta go!"

"Don't sweat it, Carla. You were technically off work and at your home. So..."

"Oh my God! I am so embarrassed. I'm sorry, Amber." (Carla starts walking quickly to the elevators).

"Ok, Carla. Try to have a good day. Don't worry. I'll take care of your schedule." (Carla frantically pushes the elevator close door button). "Thanks, Amber." (Carla looks down to conceal her face as much as she can as the elevator door closes).

Chapter 3

Meeting in the Ladies Room

"How is it going today Leah?"

"Oh, just fine Mej."

"You look like you got something on your mind."

"No, no, no." (Standing next to her office window and looking down at cars passing by). "I just can't wait to get out of this office." (Turning around to face Mej). "I am so ready to just exhale and let my hair down!"

"Wow! You must have something big planned for later on, Ms. Thang?"

"As a matter of fact, I do! Several of the girls from the Greenville office are coming in today and we are going to that new jazz restaurant on Main Street. Ummm, I think it's called Lena's."

"That sounds really nice. Hmmm, when did it open?"

"Oh, it's been open for about two weeks now."

"Well, I hope you girls enjoy yourself."

"Oh for sure..." (Looking straight into Mej's eyes). "Hmmm, why don't you come out and hang with us, Mej?"

"Oh no way!" (Shaking his head). "And be a third wheel? No. I think I'll pass this time, Leah."

(Come on now. Bring your fine chocolate ass out! All I need is to get your ass out and your ass is going to hit this pussy! I been watching your ass for months. Fuck! If we weren't in the office, I would bend over my desk and throw this skirt up and have you push that dick all up in this ass! Hell, I didn't wear any panties and this pussy is already moist just talking to you...).

(Placing his hands on Leah's shoulder) "Leah!...Leah!"

"Oh...uh...yes, Mej?"

(Waving his fingers in Leah's face). "Come back to us, come back to Earth."

(Cum in my muthafuckin mouth niggah!) "Oh, I'm so sorry. I was just thinking about going down to the cafeteria for a choco, I mean Chico-stick. What were we talking about?"

(Placing both hands on his head). "Your girls night out. Duh!"

"Yes, oh yeah! Come on Mej, you got to come! It'll be a really nice time."

"Well..."

"Come on, the girls from Greenville are fine! And this one named Twalla, oh my God! The ass on her, you can bounce a quarter off that ass!"

"You act like you might like..."

"Don't even go there! I have no problem giving a woman props when she looks good."

"Yeah, you're right, I was just kidding." (A big sigh) "Ok, ok then, Leah, I'll come by and at least meet my coworkers." (With a smirk on his face). "I remind you, this is strictly for professional networking. Hmmm...I do have a need for a quarter bouncing apparatus..."

"Ha, ha! You are too silly!"

"Well, I'm just saying..."

"Ok, crazy, well we will be there around 8:30."

"Sounds good, Leah, see you then."

(Leah's phone rings). "Leah Strom speaking."

(Mocking Leah in man's voice) *"Leah Strom speaking."*

"What! Who is...Twalla! Stop playing around, girl!"

"Ha, ha, ha! Girl, I always get you with that one."

"Whatever! I knew it was you."

"Yeah right! You know I got you. Go ahead and admit it!"

"Ok, ok. Yeah, you threw me off a little. Ha, ha, ha. Anyway, what time are you girls getting here?"

"Well...we're already here!"

"What? You must have left the office early."

"Yeah we did. We took some extra time last night to finish up some things for our meetings in hot-lanta! We couldn't wait to get down here, girl."

"Shoot! I need to hurry up and get out of here then."

"No rush. We still have to check into our hotel. And you know we got to shower and change before we go out. You know we got to be fly and represent in the ATL!"

"Ha, ha, ha. How could I forget? Ms. Twalla is got to be on point. No matter if you are cleaning the house or the yard..."

"Stop it, girl! You know I ain't that bad...ok...well maybe. Ha, ha, ha."

"That's what I thought. Um hum. So who all came down with you?"

"Oh, three other sisters from the IT department. Barbara, Georgette and Renee..."

"Hmmm. I don't think I met them before."

"Well they all are cool. You'll like them. They like to chill when we off work and take care of business when we on the job."

"Ok, that sounds good. I know if they're your friends, then they're already cool with me. Are they married?"

"All single, girl! They all looking to see what's up with the brother's in the "A"!"

"Oh really? Well, there should be plenty at the Lena's jazz café I told you about."

"Oh yeah! I read some of the reviews online. Looks like a real cool spot."

"Yeah it is. Actually, I have a frie..." (Oh no girl! I better not tell them hungry bitches about Mej. That's all mine!) "I mean, there should be a lot of guys there. So you girls should have a nice time."

"Um hum. You're up to something, Ms. Strom."

"Who me? No, girl. Not at all."

"Yeah right. I know when..."

"Anyway, what time are we meeting down at the café?"

"Well, we just pulled into valet parking at our hotel. So after we check in...ummm...I think we'll be there in about 2 hours."

"Perfect! I'm going to wrap things up and head home and get ready as well. Hmmm...how about I pick you all up so that you don't have to worry about getting directions?"

"Girl, you know that's fine with me. It's been a while since I been down here. And you know the landmarks have probably changed..."

"Oh yes, I know. You drive by landmarks! Ha, ha, ha."

"Is there any other way?"

"Yes! But never mind. I'll pick you guys up around 7:30."

"Cool. We will see you then."

"Ok, I will...wait, wait! What hotel are you guys staying at? Ha, ha, ha. I might need to know that."

"Ha, ha, ha! Girl, we are at the Exnicious Hotel off of West Peachtree Street. We'll be waiting in the lobby."

"No problem, see you then. I will be driving my Lexus SUV."

"Ok. Talk to you later." (Twalla hangs up the phone).

(Leah and her co-workers are sitting at the back table in Lena's jazz café having drinks). "Twalla, do you hear that! Oh, girl that is my jam. That cut is so damn smooth!"

"Oh yeah. Najee is definitely one of my favorite jazz artists. I am gl–"

"Whew! Jazz makes me so damn hot! Oh, did I say that out loud? Ha, ha, ha."

"Leah you are so crazy, girl, but this is a nice spot! Thank you for showing us what life in the ATL is all about girl."

"Oh don't even mention it."

"Well, you know Greenville doesn't have anything like this! This is really, really nice."

"And the men, oh my God! The brothers up in..."

(Twalla turns to her left in shock as she responds to Renee). "I know I didn't just hear what I think I heard!"

(Renee laughs and smiles). "Ha, ha, ha."

"Oh, cat got your tongue! You know that you never say anything about men."

(In a defiant voice). "Well, just because I don't mention anything, doesn't mean I'm not getting..."

"Whoa, whoa, whoa! TMI! TMI!"

"Too much information!"

(They laugh).

"Soooo...what about the men here?"

"What do you mean?"

"Like, I mean are they friendly? Stuck up? Or what?"

"Well, I think they're actually pretty cool. I mean they ain't gonna walk up to you and give their resume, but they will definitely holla."

"Yeah, they'll definitely do that. When I went to the ladies room, I got stopped twice on my..."

"Shut up, Twalla! You don't count. You know why they were hollin at you."

"But..."

"Twalla!"

"But..."

"Twalla! Go on with that!"

"But come on, Renee. Can't I have a nice personality?"

"Yeah, but I'm just saying."

"Ha, ha, ha. Well momma always said, 'We got to use what we got, to get what we want!'"

"I heard that. Ha, ha, ha. Stop hating, Renee. You know the bitch got ass!"

"Yeah, I know. Shit just ain't fair!"

(The table laughs).

"Anyway...Leah, did you invite anybody from the office? Uh...like, men!"

"As a matter of fact I did. I told one of the guys I knew to invite some of his boys (bitch you are lying...). "I don't know if he's coming, but if he comes through I'll invite them over and get a bigger table."

"All right then! I hope that niggah comes through..." (Renee licking her lips). "...with his boys!

(Yes, I do. I really hope he does). "We'll see. I told him we would be through around 8:30." (Leah looks down at her watch.) "Hmm...we got about...15 minutes."

"Ok, girl. In the meantime, I'm going to get my drink on!"

"Sounds good to me."

"Waiter?" (The waiter stops to take their drink orders. Leah keeps turning her head looking across the room for Mej.) (Damn! Where is he?)

"Leah?...Leah?"

"What?"

"What are you drinking?"

"Oh, oh. Just get me an Amaretto sour." (Leah looks around gain for Mej. She grabs her glass to take a sip of water and almost chokes as sees Mej come in the door.) (Finally! His tall, fine, chocolate ass gets here. What the! All right you little ho-stess bitch! Stop all your damn flirting. That niggah is taken...oh shit! I can see his smile all the way from here. Unnh! Shit!)

(Leah closes her legs tighter).

(My pussy is on fire! His fucking smile starts my shit to flowing. Damn...).

"Girl what's up with you!"

(Choking and stuttering)

Cough! Cough!

"Umm...uh...nothing."

"Nothing my ass. You act like you seen a ghost or something."

(Oh no! This mutha fucka real!...I hope they didn't see him.)

(Gaining her composure.) "Oh, I wanted to intr... (Fuck that! I am not introducing these ho's to that fine ass niggah! Every bitch for herself!).

(Leah tries to throw off Twalla and the girls by keeping and eye on Mej and turning back to them periodically). (Ok, I don't think they saw him...good! He sat at the bar.) "Oh, I just had something stuck in my, my throat."

(In disbelief). "Right...whatever you say, girl. Did you think we were born yesterday? You up to something."

"No seriously, I'm good. I just had the water go down the wrong way." (Taking a deep breath. I got to get over there without these bitches knowing). "Umm... I'll be back." (Pretending to still be choking).

Cough! Cough!

(Leah stands up covering her mouth with a napkin). "I'll be back."

Cough!

"I going to run to the ladies room."

"Ok, girl, you ok?"

Cough!

"Yes."

"We will be right here then. Call me if you need any help?"

"Thanks."

Cough! Cough!

"Oh, cover my drink with a napkin when it comes."

Cough!

"I'm paranoid about things getting into my drink."

"No problem."

(Leah pushes her chair in and grabs a waitress passing by).

Cough!

"Excuse me? Where is the Ladies room?"

"Oh, just go around the corner of the bar and straight back, first door on your left in the hallway."

"Ok, thanks." (Leah heads to the bar to see Mej. She continually looks back to ensure that the girls don't see her.)

"Good. They shouldn't be able to see me now."

(Leah stops at the opposite end of the bar as Mej looks off towards the door and around the room looking for her).

(Look at him sitting at the bar looking all GQ with one foot on the bar stool and one on the floor. All dignified with one hand sitting on his knee. Unh! Damn that shit turns me on! I didn't think I could get any wetter tonight. Shit! Un, un, unh! I'm bringing my best... Oh, wait a minute girl! That is just naughty.)

(Leah looks on at Mej with a devilish grin.)

(Ha, ha, ha. You are one trifling, nasty bitch...and I love it!)

(Leah walks toward Mej's end of the bar. Mej is looking away as she approaches. As he turns and recognizes Leah, Leah traps his hand on his knee with her pussy and gives him a big hug).

"Hi, Mej!" (As she leans in closer). "I'm glad you could make it!"

(Stuttering and afraid to move his hand). "No...no...th-ank you! This spot...is real-ly n-n-ice! (Taking a deep breath.) Whew! It's really good to see you! (What the fuck! Does this girl know my hand is directly on her pussy! She has to fucking know! I can feel her silky fine pussy hairs. Yep...yep...she don't have on panties!)

(Leah continues to hug Mej and knows he is about to burst in to flames. She squeezes tighter, enjoying every second as he tries to figure a way out.)

(In a seductive voice). "I'm glad you like the spot, Mej." (Soft moan) "Hmmm...you smell so good, Mej."

(Oh fuck! I'm done. A sexy voice is my weakness. My dick is hard as a rock! Are you kidding me! Do I like the spot! I have a juicy...ok...ok...try and hold it together). "Thank you, Leah. You smell really good as well."

"Thank you, Mej." (Leah releases her hug but keeps his hand trapped with her pussy).

(Mej is at a loss for words so he just compliments Leah on her appearance. He tries to avoid eye contact to conceal his nervousness). "You really look nice tonight, Leah. You smell so good."

(Leah lets Mej's hand go free). "Thanks...ha, ha, ha. Again. You seem a little nervous, Mej? Are you ok?"

(Shaking his head signifying yes while looking around). "Yes, yes. Oh yeah, I'm fine."

(Leah glances down between Mej's legs and see a clearly defined bulge in his pants.)

(Mmmm...that looks real tasty. I can see the head and the shaft clearly. Oh yeah, nice size.)

(Licking her lips) "Oh my! What do we have here?"

(Mej wants to close his legs to conceal his hard on but Leah is standing in between them. He starts sweat and fidget with is collar.) "Is the AC on in here? It's getting a little hot!"

"Ha, ha, ha! You are so funny, Mej. You know why you got hot."

"Yeah I do."

"Well let me get closer and ask you something." (Whispering). "Did you like the feel of that juicy, hot, wet pussy?"

"Oh yeah, it felt so damn good!" (I knew she did it on purpose). "Wow! You did that on purpose?"

"Oh yeah, baby." (Looking directly into his eyes). "I've been looking for this opportunity for several months."

"Damn, I didn't have a clue. You are so unassuming."

"Oh little ol' me?" (Slight chuckle). "He, he, well...when you know what you want, you go for it."

"That's for damn sure! Shit! I was about to cum on myself just sittin here."

"Oooh, oooh. Don't waste that precious cum like that."

(Mej clears his throat). "So, umm, what do you have in..."

(Putting her hand up to his mouth).

(In a soft voice). "Shhhh, shhh, baby. You wanna feel this pussy again don't you?"

(Mej nods and puts his hand on his knee waiting for Leah to hug him as she did before).

"Oh no, baby, not like that. I want that hand all up in this pussy. Turn towards the bar so no one can see."

(Leah scoots in beside Mej). "Give me your hand." (Leah slightly lifts the front of her skirt while facing the bar. She pulls Mej's hand directly on top of her pussy). "You feel that?"

"Damn! You don't have on any panties! I knew you..."

"Give me your finger."

"Oh shit, that is so hot and juicy!"

"Move it in and out. Unnh!...Unnh!...Oh that feels so good, Mej."

"Oh my God, Leah, I'm as hard as a diamond drill bit."

"Umm!" (Leah eyes start to stretch as she enjoys Mej's finger in her pussy). "You want to fuck this pussy don't you?"

"Hell yeah!"

"You want to slide that dick in and out of this pussy."

"Oh Lawd yes!"

"Lets get out of here, Leah and go back to my place. I want you so bad, baby."

"Oh that sounds nice. But you know I got my girls here."

"Oh shit! That's right. Damn! I guess we can meet after..."

"Hmmm! I got something even better." (Leah pulls Mej's hand from her skirt and stands up to lead him towards the ladies bathroom). "Come on. Follow me."

"Where we going?"

"Just come on."

(Leah and Mej are standing in the hallway in front of the bathrooms). "Stand right here while I check the bathroom."

"But...but..."

"Hold on, I'll be right back."

(Damn, I can't believe I am contemplating fucking in the women's bathroom. Fuck it! Leah is fine as hell and that pussy is hot like fire!)

(Leah stands at the door of the ladies bathroom with it slightly open. She leans out and waves Mej the come in). "Ok, Mej. Come on. The coast is clear."

(Mej continues to look around for any one coming). "Come on! Hurry!"

(Mej hurries into the bathroom. His heart is running like a car engine. He paces back and forth near Leah.) "Whew! I cant fucking believe this. Damn!"

"Calm down, baby. Look, nothing to worry about. See? The stalls go all the way down to the floor and they lock from the inside."

"I'm still nervous as hell!"

"Shhhh! It's all good, baby." (Leah goes into the end stall furthest away from the door. Mej follows but stops short of the door).

"What are you waiting on? Get that dick up in here. Hurry! Before someone comes in!"

(Mej moves into the stall and closes the door behind him. Leah pulled up her skirt and bent over and placed her hands on the handicap rails in the stall).

(In a low voice). "Oh shit! I've died and gone to heaven. Damn your ass is so round and smooth! Unnh! And the pussy lips peeking back at me. Shining and glistening with pussy juice all over them." (Mej reaches down and wipes her pussy with his full hand).

"Ummmmm....oh shit, that feels good!"

(Mej places his whole hand in his mouth and licks her pussy juice off them). "And it tastes good too! Damn, your pussy tastes good. (Getting goose bumps. Oh shit. I have to be honest. I may not last 30 seconds up in that shit. But I gots to have it).

"Lock the door. Hurry up! Pull that dick out and hit this ass!" (Mej quickly fumbles with unbuckling his belt. His dick is so hard that he pushes it down in order to slide his pants down). "Oh my goodness! My pussy is throbbin! I need to feel that dick inside me."

"Yeah baby. I'm ready for that pussy." (Leah looks back and grabs Mej's dick).

"Oh yeah! Damn, that is a nice, phat dick."

"Ooooh...ohhhh..." (Looking towards the ceiling). "Oh damn. Your soft hands." (Mej reaches out to feel Leah's ass). Your soft ass. Soft pussy. Damn girl! I'm going to explode."

"Oh no. Not yet, baby." (Leah keeps one hand on the rail, turns around, and puts Mej's dick in her mouth).

Slurp!

"Ummmm!"

Slurp!

"Ummm!"

Slurp!

"Oh Leah! Oh Leah! Suck it baby!"

"Ooh, this dick tastes good! Ummm...ummm..."

Slurp!

"I like..."

Slurp!

"...the way..."

Slurp!

"...your dick feels..."

Slurp!

"...In the back of my throat! I can feel each vein with my lips!"

"Shit, baby! This feels so good!"

Slurp!

"Ummmm!"

(Leah pulls Mej's dick out of her mouth).

"Oh my pussy gets so hot when I suck a good dick! Unnnh!"

(In a loud voice). "Oh hell yeah! Girl, that feels so damn good!"

(In a low but slightly concerned voice). "Keep it down, Mej. Someone might come in!"

"I don't really give a fuck right now!"

"Damn! You just made my pussy so fucking hot! I love that rough talking shit!"

"Oh you do, huh! Well, turn your ass around and get ready to ride this dick!"

"Ummm!"

(Leah flips her skirt up and places her hands on the rails in the bathroom stall). "Oh shit! You think you can handle this pussy?"

"Oh yeah! I'm about to tear that shit up!"

"You gone beat it like you stole something!" (Leah starts to wiggle her ass and grind in a circular motion). "You going to cum all up in it!"

"Hell yeah!" (Leah reaches back and grabs Mej's dick and pushes the head into her pussy and pulls it back out). "Unnnh! Damn, that pussy is hot!"

"You sure you want that?"

"Fuck yeah!"

"You promise to cum all up in it!"

(Heavy breathing). "Yes, I promise."

"Well say, 'I want to cum all in Leah's...'" (Mej removes Leah's hand from his dick and rams his dick inside her pussy).

"Unnnnh! Oh shit, niggah! Unnnhh!" (Mej reaches down and grabs a hand full of Leah's hair). "Unnnhh! Oh, Mej! That dick feels so good! Unnnnhh!"

"Whew! Fuck! Girl this pussy is good as hell! Unnnh! Unnh!"

"Oh shit, smack my ass! Smack!"

"Oh yeah! Unnnh! Oh shit! I love the way you pull my hair! Unnnh! Unnnh! Pull that shit out!"

"Oh, baby! I'm about to cum, baby! I can't hold it anymore!"

"Unnnh!" (Between breaths). "Let that shit go niggah! I'm bout to cum too."

(Rapid thrusts).

"Unnnh!"

Plop!

"Unnh!"

Plop!

"Unh!"

Plop!

"Cum all up in this pussy!"

(The bathroom door suddenly swings open. Two women are talking as they come in. Mej and Leah stop in the middle of a thrust. They both cover their mouths trying to muffle any sound. Mej begins to hold his breath to stop himself from cumming).

(Both girls are standing at the sink fixing themselves up at the sink.) Girl, did you see that crazy-looking guy with those tight purple jeans on with matching shirt and shoes?"

"Ha, ha, ha! Hell yeah. What in the fuck was he thinking?"

"I know. He came up to me talking about, 'Let me buy you drink sweety pie.'"

"What!"

"Yeah, some old tired shit like that. Talking about, 'I can see myself marrying you baby.'"

"Girl you lyin!"

"No, I'm not. Ha, ha, ha!"

"Marrying you? He must be drunk as hell."

"You got that right."

(In a barely audible voice, Mej covers his mouth and tells Leah that he is about to cum).

"I am about to cum baby! I can't hold it! I'm trying! Oh shit!" (Mej cums so hard in Leah's pussy that she cums at the same time. Mej's stomach muscles tighten as he grabs one of the rails to keep his balance. Leah feels the tight grip on her hair weaken as Mej fights to stay on his feet while his dick throbs from cumming inside of her).

(A muffled scream).

"Unnnnnnnnh! Oooh! Oooh!" (Leah fights to keep her body still to avoid aftershocks from cumming so hard). (Please don't move! Don't move...Ohhhhhh...)

"Unnhhh!"

(One of the ladies turns to the other and looks back at the stalls). "Did you hear that?"

"Yeah, it sounded like someone grunting and screaming." (Mej and Leah stay perfectly still with his dick still inside Leah's pussy).

"Shhh! Must be the stall on the end; it's the only one that's fully closed." (Placing her hand to her mouth and tip-toeing to the end stall).

"Are you ok in there?"

(Leah responds breathing hard). "Oh...yeah! Thank you. Something from dinner didn't agree with me."

"I definitely understand, girl. Sorry to bother you. Just wanted to make sure you were ok."

"No...thank you very much. I appreciate it."

"Ok then. Glad you're ok." (The two women continue their conversation and leave the bathroom).

(As soon as the door closes, Mej pulls his dick and uses his hand to catch and cum dripping from Leah's pussy). "Hey, give me some tissue."

"For what?" (Leah bends over and quickly sucks every drop of cum off of Mej's dick and hand).

"Ooooh! Ooooh! Ooooh! Oh my goodness! I guess I don't need any tissue."

(Leah wipes herself off and fixes her clothes. Mej pulls up his pants and switches places with Leah).

"Ok, stay in here. I'm going to check to see if anyone is coming. When I signal for you, just come right out and go directly into the men's bathroom."

"Ok, babe. Got it."

(Leah looks around outside the door and beyond the hallway for anyone coming. She rushes back to let Mej know that it's all clear).

"Baby! Come on!" (Mej rushes out in the hall way. Leah starts to walk back out to the table when she feels a tug on her arm).

(Mej turns Leah around and brings her close to his chest and begins to kiss her).

"Thank you, Leah."

"Oh, my pleasure, Mej."

"I don't think I'm going to meet your friends tonight. Whew! You got me weak girl. And you know, I don't even care about that. I'm taking my ass home to sleep."

(Blushing). "Ha, ha, ha! You are just saying that Mej."

"Oh no, baby. I can't wait to see you again. I will definitely be calling you. I just didn't know. But I know now."

"Um hum...well, I will be waiting for your call, Mej." (Leah turns and rubs her ass on Mej's dick).

"Oh shit, girl! Don't play."

(They both laugh).

"Ok, baby. Let me get back to the girls. I'll see you later."

"Ok, baby. See you." (Mej goes to the men's bathroom to check himself over and heads home. Leah returns to the table with the girls).

(All the girls peer at Leah as she approaches the table).

"Where have you been, heifer!"

(With a wide grin). "Oh my, what harsh words!"

"Harsh my ass! Yo ass been gone for a long time. We were about to send out a search party for your ass."

"Twalla, come on now. I wasn't gone that long. I had to..."

"You wasn't gone that long. You wasn't...girl, it's been..."

"I just couldn't stop coughing. And then I had to fix my make-up and take care of a wardrobe malfunction."

(Rolling her eyes in disbelief). "Oh really...a wardrobe malfunction? (A sarcastic laugh). "Ha, ha, ha. So...did you get it fixed?"

(With a devilish smirk). "Umm hum! Most certainly." (In ways you will never know).

Chapter 4

Health Nut

"Thirteen!"

(Rapid urging).

"Come on, come on, come on! Fouuurteeeen! Push it!" (Ryan leans in closer with his fists clinched urging her to push).

"Puuuuuuussh!"

(Straining voice as she pushes the weight up).

"Arrrrrrrrrrrrrrrrrrrghh!"

"Come on, you can do it! Just one more! Fiffffffffffffffteeeeen!"

"Unh!" (Placing weights at rest and exhaling) "Pssst! Psst! Whew! Damn! That was tough!" (Long exhale). "Psssssssssssssst! Hey!" (Ryan turns around). "Thanks for pushing me."

"Oh, no problem. I knew you could do it." (Smiling). "Sometimes a little push is all you need."

(Extending her hand and standing up from the seated bench press machine). "Yeah, I see that. Oh, I'm Frenchie by the way."

(Hesitating and then putting his hand out). "Oh...excuse my manners, I'm Ryan."

(With an inviting smile). "Nice to meet you, Ryan."

"Oh my pleasure!" (Shifting his eyes down to the small bead of sweat trickling down from Frenchie's neck into her breast cleavage. Ryan continues to shake her hand as if in a trance).

(Frenchie likes the attention but starts to pull her hand free). "Yes...uh...very nice to meet you. Thank you. Can I have my..."

"Oh, oh! I'm sorry. I must have been day-dreaming."

"Ha, ha, ha. To say the least. It's no problem."

"Good, good. Hmmm...Frenchie...interesting..."

"Yes?"

"No, no. I was just thinking...I mean a very interesting name..."

"Oh, ok..."

"Never actually knew anyone with your name. It's actually really cute." (Actually it's really sexy! Damn! Her ass is fine).

(In a soft, girlish voice). "Thank you, Ryan." (You ain't slick brotha. I saw you all in my breasts. Ha, ha. Well, you ain't half bad yourself). "Ha, ha, ha."

"So, are you new around here? I come in the gym five times..."

"Yeah. This is actually my first week. I used to work as a patent attorney for Mary Magdalene."

"Oh wow! That's a huge tobacco company. They have a lot of really interesting products."

"Yes they do. But...I felt like sometimes we just had too many. I felt like we were losing focus."

"Oh really? Was that the reason you left?"

"It was a part of it, but I just felt it was time for a change."

"Hmmm, I can feel you on that...so how do you like it here so far?"

"I really like it a lot. The work has been exciting and very challenging." (Smiling). "You know, I actually enjoy work much more now."

"Yep. I can see that."

"Also, I like the work flexibility and the opportunity to move into new areas."

"All right then. Can't blame you on that. I like a woman that knows what she wants." (Looks at the clock on the wall). "Oh, I'm sorry. I'll let you get back to your workout Ms. Frenchie. Ha, ha."

"Oh, no rush. I enjoyed the chat. Actually, I appreciate the stall. Ha, ha, ha."

"I did as well." (Ryan bends down to pick up Frenchie's bottle of water to hand to her).

(Grabbing her water and smiling). "Oh, thanks for that, Ryan. It was really nice to meet you."

"You too, Frenchie. See you around." (Ryan doesn't move as he watches Frenchie walk across the gym floor). (Ummm...that Frenchie is really sexy...shit! Perfect ass and pefect tits, whew! I wonder if she's married or has a boyfriend. I didn't see a ring, but that doesn't mean she didn't leave it in the dressing room. Unnh! What am I thinking? She can't be single looking that fine...).

(Ryan gets a tap on the shoulder). "Excuse me?... Excuse me? Can I get to the machine, bruh?"

"Oh, oh. I'm sorry. Yeah, yeah. No problem, dog."

"Thanks, man." (Ryan moves out of the way of the seated bench press and goes to the free weight bench press).

(Ryan continues to fixate on Frenchie from across the room). (Un, unh! Damn that black cat suit is screaming! Meoooooooowww! I would tear...what the fuck! Oh hell! Don't do it! Don't do it! Yeah baby, bend that ass over. Stretch it out! Touch those toes!...Unh!).

(Under his breath). "Damn, that ass is juicy. That pink leotard going down the center of her ass..." (Putting the side of his fist to his mouth). "Oh my goodness! I should just walk up behind that ass and grab those hips and slide this dick in! Unnnh! Nice and slow...ha, ha. I wonder if she would mind..."

(Frenchie catches Ryan staring at her). "Damn! Busted!"

(Ryan quickly turns to continue his workout).

(Um hum...caught yo ass looking. Ha, ha. I seen you all up in this ass when I bent over. Men...fucking men! So damn simple! Ha, ha. Well, not that simple. I guess I did bend over purposely when I saw you facing this way).

(Frenchie watches Ryan as he completes a set on the bench press. She starts to stare at his crotch as he lies down on the bench. She starts to do bicep curls with the 5 lb weights to pretend as if she'sn't looking at Ryan).

(Mmmmm...not bad, not bad. You have a nice package there, Mr. Ryan. I should walk over there and straddle your ass and ride you off into the sunset. Unnh!).

(Licking her lips). "Yeah...we gonna be fuckin' soon...real soon. (Frenchie places the weights back on the rack and decides to walk over by Ryan to give him a little more to think about.)

(Hell! What do I have to lose? I can tell he's definitely interested. I haven't fucked in 2 weeks! That's too long for me. I really just need a good nut! All this damn moving...arrrrrrrrrrrrrrgh!)

(Frenchie stands directly in front of Ryan's head as he struggles to push up 300 lbs of weights. She pulls up the tops of her leotard tighter to emphasize the "camel toe" formed by her pussy through her clothing. Ryan doesn't notice her until he rests the weights on the bench bar catch. Ryan's eyes bulge as he notices nothing but pussy staring him in the face.)

(Clearing his throat after sounding squeaky). "Hieeeee...uh, uh, uh ummm. I mean, hi, Frenchie." (Damn, damn, damn! Look at that phat ass pussy! Please sit down on my face, please! I ain't movin. Fuck it!)

(Ryan lets out a sigh while dropping his arms to the floor to show Frenchie he just needs to rest for a second before getting up).

"Whew!" (Ryan continues to look up at Frenchie's pussy as in a trance.)

"What! I know you ain't tired lifting that little bit of weight. Ha, ha, ha. I know you can do better than that. My grandma could...Ryan!...earth to Ryan. Did you hear what I said?"

"Oh, oh. Uh, um. Hi, Frenchie. I must have been daydreaming or something. I apologize. What did you say?"

"I was saying," (Yeah, I know what your ass was dreaming about), "that you can't be tired from lifting..."

"That little bit of weight? Ha, ha!" (Ryan comes to a sitting position). "See I told you I was listening."

"Rigggggght! I think I have an idea of what you were you thinking about." (I think you were like will she sit that juicy pussy on this face. Ha, ha.)

"Actually, I was thinking about my 9 AM meeting."

"Oh, I see. Mr. Workaholic is always thinking about work. Hmm...I guess that is the way to be successful around here, huh?"

"Naw, baby...sorry, I mean it ain't nothing special."

"Oh please." (Pulling on a strand of her hair). "It's ok Ryan. No harm done. But I say that about you since folks have told me how fast you've moved up the company."

"If you want to call it that."

"Geez, you are so modest."

"Ok, ok. You're right. I'm proud of my accomplishments. I thank you for that." (Ryan stands to his feet and places one hand on the end of the weight lifting bar. He thinks if they finish up soon, they could perhaps do breakfast to get to know one another better). "So...French. Are you about done working out?"

"Nope. Not just yet. I was headed into the aerobics room in a few to work my abs."

(Looking down at her stomach). "What work? You have a damn six-pack, girl!"

(Blushing). "Ha, ha, ha. Thank you, thank you. But, I have to keep it this way."

"True that, true that."

"Did you have something in mind?"

"In mind? Oh. Oh nothing important. Just thought maybe we could do breakfast."

"Oh that sounds really good. Give me 15 minutes and I'll be ready to go."

"Sounds great. I got a few leg lifts to do and I'll be waiting out here for you."

"Great. Be back in a few." (Frenchie starts to slowly walk by Ryan as she heads for the aerobics room. She stops and purposely turns as looking at the clock making Ryan's forearm rub her ass coincidentally). "Hmmm...it's 7:45. Ok...see you at 8:00."

(Stuttering). "Um...O, O, O, Ok then." (Wiping his forehead as she walks into the aerobics room). "What the fuck! That ass was soft as a mutha-fucka! How in the hell am I suppose to do leg lifts after that!"

(Walking towards the leg lift machine, Ryan sets the weight at 200 lbs). "Screw this man! I can't concentrate after that. I'm going back there to check her out. Hell! I got to say something to her. She being new, you know somebody is going to jump on that with the quickest. The girl is stacked. Again, I have nothing to lose." (Ryan picks up his towel and water and heads for the aerobics room).

(Ryan sees Frenchie in the mirror doing crunches as he walks through the door to the aerobics room. He sets his towel and water bottle in the corner next to Frenchie's gear). "Hi French! How's it going?"

(Breathing hard as she keeps doing crunches). "I'm on..." (Exhale), "my second set..." (Exhale), "of crunches."

"Oh ok. Don't stop. I just wanted..."

(Large exhale) "Whew! Oh, you need something?"

"No, no. I just didn't want you to get out of here without getting your information." (Ok. I'm lying. I just want to admire your fine ass).

"Oh really! Ha, ha. One!" (Frenchie begins her third set of crunches).

(Exhale) "Two!" (Exhale) "Don't worry..." (Exhale) "I won't..." (Exhale) "leave..." (Exhale) "Six!"

(Frenchie finishes her third set of crunches. She continues to lie on her back looking over at Ryan who counted her every repetition).

(Breathing hard) "Whew! That felt good."

"That felt good? Ha, ha, ha. I see how you keep it all together."

"Yeah. You can get nothing out if you don't put nothing in." (Frenchie climbs to her feet slowly pushing herself up).

"Well, I can't argue with that." (Ryan tilts his head in wonder as he looks at Frenchie). "Hey, um...didn't you have on a leotard in the weight room?"

"Ha, ha, ha. Yes I did. You are very observant."

"Well... Frankly, it was hard not to notice. I mean all I can say is Dayumn!"

"Ha, ha, ha! Ha, ha, ha! That's funny. Well, I just got a little hot and slid it off."

"Oh my goodness! They come off that easy."

"Most certainly. Easy access baby!"

(Oh hell! Why did you go and say some shit like that! I might nut on myself. Be cool man, be cool). "Easy access huh?"

"Oh yeah. For just that reason." (With a devilish grin). "When things get a little hot."

"Ha, ha, ha."

(Frenchie places her arms straight above her head to begin stretching out her body from her work out.) "Ummmmmmmmmmmmm..." (Exhaling). "Unh! I still feel tight in my lower back. Hey Ryan I'm glad you came back here."

"You are?"

"Yes, your timing is perfect. I could use your help to stretch my lower back. Do you mind?"

(Smiling as if he hit the lottery). "Oh, no problem, Frenchie! Just tell me what to do. I'm at your service."

"Ok then. Grab my arms at my wrists. (Frenchie turns her back to Ryan. He grabs both of her wrists leaving some distance between his dick and her juicy ass).

"Like this. That's not too strong?"

"Oh, you hurting me, daddy!"

(Ryan loosens his grip and steps to Frenchie's side while continuing to hold her wrists). "I'm sorry, Frenchie. Is that too much?"

"Ha, ha. You're fine, Ryan. I was just playing around."

"Hah! Girl, stop playing so much."

"Ok, ok. I apologize. As you can see, I can act a little goofy sometimes."

"I'm good. So, what do I need to do now?"

"When I say go, just pull up on my wrists until I say stop."

"Ok Frenchie, that's easy enough."

"Go!"

(Ryan pulls up and notices Frenchie is providing resistance to maximize the stretch). "Oh my! Girl, you're pretty damn strong!"

"Well, I do work out five days a week."

"Oh, I can tell. You look great!"

"Why thank you! Ummmmmmmm....stop!"

"Go!"

(I need to get his ass closer. Need to validate the contents of his package. Ha, ha).

(Damn, her body is so fucking tight. Look at that perfectly sculpted ass just reverberating as she stretches! Mmm, unh! Oh it looks so delicious).

(Frenchie begins to back up onto Ryan as if it is a part of her stretching).

(Let's see what you got, big boy).

(Oh no! Oh no! Please don't back up! Please! Please! Ummmmmmm...Oh my goodness. That ass is so soft! Oh my God).

"Yeah. That's working better. You all right, Ryan?"

(Ryan is trying to keep his composure). "Oh...Umm. Yes." (Is she serious!...No!...Don't do it boy! Don't get hard, don't get hard! Damn!)

"Ok, that's good. Ummmmmmmmmmm..." (Ok then. The dick is nice. Real nice. Mmmmm...nice and hard).

(Fuck it! Too late now! I guess I can't blame you. All of that USDA prime certified rump roast in front of you! I know she feels my dick throbbing against that ass).

(Frenchie slowly winds her ass on Ryan's dick but pretends as if she's continuing to stretch). "Oh yeah. Ummmmmmmmmmm! That feels real good. I haven't been stretched like this in a while."

(Ryan is about to explode. He can't believe Frenchie hasn't said anything about his dick poking her in the ass).

(Fuck this. She has to know. I going to see what's up).

(In a deep voice) "Hey, French, are you starting to feel more relaxed?"

"Oh yeah. I'm definitely getting there."

"Good, good...well, put your arms down. Let's try something a little different."

"Ok." (Go for it niggah). "Be my guest."

(Ryan starts to massage Frenchie's shoulders while keeping his dick on her ass.) "You feel that?"

(Deeply inhaling). "Ohhhhhh yeeeeeeeah. That feels really good, Ryan."

"Good. Let's get all that stress and tightness out...just relax..." (Breathing in deeply). "Sssssssss...yeah, there you go. You're loosening up, baby."

"Ooooooooooh!" (Oh my goodness! My pussy is getting so moist!). "That feels so good. Ummmmmmmm...you have very strong hands. Unnnnhh...I hope you don't mind the sweat."

"Baby. I hope you don't mind me calling you baby."

"I love it, Ryan. Don't stop."

"Good, baby, good. I didn't even notice any sweat." (Ryan bends over and licks the sweat off the back of Frenchie's neck—a slow, long lick with the tip of his tongue). "Mmmmmmmmm...yeah that's what I'm talking about."

(Frenchie gets goose bumps and chills down her spine) "Woooo, wooooo, wooooo...oh shit boy! That's my spot! Damn that's my spot. Ummmmmmmmmmm..."

(Ryan looks around to see if anyone is coming. There appears to be no one near them. Ryan works his hands down Frenchie's biceps to her hips. Massaging gently all the way down).

"Ummmmmmmmmm...that's it. Ummmmmmmmmmm...work those hands, baby."

"Oh you like that, huh?" (Ryan squats down with Frenchie's ass in his face. He begins rubbing her lower back and then finally that juicy ass).

(Large exhale). "Wooooooooooo...girl, this ass! This ass right here! Oh my goodness. Damn! It is so fucking soft!" (Ryan slide his hands in between Frenchie's, thighs rubbing from there down to her ankles).

"Umm...umm...oh shit! Please don't stop. Unnnh! My pussy is on fire!" (Frenchie can't take it anymore. She grabs Ryan's hands and pushes it up against her pussy). "Unnnh! Grab that shit niggah! Unnnh!"

(Ryan can't believe what's happening.) "Damn! This pussy is so wet!" (Ryan comes back to his feet. He notices that Frenchie's cat suit has only two snaps underneath limiting him from feeling the inside of Frenchie's pussy. Ryan unsnaps the cat suit). "Oh yesssss. There it is. That mutha-fucka is so juicy." (Ryan slides one finger slowly inside Frenchie's pussy).

"Unnnnnnnnnnnnnnnnnnnnh..." (Placing her own fingers in her mouth). "Ummmmmmm...that's what I've been waiting on. Unnnnnnnnh...that's it. Probe that pussy."

(Ryan licks his fingers). "Mmmmm... That pussy tastes good. Shit! I want to taste it."

"Shit! I want you too. But, I gotta have that dick now!" (Frenchie reaches back and grabs Ryan's hard, throbbing dick through his shorts). "That's what I need. Put that shit in!"

"Umm! Fuck girl! I'm about to cum already!"

"I don't fucking care! Just cum in this pussy!" (Breathing hard). "Come on Ryan! It's been..."

(Ryan slides his shorts down while Frenchie wiggles and slides the cat suit up her body revealing her naked ass). "Bend over girl. Touch those toes! Thank you, Jesus. Look at all that ass." (Ryan reaches underneath Frenchie to get a quick taste of Frenchie's pussy on his hand. He licks it off. He then takes his dick and beats on Frenchie's ass like beating on a bass drum).

"Come on niggah! Stop teasing me! You know how I want you to beat this ass! Fuck me niggah! Fuck me until it hurts! Cum all in this pussy!"

(Oh my God! I can't believe this is about to happen).

(Ryan bends slightly to line his dick up with Frenchie's pussy. Frenchie starts to moan and shake slightly with anticipation).

"Unnnnh...oh shit! Come on now!"

(Grabbing the sides of her small waist, Ryan's dick slides right into Frenchie's wet pussy). "Ummmm! Oh shit! This pussy is hot! (Don't move niggah, don't move!)

(Ryan breathing hard and fast). "Woo, woo, woo, woo!"

(I'm about to bust my load! Come on now! Concentrate!)

"Unnnnnnhh! Oh that dick feels good! Ummmm! Push that dick Ryan! Ummmm!"

(Ryan pulls his dick out to keep from cumming. He plays with the outside of her pussy with the head of his dick).

"There we go!" (Large exhale). "Wooooooooo! I'm ready now." (Ryan starts to pull back on Frenchie's waste with long, hard, deep strokes).

"Unnnnnnnh! Yesssss! Unnnnnnnh! Yesssss! Oh hell yes! Unnnnnnh! Beat that shit! Beat it! Unnnnh! That's what I am talking about, daddy! Give mommy what she wants! Unnh!"

(Ryan can't stop admiring Frenchie's perfect ass recoiling with every stroke) "Oh yeah! Sssssssss....yeah baby! Oh, look that ass! Ummm!"

"Fuck your ass niggah! Fuck it!"

"Shhhh! Shhhh! Baby, don't forget we're..."

(In a lower voice). "Right baby, right. Unnnh! Oh this is good! Oh shiiiiiit! I'm about to cum! Keep it right there baby! Keep it right there! Unnnnnh! Oh shittt!"

"Cum baby! Cum baby!"

(Ryan pulls out and pulls up his shorts).

(Whispering) "Baby! Fix your clothes! Someone is coming!" (Ryan walks to the mats to pretend as if nothing was going on).

(Frenchie quickly pulls her cat suit down. As soon as she heads to pick up her things, a group of people enter the aerobics room). "How you guys doing?" (Fidgeting with her towel). "So you guys have class in here?"

"Yeah, we are in the 8:30 aerobics class."

"Oh ok, we'll be getting out of your way. We were just doing some crunches and just finished. You guys have great class."

"Ok, thank you very much."

"Come on, Ryan. Let's get out the way."

(Ryan picks up a mat and carries it out of the room with him). "Ok, just taking this mat back outside the room."

(Frenchie and Ryan stand outside the aerobics room). "Why do you have that mat?"

(Ryan slides the mat down slightly revealing that is dick was still hard). "Now do you see why?"

"Oh wow!" (Loud laughter).

(Some members of the aerobics class look out the door at Frenchie and Ryan to see what was going on and return focus back to the class).

"Shit! I was almost there too. Arrrrrrrrrrrrrrrgh!"

"Shit! I was there from the jump! My dick is still throbbing!"

"Well, only one way to take care of that. I guess we are going to have to..."

"Finish what we started! Hell yeah! You'll be getting an email invite as soon as I get back to my desk for another workout session!"

"Hmmmm...great minds think alike."

"Ha, ha, ha! Oh yeah. Welcome to the company!"

Chapter 5

A Mountain reTreat

(Jackson enters the conference room where Lyn is sitting on the ledge peering through the blinds at cars passing by below). "Hi Lyn, aren't you glad it's Friday?"

"**H**ell yes!" (Releasing the blinds and turning to face Jackson). "This week has been long as fuck! I'm so serious...I mean I was like trying to make the clock hands move..."

"Whoa, whoa, whoa! Tell me how you truly feel! Ha, ha, ha."

"Jackson! Don't laugh." (Slight chuckle). "He, he. I'm serious."

"Ok, ok. I feel you. I was just playing. I can wait to get out of here too...hey! Look at it this way. We have a couple more hours before the weekend and it's off to Mt. Kipwah! I always like the time away from the office to just relax without an email or a text message or anything."

"That's right! I totally agree. I can't wait for the fresh air. Especially sitting out in the hot tub sipping on wine. And..."

(Thinking of Lyn in her bikini the last time they were in the hot tub with there spouses). "Yes, yes. The hot tub. Yeah, that is really relaxing."

"You got me all excited Jackson! Thanks for reminding me about this weekend. It's always fun when Kale and I hang out with you and your wife."

(Looking disgusted) "Arrrrrgh!...I just hope she doesn't dampen the mood with all that negativity and complaining." (In a female voice) "*Why we got to go to the mountains every year? Who wants to be in all those bugs? Wanh! Wanh! Wanh!*"

"Ha, ha, ha! Jackson you're so funny! I believe that's why we work so well together. Don't mind your wife. She'll be fine. She may actually surprise you."

"Well, you're probably right. I'm sure Kale will be his usual bright-eyed and bushy-tail self as well. He, he, he."

"Oh you had to go there."

"Well..."

"Ok, ok. You got me there. Well, I guess we will have to see."

"Yes we will. I guess we have that in common amongst our spouses."

"Yes we do. Oh well, nothing we haven't seen before."

(Jackson and Lyn laugh together).

"You know, Jackson, I wonder if...never mind. (Lyn briefly thinks about how things would be if her and Jackson were a couple).

"What do you mean you wonder?"

"Oh nothing. Really...it was nothing."

"Well, let's just hope for the best—a very quiet and peaceful weekend."

"Amen, brother!"

(Standing at the bottom of the stairs). "Penny! Are you ready?"

(Yelling downstairs). "Give me 5 minutes!"

(Are you kidding me? I gave her 2 damn hours notice and she ain't ready yet? Damn, damn, damn! That's why I hate going places with her. It's the same fucking thing every time!) "Ok, ok. I'll be waiting outside by the truck."

(Irritated) "Good! What is the freakin rush!"

(Under his breath as he opens the front door).

(I am so sick of this shit! Can we go to one place on time? And, it's not like I didn't give her notice).

(The door slams shut as Jackson walks outside).

(Yelling from the top of the stairs) "Stop slamming the freakin' door!" (Penny turns swiftly and goes back in the bathroom to finish getting ready).

(Jackson stops momentarily after Penny's scream, but continues to the truck since he could not make out the sound he heard. Jackson leans against the hood of the truck.)

(Deep sigh) "Whatever. Same ol' shit."

(Jackson grabs his phone to check the last night's high school football scores.)

"Oh my! Mann clobbered Byrnes! I bet Johnson threw for..."

"Ring!" "Ring!"

"Hello? Jackson Siebe."

"Is a punk!"

"Ha, ha, ha. What's up, black!"

"Nothing much big brotha-all-mightee! He, he. I got the family reunion letter today and wanted to know if there was anything else you needed me to do?"

"Naw, girl. It's all good. Just have to wait on folks to send their funds in...on time!"

"Ha, ha, ha. You know our family is going to wait to the last minute."

"Yeah, I know. I was just trying to be optimistic."

"Uh yeah... Right!"

"He, he. You always tell it like it is. Anyway, how are things going with..."

(Penny opens the front door and peeps out tell Jackson she's ready). "Jackson!"

"You and baby 'D.'"

"Jackson!"

"What, Penny!"

"Oh, I know you didn't raise your voice at me!"

(In a low monotone voice) "What, Penny? Hey sis, I got to run. We are headed up to the mountains for a weekend get-away."

"Yes, I heard. You go tend to your lovely wife." (Loud laugh) "Ha, ha, ha!"

"I'm ready. My bags are at the top of the stairs."

"You know you wrong for that girl. I'll talk to you later. Bye."

"See ya." (Jackson and his sister hang up the phone).

(Penny stares at Jackson as he walks toward the house past her to get Penny's bags). "Who was that?"

(Sarcastically) "It was my girlfriend."

"Your what! Don't play with me, Jackson."

"You know that was my sister. Don't trip. Just go to the car. I will be right there."

"You play too damn much."

(Walking up the stairs). "Yeah, yeah, yeah. Is this all?" (Shut your fucking mouth, Jackson, you know that's more argument).

"Is this all? What do you mean is this all?"

"Nothing, nothing. Could you go to the truck, dear?"

(Under her breath) "Um! Whatever Jackson." (Walking out the door). "What is all the God damn rush? Are we running to a fucking fire?" (Big sigh as she plops in the passenger seat of the truck).

(Exhaling) "Puuuuuuh... Here we go. Another exciting adventure." (Twirling her index finer around in the air). "Whoop-dee-do."

(Jackson temporarily puts Penny's bags on the side walk to lock up the front door. He places the bags in the trunk and get's in the truck with Penny).

"All right baby. Are we ready to roll?"

(Non enthusiastic voice). "Yeah, Yeah. Let's go." (In a muffled voice). "What's the fucking rush! They probably won't be there on time anyway!"

"What did you say? "

"Nothing, nothing." (Penny looks out the passenger window shaking her head).

"Oh, it's more than nothing. I know that look. Here we go all ready. The complaints have begun." (Damn it! Shut your mouth Jackson).

"What did you say?"

"I'm glad the Saints won."

"What the fuck ever! You know you didn't say that."

"It's all good baby. Let's just go enjoy our weekend."

"Yeah, whatever."

(Jackson turns the volume up slightly on the radio and backs out the driveway. He sings along with an old cut from the SOS band) .

"As long as I...can be your number one, you still can have your fun..."

(Penny pulls a book out of her purse and starts to read as Jackson shifts the car in drive and heads to Mt. Kipwah)

(Underneath the radio and Jackson's singing) "Hmmm...Relationship Physics: The Science of Marriage. Sounds interesting. Humph! Something Jackson should definitely read. He, he."

(Sound of gravel against the truck tires). "Well shut my mouth!" (Penny slightly startles Jackson).

(Slight wobble in the truck) "Wha...what's wrong!"

"Awe, Jackson! You are such a scaredy cat! I'm just surprised Lyn and Kale are all ready at the cabin. That's definitely a first!"

(Tell her she's right). "That's right, dear. You are so..."

"Like last time we waited forever for them to..."

"Meet us at the beach. Ha, ha, ha. You are so right about that."

"I know I'm right." (Bringing her voice down and covering her mouth from the front). "And what about Kale taking forever to cook those nasty burgers!"

"Yes, honey." (Forcing a slight laugh) "I do remember that."

"Yeah, yeah, and Lyn...she kept talking about that dance club all day."

(Excited) "Oh you mean the Splash and Wave club right on the beach! Yes..."

"What! You act like you liked it. She kept wanting us to go all day! She really gets on my nerve with stuff like that!"

(Turning his head quickly to Penny). "Baby, didn't you think that was fun?"

"Noooooo! I mean...what is fun about it? You have..."

"Don't you think that..."

(Looking at Jackson out the corner of her eye). "Married couples in a club? What can married people do in a club?"

"Well, they can..." (Jackson roll his eyes out of Penny's view. He decides to drop the argument). "Hmmm...I see what you mean, baby." (Just like Lyn and I discussed...a big ball of negativity!)

"And another thing..."

(Cutting her off before she continues). "Ok, ok, baby. We're here."

(Penny gives Jackson a dirty look). "Humph!"

(Jackson ignores Penny's reaction) "Look, look. There's Kale coming from around the side of the cabin." (Jackson hits the auto window switch on the truck door letting his window down as he slowly pulls into the parking space bringing the truck to a stop).

(Kale notices Jackson and Penny's truck. He drops some trash in the dumpster beside the cabin and walks over to the truck and sticks his hand through the window to shake Jackson's hand). "How you doing, bruh?

"I'm good man. It's good to see you."

(Kale places both hands on the windowsill of the truck while standing with a slight bend in his back looking across and acknowledging Penny). "Hello, Penny! How is the boss of the family doing? He, he."

(Penny looks around Jackson and sarcastically responds to Kale). "Ha, ha! I'm blessed and highly favored! I'm just looking forward those fantastic burgers again!"

(Jackson gives Penny a funny look). (What in the world! Why is she getting him started?)

"Ha...ha! You want to go there huh? Those burgers weren't my fault."

"Ha, ha, ha." (Under her breath) "Yeah, whatever. I hope your ass went to cooking class."

"What's that?"

(Jackson jumps in). "It's all good, man."

"Jackson, it's fine. I was just playin' around." (Penny takes a sip of bottled water and asks Kale about Lyn as if nothing happened). "So where is my best girl Lyn?"

(Yeah, where is my girl Lyn).

(Kale is still slightly upset. But decides to drop the conversation). "Well, she should be in the kitchen cooking up her famous baked beans."

"Oh ok. You think she needs any more help?"

"I think she's about done. But I could really use some help setting the table in the back if you don't mind?"

"Oh no. I don't mind at all."

"Good. Come on around back to the grill." (Sarcastically) "I'm just about to take those famous burgers off the grill."

"Ha, ha, ha. Ok, ok Kale. I coming."

(Kale trots around to Penny's door to let her out followed by Jackson getting out of the truck and opening the door to the backseat. Penny gives Kale a hug as she exits the truck). "Good to see you again, Kale."

"You too, Penny."

(Kale looks at Jackson to ensure that it's ok for Penny to help him out) "Ooops! Hey Jackson, is it ok if I borrow her for a minute? Sorry about that."

(Please take her with you). "Oh man, please. You know that ain't a problem."

"Thanks, man. Come on, Penny. Follow me."

"Ok, Kale. Lead the way...Oh, oh, Jackson? Could you drop the items in the backseat at the kitchen?"

"No problem, honey."

(Penny and Kale takeoff for the back of the Cabin. Jackson realizes that he doesn't know where to go)/ "Hey, Kale!"

(Kale and Penny turn back towards Jackson). "Yeah, man. What's up?"

"Ohmmmm, which cabin are we in?"

"Ha, ha, ha. My bad, bruh, my bad. We are in cabin 29-W. Your guy's bedroom is first door on the right. The kitchen is on the other end of the hall. Last door on the left." (Kale and Penny continue around the side of the cabin headed toward the back patio).

"Thanks, man." (Jackson grabs the items out of the back seat and walks into the cabin and then to the kitchen).

(I am glad those two are gone. They really deserve each other. I can't wait to see Lyn).

(Jackson tip-toes into the kitchen while Lyn is bent over checking a pie in the oven. She's wiggling her ass dancing to a tune on her Ipod).

(Mmm, unnh! Look at that phat booty. Shit! I wish I could...wait a minute. I shouldn't be thinking this way).

(He takes a quick look out the window to be sure that Kale and Penny didn't see him eying Lyn. Jackson sets the items from the truck on the table quietly and rushes up behind Lyn as she closes the oven door and turns around).

(Lyn jumps)

"Woo!" (Breathing hard) "Oh goodness!" (Placing both of her hands up to her chest over her heart). "Hi Jackson, you startled me!"

"I'm sorry. I didn't mean to scare you. You probably didn't hear me since you were jamming so hard. He, he."

"Yeah right! That's why you snuck in...but it's good to see you. Um hum." (Breathing more calmly). "I didn't know you guys were here all ready!" (Lyn walks over and gives Jackson a strong embrace and kisses him softly on the neck).

"Ummmm..." (That felt good). "It's good to see you, Lyn. You are looking great as usual."

"Oh, Jackson, stop it!" (As she gives Jackson a light pat on the chest) "You are just too funny! Ha, ha, ha!"

"Well you know, Lyn, ever since we talked Friday, I've been looking forward to coming up here."

"Me too...so where's Penny?"

"She's outside with Kale by the grill." (Looking through the window).

"Oh that's good! Those two need to hang out together."

"You're kidding! I was thinking the same thing."

"Nope. And you know Kale kept complaining that I was rushing him out the house."

"Oh wow! That is unbelievable. Are they trading notes?"

"Ha, ha, ha! They must be!"

"Incredible! You are so right, they should be together." (Jackson shakes his head in disbelief that his wife and Kale are so similar).

"Anyway...you're going to love your bedroom."

"Oh really? I haven't seen them yet."

"Yep. This cabin was a last minute change. It actually has a large Jacuzzi tub in both of our rooms."

"Oh damn!" (What am I getting excited for? Penny ain't gonna do nothing). "Nice."

"Hmmm, you look like you're not excited."

"Oh, I was just thinking about...nevermind. So what's all left to cook?"

"Well, I just finished making the baked beans and the potato salad. Last thing is the pie..."

"Potato salad? Oh, girl, what do you put in that potato salad?"

"Well..."

"Oh, if you tell me you'll have to kill me?"

"Ha, ha, ha. Hmmm...that's for me to know and you to find out."

"Uh huh. I figured that. Actually, everything you touch has always been delicious!"

"Why thank you, Jackson. (Lyn turns around to check on the pie in the oven. Jackson watches her ass as she reaches into the oven to test the pies filling).

(Why does she keep doing that? I would love to feel that ass. Dayum!)

(Lyn takes the pie and wants to set it on the cooling rack on the shelf to the right of stove). "Jackson? Could you help me put this pie on the rack? Kale put the rack up here and I can barely reach it. I just don't want to drop it."

"Here I come." (Jackson stands directly behind Lyn right up against her ass). "Let me help you with that."

(Lyn can feel Jackson's body and dick against her ass as he reaches around her to lift the pie up to the rack).

(Damn that feels good). "Thank you so much, Jackson."

"No problem, baby. It was my pleasure."

(Did he realize he called me baby?)

(Did she realize how soft that ass is? Damn! Oh my God! Kale is a...)

"Jackson?...Jackson?"

"Um, yes. Sorry."

(Grabbing the baked beans). "Stop your daydreaming. He, he. Let's get this food outside. The burgers and should be ready by now." (Lyn pushes the door open with her foot while holding the baked beans). "Hey, grab the potato salad out of the refrigerator."

(Jackson grabs the potato salad from the refrigerator).

"Okay, Lyn, I'm right behind you."

(Penny and Kale turn to the door as they see Jackson and Lyn come out the door to the patio) "Hey guys, are you ready to eat?"

(Penny jumps up to grab the pan from Lyn). "Most definitely. Let me help you with that." (Penny sits the pan of food she grabbed from Lyn onto the side table near the rest of the food. She turns back around to give Lyn a hug and a peck on the cheek). "Hi, Lyn. I'm so glad to see you!" (Jackson stands with his pan of food to see if Lyn wants him to put in the same place).

"You too, Penny! It's been a while. I enjoy our little..."

(Kale is irritated by the time it took Lyn to get the food ready) "Yes, it has been a while. It's about freakin' time, Lyn. I had these burgers ready for a while!" (Lyn, Penny and Jackson are confused why Kale is so upset).

"What! Are you kidding me? I had several things to make and..."

(Jackson sets his container down and jumps in to divert the ensuing argument). "Hey...hey. Everybody let's just sit down and eat this delicious food." (Penny takes a seat adjacent to Kale who is already seated at the picnic table for four followed by Lyn yanking the chair back and plopping down in the seat with arms folded. Jackson waltzes around to his seat and sits down). "Ok. Let's enjoy ourselves, people.

We really have a lot to be thankful for. Starting with great friendship..."
(Jackson looks around at everyone and notices that Lyn is still upset. He
decides to proceed with blessing the food). "Let's all join hands. Bow
your heads. Let me first thank these two great cooks for preparing such
a delectable meal. May this meal provide nourishment and strength for
our bodies as well as foster a weekend of fellowship and love for one
another. In his name we pray."

(All together) "Amen."

(Lyn is still upset at Kale's comments. Kale is trying to play off the
fact that he has upset Lyn. Everyone starts eating).

"So, Lyn, what did you put in this potato salad girl? It is off the
chain!" (Kale frowns at Penny's comment).

"Thank you, Penny, I'm glad someone enjoys it!" (Lyn rolls her
eyes at Kale).

"No complaints out of me. It's good as always."

"Thank you, Jackson!" "

"Well, it should be good—you took long enough!" (Kale leans into
the table). "Why can't you just do what I ask? It's real fucking simple.
We had a specific time..."

(Lyn jumps up and thrusts her hands down beside her body and
walks back in the kitchen without saying a word).

"See! Just get up and run away. She's all upset now. All I asked for
was to have it done on time! See Penny, that is what I'm talking about!"
(Penny just stares back at Kale as he continues arguing about Lyn). "She
knows I'm right, so that's why she walked away!" (Jackson is about to get
up and check on Lyn when she comes back out to the deck) "Kale, I'm
going to take a walk." (She mutters to herself). "Before I kill your ass!"

"Go ahead, no one is stopping you!"

"Girl, don't go." (Penny quickly peers at Kale). "Aren't you going
to finish your food?"

"No. I just don't feel too hungry right now."

"Ok then. I'll put it up for you in case you're hungry when you get
back."

"Thank you, Penny." (Lyn stares at Kale). "I really appreciate it!"

(Kale looks away from Lyn). "Whatever. Just go."

(Lyn starts to walk around the side of the cabin, but stops when
Penny suggests that Jackson accompany Lyn. Penny looks over at

Jackson while placing her hand on his forearm). "Honey, why don't you go with her. It's getting a little dark."

(Jackson is shocked that Penny would make such a kind suggestion).

(Is this a trick question?) "Huh? You sure you don't won't go, baby?"

"Yeah, I'm sure."

(Jackson looks at Kale) "Go ahead, Jackson. If you don't mind."

"Not a problem...ok Lyn, let's go before it gets too dark."

(Jackson and Lyn stop briefly in front of the cabin while Lyn squats to retie her tennis

shoes). "Now you see exactly what I'm talking about, Jackson. He takes the smallest things and just blows them up. For no fuckin' reason!...I mean, come on a few minutes..."

"Yeah. I really see what you are talking about...he, he..."

"What are you laughing at?"

"No, it's just funny how I thought I was the only one. I'm like...is that Penny in a male body?"

(Lyn laughs loud as she stands after tying her shoes) "Ha, ha, ha! You are joking..."

"I wish I was. It's so similar with me and Penny".

"Oh really? So how do you deal with it?"

"That's easy. I just simply ignore it."

"Hmm...I guess I'm going to have to try that approach."

"Yeah. Give it a try. It is the only way to keep your sanity...so, are you all ready to go?"

"Good to go."

"All right then, let's leave all the negativity on the patio and enjoy this walk and fresh air."

"That sounds good, Jackson." (Lyn turns to Jackson quickly, giving him a quick hug and kiss on the cheek). "Let's go!"

(Clearing his throat). "Uh um! Wow Lyn! That was really nice!"

(Lyn and Jackson begin walking up the hill away from the cabin. They proceed around the bend out of view of the cabin).

"Oh really?" (Lyn comes to a stop).

"Yes really. (You just don't know how much you turn me on Lyn. Just a little kiss. Unh!)

"Well, step over here." (Jackson stops 2 feet from Lyn) "Nooooo..." (Soft voice). "Come closer."

(Lyn tip-toes up to Jackson and wraps her arms around his neck and pushes her tongue down his throat).

"Mmmmmmmm!" (Jackson stands motionless after letting his arms fall to his sides).

Kiss!

"Mmmmmm!"

"Whew! Damn, Lyn! You don't know how long I've been waiting on that."

"Me too! I was a little nervous. I'm like...should we be doing this? It feels so good, but I know it's wrong...but when I sensed how you felt from my kiss on the cheek, I went for it."

"Mmmm, mmnh! I'm so glad you did. You make me feel...like...fuck it! It's just good."

(Soft chuckle) "He, he. The feeling is mutual. I just feel like we are so perfect for each other. Why couldn't we have met before we..."

(In unison) "Met our spouses. Ha, ha, ha."

"That's funny. We were both thinking the same thing." (Looking into Lyn's eyes). "I've said it the very first time I met you." (Jackson places his hands onto Lyn's hips).

(Soft voice staring up at Jackson). "What did you say baby?"

"I said, we connect very, very well." (Jackson starts to give Lyn a kiss when they notice the lights of a car coming around the bend. They both quickly drop their hands and stand off to the side as the car passes by).

(After the car clears the hill, Lyn and Jackson look around nervously to make sure everything is all clear). "Whoa. That was a close one."

"Yeah. What were we thinking being so close to the cabin." (Jackson and Lyn continue their walk). "Kale would kill me if..."

"Hey, hey, don't go that far. Think of it this way: they're busy playing negativity warfare."

"Ha, ha, ha. Yeah, I bet. They're back there having a blast. You're so crazy...negativity warfare. Ha, ha, ha."

(Jackson and Lyn come upon a set of picnic shelters after they have been walking for more than thirty minutes). "Hey, let's stop over here for a minute at these picnic tables."

"Sure. You're going to have to lead me over. I can barely see back there."

"Grab my hand." (Lyn grabs Jackson's hand and follows him back to the picnic tables furthest away from the road). "Have a seat here." (Lyn sits the side of the table with her feet dangling as Jackson stands in front of her leaning against a support post).

"Thank you, Jackson."

"For what?"

"For walking with me and stepping in at dinner trying to diffuse the situation."

"Oh, Lyn, you know that's no problem. You don't have to..."

"Yes, I do. I just want you to know that I appreciate it."

"You're welcome." (She should know by now that I care about her a lot).

(Lyn looks back to the light post by the road). "You know what's interesting?"

"What?"

"How when I was standing at the road, I couldn't see shit over here. Now it's as clear as day over by the road. Did you notice that?"

"Yes, I did. The difference is that I closed my eyes and looked away from the light so my eyes adjusted quicker."

"Hmmm...wow! I learn something new every day."

"Um hum. I think we have learned a lot about each other today..."

"Whoooooo! Whooooo!"

(Lyn jumps off the table and grabs Jackson around his waist while placing her head in his chest).

(Whispering nervously). "What was that! Did you hear that!"

(Jackson places his hand on the side of Lyn's head to confirm to her she's safe with him). "It's ok, baby, it's ok. It's just an owl." (Jackson bends his neck down and kisses Lyn on the top of her head) "You're safe with me, baby."

(Lyn calms down as she listens to Jackson's soothing voice) "Ummmm...I do feel safe with you. It feels so good, so natural."

(Jackson places both of his hands in the small of Lyn's back nudging her closer to him). "Ummmm...baby, you feel so damn good. I just can't let you go." (Lyn squeezes Jackson tighter causing his right hand to slip onto her soft ass). (Shit! That ass is so soft!)

(Looking in to Jackson's eyes). "Then don't!"

(Jackson grabs the sides of Lyn's head with two hands and begins kissing her passionately). "Mmmmm..."

Kiss!

"Mmmmm..."

(Lyn starts to moan loudly between kisses).

(Jackson continues kissing Lyn while pulling her T-shirt out of her pants. He briefly pulls away to pull her shirt over her head. He tosses it onto the picnic table).

(Breathing hard) "Oh yes. Yes, yes. Those are nice."

(Jackson flips out one of Lyn's breast and begins to suck it) "Ummm..."

Suck!

"Ummm..."

"Suck that tittie, baby! Ummmm! Bite it! Ummmm! Bite that shit! Ummmmmmmm!"

(Jackson reaches around to undo Lyn's bra) "Hell yes! Look at those juicy tits! Ummm!"

Suck!

"Ummm!" (Jackson takes one hand and slowly eases it into Lyn's tights). "That's what I'm talking about. That pussy is wet as hell!" (Jackson takes some of Lyn's pussy essence and begins to massage her clit).

(Light moans) "Ummm...ummmm... ummm... oh, Jackson...that feels so good. Ohhhh...ummm...stick your finger in me baby..." (Jackson pushes his middle finger deep into Lyn's pussy). "Unnnnh! Unnnnh! That's it. Deeper! Unnnh! Deeper! Unnh! Oh my God! Jackson, that feels so good!" (Catching her breath) "Whew! I am literally on fire! Unnnh!"

(Breathing hard) "Hunh? What did you say?"

"I need you to put this fire out! Unnnh!"

"That's what I thought you said!" (Jackson pushes Lyn's tights down to her ankles. He reaches behind her for her T-shirt spreading it to the edge of the picnic table). "Hold on to me." (Jackson helps Lyn sit on the edge of the table). "Now lay back..." (Jackson stands back for a second to just take in the site of Lyn's pussy lips being squeezed between her thighs and her ankles bound by her tights). "Damn! Look at that phat pussy! Oh yes, sir! That is a beautiful fucking site! I gots to get a taste of that!"

(Jackson grabs the center of Lyn's tights at her ankles with one hand and uses the other hand to spread open her pussy. He takes his tongue and begins gently suck on Lyn's clit).

"Unnnh!"

Slurp!

"Oh shit, Jackson! Unnh! Shit! Shit! Unnnh! I'm about to fucking cum! Fuck! I can't...unnnh! Not this...unnh! Quiiiiiiiiccck! Oh! Ummmmmmmmmmmmmm! Damn! Oh my God!" (Breathing hard) "Shit! Mutha-Fucka!" (Rapid Exhaling) "Woo! Woo! Oh hell! Shit! Kale, never does that!"

"What! No wonder your ass came so quick!" (Jackson lets go of Lyn's tights so that she can get down of the table).

"What the fuck are you doing?"

"I was letting you..."

"Oh no the fuck you ain't! You are going to give me some dick niggah! Come around here and let me taste that dick." (Jackson moves around to the side of the table so that Lyn can suck his dick. Lyn reaches over and pushes Jackson's pants down). "Now put that dick in my mou... Urrgh!"

Slurp!

"Mmm..."

Slurp!

"Oh, Lyn!" (Sucking air threw his teeth). "Sssssssssssssssssssssss! Umm! That's it! Suck on daddy's dick. Ummm!"

Slurp!

"Mmmmm! That's what I like."

Slurp!

"Mmmm!"

(Lyn keeps the dick at the back of her throat while twirling her tongue rapidly around Jackson's shaft). "What the fuck baby! Damn! You about to make me cum! Oh God! Unh! Unnnh! Unnnnh!" (Jackson's dick is throbbing).

(Lyn pulls her mouth off of Jackson's dick). "Oh no, baby!"

"Oh, no! Oh no what?"

"Momma wants you to put all that cum in this ass!"

(What the fuck).

"Oh, do you need directions?"

"Fuck it!" (Jackson moves to the end of the table. He grabs one of Lyn's ankles with his left hand and places his finger inside her pussy to lube up her asshole). "Mmmmm...yeah, let me feel that asshole!" (Jackson slowly slides his finger in Lyn's ass).

"Ooh! Yeah, daddy! Get that ass right!" (Jackson continues sliding his finger in and out of Lyn's ass). "Umm...yes...umm...yes...come on, baby. Plug that ass with that dick!"

(Jackson releases Lyn's ankle and uses his other hand to put more pussy juice on his dick. He grabs the head of his dick and slowly begins to slide his dick in Lyn's ass).

"Oh, oh, oh, oh, oh, oh baby! Ummmmmmmm..." (Rapid breathing). "Woo! Woo! Woo! Don't move, don't move!"

"I got you baby! I got you! Relax that asshole!"

"Oh fuck, baby! Your dick is filling my ass up!"

"There you go. You ready now. (Jackson grabs Lyn by her ankles and starts to fuck her in the ass harder and harder).

"Unnnnnnh! Unnnnh! Unnnh! Deeper! Unh! Faster! Unh! Unh!"

Plop!

"Unh!"

Plop!

"Tear that shit up! Unh!"

(Jackson looks down at Lyn's ass jiggling on every stroke) "Damn! Look at that ass!"

"Unh!"

Plop!

"Shit! Unh!"

Plop!

"Oh baby! Rip that ass! Oh yeah niggah! I feel you! Unh! Unh! Unh! Give me that cum!"

"You want it baby! Unh! You want it! Oh shit! I am about to...unh!"

"Give me shit baby! Fuck me!...Fuck me!"

Oh! Oh! Oh! Oh! (Jackson braces himself as he explodes in Lyn's ass). "Arrrrrrrgh!" (Rapid breathing) "Whew! Woo! Woo! Woo!"

"Yes, baby! Yes! All that hot cum in that ass!"

"Whew! Lyn, that was hot! Oh my goodness! Your ass is so good."

"Oh shit! Catch it! The cum is dripping out my ass."

"Got it, baby. I got it." (Jackson wipes the cum on the side of the picnic table). "Damn, that was close. He, he."

"Yeah. Kind of hard to explain cum on my shirt from just taking a walk. Ha, ha." (Jackson helps pull Lyn's tights down. Lyn stands up and pulls her tights up the rest of the way). "Ooops, you got a little drip there." (Lyn grabs Jackson's dick and wipes off the cum residue).

"Mmmm. Thank you, baby. That was the fucking bomb!" (Jackson helps Lyn to with putting her T-shirt back on).

"No. Thank you, Jackson. You don't know how much I needed that." (Lyn walks up to Jackson and give him a light kiss).

"Muah!"

"Mmmm...one more. Muah! Ok, we better get back. You know they're probably looking for us." (Jackson and Lyn make a quick stop by the community restrooms to straighten up before they get back to the cabin).

(Jackson and Lyn are about one hundred feet from the cabin). "Jackson, I just want you to know I really appreciate everything."

"No problem, Lyn." (Shaking his head in disbelief of what just happened). "Whew! I mean..." (Looking down at Lyn's ass). "I should be thanking you!"

Ha, ha, ha! You're so crazy. Ha, ha, ha! Ha, ha, ha!" (Lyn slaps Jackson on the shoulder from laughing so hard. She briefly puts both hands on her knees). "Oh my goodness! My stomach is hurting! You are killing me with that look!" (Jackson and Lyn are unaware that Kale and Penny are watching them as they approach the cabin).

"No for real!" (Jackson gestures with his hands as taking a bow). "That was truly my pleasure."

"He, he, he. Whew!" (Regaining her composure). "Likewise...you know, come to think of it, I haven't come like that in all the years I have been married."

"Really, you got to be shittin me!"

"No shit!"

"Damn, I can't believe Kale doesn't sleep in that pussy, and especially that ass!"

"Yeah, that's all he does, is slee..." (Jackson nudges Lyn to change the conversation because Kale and Penny are both standing in front of the cabin awaiting their return) . "Honh?"

"Hey, hey. Watch it." (Jackson tries to play it off since he knows that Kale and Penny are probably both upset). "Hey guys!" (Penny is standing with her arms folded looking at Jackson while Kale just is holding one hand under his chin with one finger over his lip). "Everything ok?"

(Penny starts to scan Jackson up and down). "Is everything ok? Is everything ok? Where the hell have you two been?"

(Jackson takes offense to Penny's comments but knows he has to diffuse the situation). "Baby, we discovered a nature trail on our walk and decided to explore it before it got too dark. The funny thing is we had trouble getting off the trail as we lost daylight. Sorry about that. I thought I could remember our way back."

(Kale thinks the story is valid but wants to know why Lyn was laughing hysterically). "Ok then. What was all that laughing about, Lyn?"

"What laughing?"

"You know what laughing! I saw you when you were walking up."

"Oh that. Ha, ha, ha. I'm sorry. Jackson just made this funny face when he figured out we were lost. After he kept saying, 'I know the way, I know the way. I am an ex-boyscout.' Ha, ha, ha. Whew! That is just too funny." (Lyn goes up to Kale and starts to rub on him to make him feel secure). "Come here baby. You missed huh?" (In baby talk). "Come on, let's go inside. Mommy going to make it all better." (Kale and Lyn walk to the cabin passing Penny. Lyn looks back and Jackson and winks at him for covering up their secret).

"Yeah. You and Lyn are quite chum..." (Jackson puts a finger up to Penny's mouth shushing her).

"Baby, don't even say it. You have nothing to worry about. You know there is only one queen bee."

"Yeah but..."

"Don't say it. Who is the queen bee?"

"I...I...I am."

"Who is the queen bee?"

"I am baby!"

(Jackson grabs a handful of Penny's ass and pushes her toward the cabin). "That's what I'm talking about!" (Penny and Jackson head to their cabin bedroom for the evening).

Chapter 6

69 Yards to Score!

"What happened! How did we get the ball back!"

"The guy..."

"I mean, when I left the Hellcats had the ball on the 50 yard line! Now the Brims are 3rd and goal!"

"Well the guy..." (Cleo stands with her arms crossed with her eyes rolling in the back of her head).

"Did they fumble? Did they intercept the ball?"

"Like I was saying! The guy..." (Cleo puts both her hands on her forehead and gives up trying to tell Trent about what he missed before going to the bathroom).

"Go baby! Come on baby! Go! Go! Go!" (Trent grabs and hugs Cleo with excitement as the Brims score a touchdown).

(Cleo looks at Trent with a slight embarrassment as continues jumping up and down celebrating the touchdown). "That's what I'm talking about, baby girl! Can you believe it! We came from three touchdowns behind! I thought for sure it was over after half time. Whew!" (Trent raises both hands in the air and starts to high-five other Brim fans in the stands). "Yeah, baby! That's how you do it!"

"Oh you want to talk smack now huh?"

"What smack, baby! That's ball game baby! That's ball game!"

"Oh you know what I'm talking about. After halftime, you were quiet as a mouse. What, what?" (Cleo taunts Trent by putting her hand up to her ear as if she's listening out for his response).

"Oh. Ok then. I wasn't saying nothing after halftime, because I knew my boys were going to make a comeback."

"Ha, ha, ha! Whatever, niggah! You know your ass was worried. Admit it!"

"No really, I was..."

"Please, Trent! Ha, ha, ha!"

"Ok, ok, baby. You're right...But all that matters is that I won!" (Trent starts to dance the cabbage patch in front of Cleo).

"Oh, all right then. A win is a win."

"And?..."

"And what?"

"Oh don't act!"

"Oh! Oh! (Cleo covers her mouth laughing pretending as she forgot the bet her and Trent made prior to the game.) "You mean about the bet we made before the game."

"Right, right."

"So, what did we bet again?"

"Oh you got jokes today. Ha, ha, ha."

(Cleo continues to joke with Trent as she senses further frustration from him). "Oh! Oh! I remember. We bet twenty dollars that..."

"Forget it Cleo." (Trent turns to leave the stands). "Let's..."

(Cleo rushes and grabs Trent's arm). "Baby! Baby! I'm just playing with you. I remember our bet. You know I/m a woman of my word and I always cash the checks I write!"

"Girl. You're always playing." (Trent relaxes and turns back to Cleo).

"Actually, I am glad I lost the bet."

"What!"

"Yeah, I'm glad."

"But you kept saying how nervous..."

"Yeah, but I'm more excited than nervous. I couldn't let you think I was some kind of freak or something."

(Trent looks at Cleo in disbelief) "Come on, girl."

"Ha, ha, ha. Well you know I am a laaaaady!"

"Oh yeah. You're a lady. But you're a bonafide freak! Unnnnh! And I love that shit."

(Cleo places both hands below her chin with a look of dismay). "Oh my! A freak? Well, I never. Ha, ha, ha...ok, ok. Let me stop. The truth is, I've been fiending for some of that big black dick all day!" (Cleo reaches inside of Trent's mid-length leather jacket and feels his dick through his pants.)

"Oh wow, baby. That shit feels good! Ummmm..."

(Cleo tip-toes while continuing to hold Trent's dick and whispers in his ear). "You ready to hit this pussy?"

(Trent concentrates on not overreacting to conceal his excitement.)

(In a low and excited voice). "Damn baby! You know I'm..."

(Cleo releases his dick and points him up the stands to the exit as the crowd flow toward the exit has reached their row. Trent quickly straightens his jacket to conceal his hard dick and turns to exit their row). "Babe. Time to go. They're letting us out. Thank you."

(Cleo and Trent walk out of the stands to concession area and stand off to the side as folks head toward the exit.) "I can't wait for all these folks clear out the stadium. I'm about to nut all in my pants!"

"Ha, ha, ha!"

(Trent takes a deep sigh). "Damn, girl! You know you got me fucked up, right?" (Cleo looks back at Trent as if she has no idea what he is saying). "Oh hell no! Don't give me that look. You know what the fuck you doing! Like when you whisper in my ear...shit! I can't control my..."

"Who little ol' me?"

"Yes, little ol' you!"

"Ha, ha, ha."

"Yeah. Go ahead and laugh. Real funny. Real fucking funny."

"Baby, you know I'm not laughing at you. I'm glad that I turn my man on. You know that's my number one rule..."

"And what's that?"

"Ain't no other bitch going to take care of my man better than I can!"

"All right then! That's my, baby! Unnnh! I can't wait to get up in that ass."

"I can't wait either! How long is going to take for the stadium to empty?"

"Shouldn't be that long."

"Good, cause I'm getting a little chilly."

(Trent looks around for a warmer spot for them as the stadium empties). "Oh, baby, I didn't know you were getting cold."

"Not that bad, just a few chills."

"Oh, I know the perfect spot. My boy works with the stadium crew part-time and says the area near the boiler room stays pretty warm. Don't ask me how he knows that. Ha, ha, ha."

(Cleo shivers slightly). "I really don't care, baby...woooo!" (Her teeth chatter slightly). "Let's just g-g-g-go there then."

"All right, baby. Follow me."

(Trent leads Cleo by the hand to a broom closet next to the boiler room).

"Ahhhh! I'm starting to feel a lot warmer myself." (Stopping in front of the closet he releases Cleo's hand. Cleo stands behind him waiting with her arms stretched by her side trying to keep her body from shivering).

"Yeah baby, this feels good."

(Trent rubs both of his hands together before checking the door.) "Ok, here we go. Hope this door is unlocked. Yes!" (Cleo rushes inside the door as Trent is opening the door).

(In a shivering voice). "Grrr...m-m-man is cold out there!"

"Thank you, thank you, thank you God! It feels much better in here."

"Yes it does. I'll have to let my boy know he came through for me."

(Cleo stops shivering and stares at Trent for a response). "Wait a minute? So your boy knows about this."

"No, no, baby." (Placing his hands on her shoulder). "I just ask him about places to hide out."

"Oh ok. I was getting ready to say."

"Come on now, baby. You know me."

"You're right, you're right. I'm sorry. I do know you better than that." (Cleo reaches up and kisses Trent in the mouth). "Mmmm..."

Kiss!

"I know my baby. I'm just glad to be here with you."

"Same here, baby. Now walk over here."

"Ok, baby. Whoops!" (Cleo almost trips on an object in the floor). "Damn, it's dark in here! Careful, baby, careful. Just keep holding on to my arm."

"Ok. I got it. Go slow."

(Trent leads Cleo over to an old office chair stored in the closet). "Let's sit here." (Trent uses his hand to clear the chair of dust and debris. Trent removes his jacket and sits down in the chair). "Sit right here, baby." (Cleo sits down sideways across Trent's lap while lying in to his chest). "Take my jacket and cover us, baby."

"Ummmm...that feels so much better."

"You know I'm going to take care of my baby."

"Yes you do! You always..." (Cleo grabs both sides of Trent's head and begins to tongue kiss and rub the back of his head).

"Mmmmmmmmmm..."

Kissss!

(Trent takes one hand and starts to massage Cleo's breasts). "Ummmm...oh, Trent! You know that feels so..."

Kisssssss!

"Mmmmm....your breasts are so fucking soft!"

"Oooooh, don't stop, daddy, please don't stop. You know my breasts are one of my ... Unnh!" (Breathing heavy). "Hot spots!"

(Trent slides his hand down to Cleo's hips and thighs. He starts to rub the sides of her skirt up exposing her stockings). (In a deep voice). "Ummm...oh yeah. Your pussy is so hot baby. Ummm...let me taste it." (Trent slowly slides one finger into top of Cleo's stocking towards her pussy).

"Woo!...your finger is cold!"

"I'm sorry baby. You want me to stop?" (Trent keeps his hand still).

"Nooooooo! I didn't say all that." (Cleo lifts up and pushes her stockings down to mid thigh). "Oh shit! I can feel all that dick about to go up my ass!"

(Trent lightly glides his extended finger over Cleo's clit and into her pussy). "Oh damn, baby! You are flowing like Niagara Falls."

"Unnnh! I told you I was ready for you!"

(Trent takes his finger out of Cleo's pussy and puts it in his mouth.)

Slurp!

Lick!

"Ahhh! That's some good pussy." (Slight chuckle). "Ha, ha. I swear it tastes like strawberries."

"Ha, ha. I guess it's all that fruit I eat."

"Um hum." (Trent puts his finger back in Cleo's pussy and starts to penetrate her slowly with a gentle digging motion).

"Unnnh!"

Slosh!

"Ooooooooooohh! Oh fuck! What the... Unnnh! The fuck, are you doing! Ummmmmmmm! That shit is driving me crazy!"

"Oh you like that huh?"

"Ummm! Yeah baby, I love it! Fuck this! I gotta have thick dick!"

(Trent slows down fingering Cleo and stops). "Wait, baby, wait. You know we have to go to the field..."

(Cleo turns her body sitting up straight in Trent's lap. She swings her head around to Trent). "Fuck, the mutha-fucking field! You got me all..."

"Baby..."

(Cleo slightly raises her ass while standing in front of Trent. She reaches her arm back through her legs and starts to unzip Trent's pants).

"Come on, baby!" (Trent gently moves Cleo's hands and begins to pull up her stockings). "Our bet remember? The..."

"31 yard line? I got that baby. I got it! But, it's not like we can't do it again!"

"Please, baby! You know this is one of my..."

(Cleo subsides. She stands up and turns to Trent placing her finger up to his lips). "Fantasies?...Ok, baby. I'm sorry." (Cleo tip-toes and kisses Trent).

"Thank you, baby. I really want to make this special."

(In a soothing voice). "It will baby. Like I said, ain't no other bitch going to do better for my man than me."

"Ummmm...I love when you say that. I can't wait to go to the field. Ummm! Unh! I am going to..."

"Down, boy, down, boy! Let's save all that for the field...sooooo...tell me this: what is the big deal about the 31-yard line?"

(Light chuckle) "He, he, he. You don't get it huh?"

"Uh...no! You know I don't know very much about football."

"Ha, ha, ha. Ok, baby. Let me give you a clue. A football field is 100 yards long. Each team" (raising his voice) "SCORES a touchdown by reaching the opponents goal at the opponents end of the field." (She should be able to get that starting at the 31-yard line leaves 69 yards to score. Hmmm...at least I think she will get it).

"Huh? That's it!"

"Yep, that's all you get. Ha, ha, ha."

"Whatever! One of those engineering things."

"Awe...sweety, don't give up so easily."

"Please! You know I'm not good at math."

"Ha, ha, ha. It is really...shhhh!" (Whispering) "I think I hear someone coming." (Cleo and Trent stand still and listen to two men talk outside the door).

"Hey, man, the Brim's showed there asses today. Coming back from three touchdowns..."

"Yeah I know, man! They showed a lot of heart. I think they have a chance to make the playoffs if they keep playing like they are."

"Right. I mean...next game will be tough, but if they don't make dumb mistakes..."

"And they get back Ellerbe next week. That really hurt their run defense."

"That's right! They should be in good shape."

"Damn, I can't wait!"

"Me either!...Hey, man, let's get the hell out of here!"

"Cool. Let me throw this broom in this closet and we can head out." (Trent and Cleo look at each other and remain as still as possible. The door to the closet opens and the stadium attendant reaches in and props the broom beside the wall without looking or going in. The door to the closet shuts and the attendant leaves).

(Yelling down the hall). "Hey wait up, man. I'm coming." (The attendant trots off into the distance).

(Trent and Cleo breathe a sigh of relief). "Whew! That was close. I thought sure they didn't clean things up until the day after."

"They probably cleaned the concession areas or something."

"You're probably right. That makes a lot of sense. My genius baby is so smart!"

"Yeah right! I haven't figured out what the sig..."

"Crack!" "Crack!" (The sound of the stadium lights shutting off.)

(Cleo jumps into Trent's arms.) " What's that?"

"Ha, ha, ha. Oh, baby, it's ok. Nothing but the stadium lights."

(Breathing a sigh of relief). "Whew! That's really loud for lights. I thought something exploded."

"He, he, he. Naw, baby, it's our cue to head to the field."

"Oh thank God! Finally!"

(Trent peeps out of the broom closet door looking both ways to ensure that there is no one still inside). "Everything looks clear." (He reaches for Cleo's hand). "Come on baby, let's go."

"Ok, baby, watch your step. Here, grab my hand!" (Cleo steps up on a small ledge leading to the field and extends her hand to Trent). "Now jump down."

(Cleo almost loses her balance). "Unnh! Whoa!"

"I got you, baby. Not gonna let my baby fall."

(Breathing hard) "Oh no. I wasn't worried about that. Shit! I'm so nervous and excited at the same time."

"Me too, baby, me too!"

"You know, it doesn't feel that bad out here."

"Yeah, it doesn't." (Trent scans the field and the stands to double-check that they are alone. He takes Cleo by the hand and walks on to the field towards the 31-yard line that faces the jumbo scoreboard on the south side of the field).

"And this field, it feels softer than I thought. Like walking on air. Obviously not grass!"

"Nope, not grass. It's a new playing surface they put in this year."

"Oh wow! Just learned something else new about football."

"Ha, ha, ha." (Trent stops at the 31-yard line) "Here we go, babe." (Trent turns to Cleo and brings her close to his body and gives her a long kiss).

"Mmmmmmmmmmmmmmmmuah! We're here, babe!"

Kiss!

(In a light voice). "Thank you." (Trent looks in to Cleo's eyes and shakes his head from side to side in anticipation). "Un, un, unh...damn, girl. You so damn fine!" (Trent places his hands further underneath Cleo's jacket and starts gently massaging her back and then drops one hand cupping the crack of her ass). "Damn this booty is soft!"

(Cleo starts to wind her hips slowly causing Trent's dick to get harder).

(In a mellow voice). "Ummmmm...yeah, baby...rub your ass, baby...ummmmm..."

(Breathing hard) "Oh yessssss...shit baby!" (Trent reaches inside Cleo's skirt and notices that her stockings are gone). "What the fuck! How did you get your stockings off that quick!"

(Cleo smiles at Trent waving her finger back and forth letting him know that it's a mystery he will have to figure out on his own). "No, no, no...a good magician never reveals her TRICKS!"

"Fuck it then!" (Trent begins to kiss Cleo wildly. He then reaches underneath Cleo's skirt and begins to massages her clit.).

(Breathing hard). "Umm! Umm! Oh baby! Damn! Ruh-...umm! Ummmmm! Rub your pussy, baby!"

(Trent continues to kiss Cleo. He uses both of his arms to flip his jacket off. He then grabs the top of Cleo's jacket and pushes it off to the ground. He immediately reaches into her blouse to release one of her breasts from her bra and blouse). "Mmmm..."

Slurp!

"Ummm! Oh baby! Suck it! Oh my God! This feels so....unh! Unh!"

(A train sounds in the background) "Bomp!!! Bomp!!!" "Choo-Choo, Choo-Choo..."

(The sound of the train reminds Cleo that she's outside in the open and she becomes worried about being seen. Trent continues to suck her breast and starts to finger her pussy).

(Nervously) "Baby, baby! Unnh!"

Slurp!

"Yeah, baby?"

"Umm? Unnnnnnh!" (Breathing hard). "Do you...unnh! Think someone...unh! Can see ussssssssssssss! Unh!"

"Baby!" Slurp! (In a soothing voice). "Don't worry, baby... we're all alone. I promise."

(Breathing calmly). "Ok, baby, ok."

(Trent brings Cleo in close to his chest and squeezes her tight) "See baby, I got you. You know daddy going to take care of you."

"Mmmmm....damn, baby, you smell so...whoa!" (In one swift move, Cleo finds herself lying on top of their jackets facing up at Trent). "Baby! Shit! I love it when you take charge!"

(Trent quickly stands up and kicks off his shoes and removes his pants. His dick is sticking straight out. He walks around to Cleo's head and drops to his knees with his dick hovering above her forehead). "Take charge, huh? Hmmm...take charge of this dick then!"

(Cleo tilts her head back as Trent walks on his knees closer to drop his dick in her mouth). "Mmmmm!"

Slurp!

"Mmm, mmm! Shit! I love that dick!"

Slurp! Slurp!

(Cleo is so turned on by sucking Trent's dick that she starts fingering herself).

Slurp!

"Suck that shit, baby! Ummmm! Suck it!"

(Long sucks) Slurrrrrrrrrrrrrrrrp!

"Umm!"

Slurrrrrrrrrrrrrrrrrp!

(Briefly taking Trent's dick out of her mouth). "I love sucking this dick!"

Slurp! (Cleo sniffs in hard through her nose). "Fuck yeah! Put those balls all in my face!"

(As if on cue, Trent bends over towards Cleo's pussy. He pulls her skirt up slowly with his mouth. He wets and stiffens his tongue and begins to encircle Cleo's clit). "Unnnnnh!" (Cleo struggles to keep sucking Trent's dick while Trent begins to suck on her clit). "Unnnnnh! Sl-ur-up! "Unh!" Sl-ur... "Unnnnh!"

(Trent places two fingers on Cleo's pussy to spread her pussy apart. He then submerges his entire tongue inside her pussy.) "Unnnnnnnnnnnnnnnnnnnnnnh! Oh shit!" (Trent's dick pops out of Cleo's mouth. Trent goes faster in and out with his tongue). "Unh! Unh! Unh! Unh! Unh! Unh! (Trent slows his penetration to a long stroke with his tongue).

(Breathing hard) "Oh God! Ummmmmmmmmmmmmmmmm! Shit! Oh my God! I'm about to cum! Ummmmmmmmmmmmmmmmm! Oh God!" (Cleo slightly lifts her hips towards Trent's mouth to apply more pressure on her pussy). "Ummmmmmmmmmmmm! Ummmmmmmmm! Ohhhhhhhhhh..." (Cleo's stomach muscles tighten as she briefly goes silent and cums in Trent's face). "Oh God!" (Catching her breath) "Oh God! Oh God! Damn, baby, can't nobody suck this pussy like you!"

(Trent comes to his knees as he looks down at Cleo. Cleo has two hands cupping her pussy as it continues to throb). "So you like the way daddy sucks that pussy, huh?"

"Oh shit yeah! Baby, you make me lose my mutha-fucking mind!"

"Ha, ha, ha...oh shit...what are you doing?" (As Cleo jumps to her knees).

"Just being selfish, baby. I need to feel you inside me! I need all that hot cum in this pussy!" (Cleo turns her ass around and lay on the side of her face with her ass in air).

"Oh, that's not selfish baby!" (Trent walks up close to Cleo's ass on his knees. He licks the tips of his fingers and reaches underneath Cleo and strokes her pussy while placing one hand on the side of her hip) "I been waiting to tear..."

"Fuck me, niggah! Fuck the...unnnnnnnnh!" (As Trent pushes deep into Cleo's pussy). "Unnh! Unnh! Unnh! Fuck! Fuck! Fuck! Unnh! Shit! Unh! You're in my fucking stomach! Unnh!"

Smack!

"Damn this pussy is good!"

Smack! (Trent grabs a hand full of Cleo's hair and pulls her back against his dick).

"Unnh! Hurt me! Unnh! Hurt me, daddy!" (Trent goes faster and pulls Cleo's hair harder).

"Unh!"

Plop!

"Unh!"

Plop!

"Beat this pussy! Oh God! Oh shit!"

Plop!

"Make it sore! Unh!"

(Trent goes faster and faster as he gets closer to cumming). "Unh! Oh fuck! Oh shit!" (Breathing rapidly). "Oh shit! Oh shit! Oh shit! Oh shit!"

"Unnnnnnnnnh!" (Cleo clinches the jackets on the ground and grits her teeth)

(In a forceful voice through her teeth). "Hit-this-pussy-niggah! Bust-this-pussy-wide-open!"

(Trent's dick is throbbing. He is about to cum.) "I'm about to cum, baby! Umm! I'm about to cum! Oh shit!"

"Oh hell no! Unnnnh! You better not cum!" (Cleo can feel Trent's throbbing dick on the walls of her pussy). "You better not fucking cum!"

"I can't hold it, baby! Oh shit! I can't hold it! I can't...ohhhhhhhhhhhhhhhhhhhhhhhh Shi-...ummmmmm!" (Breathing hard) "Oh!" (Exhale) "Oh!" (Exhale) "Whew! Damn, baby! Shit, shit! That felt so good!" (Trent collapses on top of Cleo's ass and back).

(Breathing hard) "Whew! Time for a nap."

"Ha, ha, ha. Shit! You aren't the only one. I can't count the number of times I came."

"What! And you were telling me not to cum!"

"I know baby, I know. I just wanted to cum together." (Cleo feels an aftershock). "Ooh, ooh! Don't move, don't move. Ummm!" (Big sigh) "Oh that was so good."

(Trent raises his body up and places his hand underneath Cleo's pussy to catch any cum as he pulls his dick out. He stands up and begins to put on his pants) "Wow, no sperm to catch. Ha, ha, ha."

"Oh don't worry about that baby. You left that cum deep up in this pussy." (Cleo stands up and begins to fix her clothes).

"Ha, ha, ha." (Trent grabs both jackets from the field. They put on their jackets and head off the field.) "Let's go baby. We should be able to get out through the back fence."

(Before they walk under the chain in the misaligned fence, Cleo discusses the significance of the 31-yard line.) "Ok baby...sooooooo...I think I figured out the significance of the 31-yard line."

"Oh really?"

"Yeah, it's simple. One hundred yards minus thirty-one yards is 69."

"Ha, ha, ha." (Trent stands back crossing his arms surprised by Cleo's answer).

"Sixty-nine yards to score!" (Cleo wiggles her head and gloats in front of Trent).

"Ha, ha, ha. Touchdown baby! Damn, you got it! I knew my baby would get it."

"Ha, ha, ha. Yeah! That is one of my favorite numbers and you know..."

"Yeah, yeah! You were born in 1969." (Trent pushes the fence as far apart as he can as Cleo bends down and walks through. He follows Cleo under the fence. He grabs her hand and they trot off to their car).

Chapter 7

A Visit to HR

(Answering phone) "Felicia Tidwell?"

"Hi, Felicia, your 9:00 AM appointment is here in the lobby...a Ms. Bria Thomas."

"Ok, send her right up."

"Ms. Thomas, take the elevator to the 4th floor. Ms. Tidwell's office will be to your right, suite 403."

(In a nervous voice). "Thank you, ma'am." (Bria presses the elevator up button and nervously waits for the elevator.)

(Oh my goodness, what could this meeting be about? Nothing good ever comes out of meeting with Felicia Tidwell. Oh God! I'm so nervous!)

(Bing! Elevator door opens) "Good morning!"

(Bria in a sad voice) "Good morning, sir."

"Hmmm...not having a good day?"

(Trying to hide her nervousness). "Oh...oh no, it's ok."

"Well, I hope you have a better day."

"I hope so too." (Bria steps in the elevator. Floor 1, Floor 2, Floor 3, Floor 4...Ding!) "Ok, here we go, suite 403."

(Bria stops at Felicia's administrator's desk). "Hello. How are you?"

"I'm doing ok."

"You are?"

"Bria Thomas."

"Oh...um" (with a concerned look) "go right in." (Damn, I know this won't be good). (Bria walks in as Felicia raises her head up from her desk).

"Hello, Bria, please have a seat." (Bria sits in the lone chair in front of Felicia's desk). "Do you need anything to drink? A water? A Coke?"

"No, ma'am, I'm fine."

"Ok...well, let's get right to it. I've called you in my office to discuss some very serious code of conduct violations."

(Bria swallows hard).

"Before the company takes any action, I am required to ask you direct questions concerning the allegations set against you. Do you clearly understand the process set before you?"

"Yes, ma'am." (Shit! Shit! Shit! I'm about to lose my job. It must be about me and Oscar having...)

(Felicia in a serious voice). "Please answer each question with a simple yes or no. Understand?"

"Yes."

"So for the first question, have you ever had sex on company grounds?"

"Um...uh...yes."

"Did you have sex more than once?"

"Yes."

"Did you have sex with Oscar Levine?"

(Crying) "Yes...yes...oh my God! I can't believe I did this! I'm going to lose my job! I should have..."

"Please calm down, Bria."

(Sobbing) "But I don't know what I'm going to do."

(Felicia hands Bria a tissue) "Bria, I'm very sorry to inform you that effective today, you are terminated from the company for violations of the code of conduct, which you have not denied."

(Bria sitting in shock covering her face with both hands).

"Please return to your office and remove your personal belongings. Drop your badge and keys at the security station on the way out."

"Do you have any questions for me?"

(Sniffing) "No, ma'am."

"You are free to leave." (Bria wipes her face and leaves Felicia's office).

(Felicia sits down at her desk looking off into the distance with a blank stare).

(This is the part of my job that I really hate. If it were up to me, I would have at least given her at least one chance. The poor girl is only wants someone to love her, but went about things the wrong way. Damn! I hate these rules! But they are in place for a reason. In this case, there was no affect on her job performance—it was stellar and that will be significant loss. It'll take some time to get someone up to her performance level. If it's not one thing, it's certainly another!)

(Long sigh). "Well, it's another long day coming, what else is new! Arrgggh! Somebody take me away from here!"

(Phone rings) Ring! Ring!

"Felicia Tidwell."

"Your 10:00 AM appointment is here: Mr. Oscar Levine."

(In a broken voice while clearing her throat) "Ummm...um...send him up please."

(With a voice of concern). "Are you ok Ms. Tidwell?"

"Oh yes, just caught a little something in my throat."

"I was just checking since you other appointment just zoomed past me on her way out."

"No. No, really I'm fine."

"Ok, no problem."

"I am sending him right up."

"Thank you."

(Receptionist hangs up phone). "Mr. Levine, you can go right up. Take the elevators to the 4th floor and make a right. Ms. Tidwell's office is suite 403."

"Thank you very much, ma'am. You have a wonderful day."

(Based on the last appointment, I hope you have a better day than the last appointment).

(Phone rings) Ring! Ring!

"My goodness this phone is so freakin loud!"

Ring! Ring! (She answers in an annoyed voice). "Hello!"

"Whoa! Whoa! Baby, it's Wayne."

"Oh baby, I'm sorry." (Frustrated) "I just have had such a hectic day! Terminated two employees this morning, completely reorganizing the Research and Development organization, negotiating the new health care plan with..."

"Baby, baby, baby!" (A soothing voice) "Slow it down...bring it down a few notches. It's going to be all right."

"That's easy for you to say, you don't know what I have to deal with."

"Hold up baby, hold up! You know I am fully aware of what your job requires. That is completely unfair. If anybody knows, it is without a doubt me."

"But...you're right, Wayne." (Pulling her hair) "Oooohh! I hate it when you're right!"

"Baby, you know I don't care about being right. I am only concerned about how you feel."

"Yes, you do have a way of calming me down."

"That's my job, baby."

"Hmmm...I don't know how you do it. You put up with me when I have one of these episodes."

"Episodes! Episodes! Baby, that's just the nature of your job. And you know that no one does it better than you! Not only do I appreciate what you do, but your whole organization knows that it would be chaos without your leadership. So take a pat on the back, baby! I know it's hard to give self-praise, but you are very valuable to your company and organization."

"Thank you, Wayne, I really appreciate you."

"Like I said, baby, it's my job to take care of you. I love you, Felicia."

"I love you too, Wayne. Thanks again. I feel a little better." (In a strained voice) "I'm going to refocus and get it done one day at a time."

(I know you're still stressed, but I'll go along with what you are saying for now). "That's the Felicia I know!"

"Ha, ha, ha!"

"So, Ms. Tidwell, will I see you later on this evening?"

"Oh for sure. I will definitely need to see you after today."

"Ok then, I will see you around 7:30."

"Right. Thanks again, Wayne, I really appreciate what you do for me."

"No problem, baby, have a good rest of the day!"

"Ok, sweety, talk to you later. Goodbye."

"Bye, sugah." (Felicia hangs up the phone and takes a deep breath). "All right then, time to get back at it. I just don't have enough time in the day. Suck it up Felicia, get your ass in gear."

(Calendar notice) "bing, bong"

(Reading notice) "Healthcare negotiation meeting in 1 hour."

"Shoot! I almost forgot! Let me review the plan options one more time before the meeting." (Felicia grabs her computer mouse and searches for the file) "Hmm...ok, here it is. 2010 Healthcare Plan Options.docx." (Felicia reads through the plan).

(At Wayne's office across town)
"Hey, Wayne, where are you headed?"
"Oh, I'm going out for lunch today. It's across town, so I might be back a little later than usual."
"Hmmmmm? You sure you going to lunch, bruh?"
"Ha, ha, ha!"
"Yes! I am going to lunch. I'm actually going to make a surprise visit to Felicia's office. She's really been having a more hectic day than normal."
"Aweee...naw, I'm just kidding. That's really nice. I was just going to ask you down to the cafeteria, but I understand completely. Well, enjoy your lunch, man. I'll catch up with you when you get back."
"All right, man, I will see you then." (Wayne walks out to his car in the parking deck). "Brrrrrrh! Man it's really chilly out here! And that rain doesn't help either." (Rubbing his hands quickly while breathing rapidly). "Woo, woo, woo...these leather seats are cold! Come on car, warm up! Come on, baby!" (Wayne backs out of the parking space and exits the parking deck).
(Radio) *This is 98.9 WHYZ, home of easy listening. With the fewest commercials on the planet! Our next song is a classic blast from the past, "All out of love."*
(Radio music playing lightly in the background against the sound of the windshield wipers).
(I really worry about how stressed Felicia becomes at times with her job. I don't think she takes stress seriously. I hope surprising her at her office will calm her down and help her to relax. Hmmm... I don't know. Well, it's worth a try. Oh let me call her administrator to get on the visitor list. I don't want her to know I am coming).
(Dialing) "Hello, Felicia Tidwell's office."
"Hi, Tarsha, this is Wayne."
"Oh hi, Wayne, I'll connect you to Felicia right away."
"No, no, wait! I want to surprise her. I know she's been having a hectic day."

"Oh, oh, ok, I got it. That's really sweet. I'll put you down on the list right now."

"Thanks so much, Tarsha."

"No problem Wayne. See you when you get here."

"Sounds good, bye-bye."

"Bye."

(Singing with the radio). *"What are you thinking of?"* *"Dunh, Dunh, Dunhhhhhhh. " I'm all out of love."*

"Oh yeah, sing it, boy! Glad there's no one else around. The birds are falling out of the sky. He, he, he. Ok, there it is, Eastland Drive. Hmmm...this is my first time coming to her new office."

(Wayne turns in and stops at the guard shack). "Good morning, sir."

"Good morning. I'm looking for building 10. I have an appointment with the Human Resource Division. Wayne Tolbert."

"Yes, I see your name on the list. Sign here, Mr. Tolbert."

(Wayne signs in). "Thanks."

"All right, go down to the stop sign, make a left and park in visitor parking in front of building 10."

"Thank you very much, sir."

"You're welcome, have a great day."

"You too."

(As Wayne parks, he sees Felicia standing by her window leaning against the wall looking away from his direction. She places one hand on the glass to trace rain drops as they randomly slide down the window). "Yep, that's exactly how I feel. Just like the raindrop. Going off in unknown directions, plummeting to sudden death at the bottom of the window. Hmmmm...I don't know. Maybe I need to consider another career? Let's see. I could go into teaching, but that doesn't pay very well. Duh! That's probably even more stressful. Ok, try again. Well, I did do real estate about 10 years back. That's not that stressful. Of course though, I would have to build new clientele. Arrgghh! Like I always knew, no easy way out."

"Bing, bong!" (Felicia doesn't realize that she has 30 minutes left until her healthcare meeting. She continues to be occupied by thoughts of career changes in her mind).

(Wayne arrives at the administrator's desk).

(Whispering) "Hi, Tarsha."

"Hi, Wayne."

"Is she still in her office?"

"Oh yeah, she's in there. Her meeting to negotiate the new healthcare plan is not until 12—a little less than 30 minutes from now."

"Ok, that's perfect."

"Since I knew you were coming, I didn't fully close the door so that all you have to do is push it open. Her desk is to the left of her conference table so you should be able to sneak in if you're careful."

"You are the best, Tarsha. Thanks again."

"No problem, good luck."

(Whisper) "Ok, here we go."

(Felicia is still at the window in deep thought. She's totally unaware that Wayne has entered her office. He gently closes the door and carefully flips the lock. He slips off his dress shoes to minimize any noise).

(There is my baby over next to the window. He slides all the way around the corner so she can't see him in the reflection of the glass. As he gets closer, she notices a presence in her office and calls out for Tarsha).

"Tarsha, is that you?" (Before she begins to turn around, Wayne gently covers her eyes with his hands. Felicia is slightly startled but quickly notices that it is Wayne).

"Hey sweety, its Wayne."

(In a calm voice) "Ummm hum, I know those hands anywhere. And that Polo cologne, ummmh! That shit drives me crazy!" (Felicia wants to turn around, but Wayne constrains her).

"Not yet, baby. Don't turn around yet. Keep your eyes closed." (Wayne slowly slides his hands down lightly caressing Felicia's neck and shoulders. He begins to massage her shoulders gently while whispering in her ear.)

(With a deep inhale) "Sssswipp! How does that feel baby?"

Kiss!

"Ummmmmmmmm! Oh that feels so good, baby."

(Wayne moves his hands to the top of Felicia's torso. He spreads his fingers apart and pushes them down the sides of her body to her hips). "Oh, baby! You are really getting me hot! Shit!"

(Whispering) "Oh good, baby. I just want you to relax, baby. Take yourself away from here."

"Unnh hunh."

"Yes, away from here." (Wayne moves his hands around to the front of Felicia's skirt and pushes his fingers in to her skirt. He pulls her body back closer to him. Felicia can feel his dick throbbing on her ass).

"Ummmm! Ummm! Oh my goodness! Shit that feels good! I can feel that big ass dick beating on my ass."

(Wayne pulls his hands out of Felicia's skirt and cups both of her breasts). "Oooooh!" (Deep breath) "Whewwww! Oh God! This is...this is so damn good!" (Felicia hears a conversation outside her door. She opens her eyes nervously). "Oh shit! Is the door locked?"

"Shhh! Shhh! Calm down, baby. The door is locked. I got you." (Wayne continues to massage her breast as she calms back down).

"Ok, baby, I trust you."

"Like I said, darling, I got you. I know how important your position is as well as that you are in Human Resources."

"Yeah, because just this morning..."

(Wayne interrupts) "Shhh! Shh! Close your eyes, baby."

(Calmly) "Ok...ok, daddy."

(Wayne then takes one hand and slides it deeper into Felicia's skirt. He slides past her blouse directly to her pubic hairs.) "Oh wow! Easy access, baby."

"Mmmmm! Yes! You know I don't like wearing panties, baby."

"Yes, I do know that, but it is always exciting to discover...oh damn! Your pussy is wetter than Ruby Falls!"

"You know how you do that to me, baby. Just like turning on a faucet!"

(Waynes slides his fingers directly on top of Felicia's clit. He begins to encircle her clit with his index finger). "Unnhhh....unnnh...oh, baby! Rub mama's pussy. Rub that shit! Oh goodness, let me feel it inside." (Felicia grabs Waynes hand with both of her hands and forces his finger inside her). "Unnnh! Unhhh!" (Wayne goes deeper and presses his finger to the top of her vaginal walls). "Oh damn, niggah! Ummm! That is my fucking spot! You're going to make me cum! Ummm!"

"Go ahead, baby, cum all in my hand. Do it, baby! You can do it!"

"Unnnh! Unhhhhh!" (Louder) "Unnh!!! Ohhhhhhhhhhhhhhhhhhhh! Ummmmm!" (Gasping for breath) "Oh yes...oh yes... damn, I needed that shit!"

"Yes you did, baby, that's why your daddy came all the way here."

"Well, mommy appreciates it. But you know you ain't leaving here without cumming up in this pussy!"

"Damn baby! I love it when you talk like that. You ain't said nothing but a word!" (Wayne turns Felicia around, picks her up and carries her over to her desk. He forces her gently down onto her back. He places her legs on his shoulders. Her skirt falls back exposing half of her pussy. Felicia reaches up and unbuckles Wayne's pants, unbuttons and unzips them and lies back down. Wayne pushes his pants and underwear to the floor). "Oh yeah! Let me see that pussy!" (He flips her skirt back.) "There's my pussy! Oh yeah, that's what I'm talking about! Let me taste that phat pussy!" (Wayne bends down and begins to suck Felicia's pussy).

(In a muffled voice) "Mmmm...mmmmm...mmmm..."

Slurp! Slurp!

"Yes, daddy, suck that pussy! That shit feels so good. Let me feel that dick! I need to feel that dick!"

(Wayne stands up and grabs his dick by the base and starts to lightly beat on Felicia's clit). "Oh! You want to feel this dick huh!"

"Oh yes, baby, oh yes!" (Wayne puts part of his dick head into her pussy lips). "Ooooohhh! Oooohhh! Come on, baby, don't tease me!" (Pleading) "Put it in! Please, put it in! (Wayne grabs each of Felicia's inner thighs and slides her body forward and back on his dick) "Unnnh! Unnhhh! Unh!!! Oooooh, niggah! You said you..."

(A knock at the door freezes them both in their tracks) Knock, knock!

(Catching her breath) "Uh um...who is it?"

"It's Tarsha. You have 5 minutes until your next meeting."

(In a low surprised voice). "Oh shit! Damn, I forgot that I have the healthcare meeting." (Wayne and Felicia both scramble to clean up and pull themselves together). "Oh yes, thank you Tarsha. I was just getting some things together before the meeting. Thanks for reminding me."

"Ok, Felicia, no problem. Damn! Damn! Damn! That shit was so good!"

"I'm glad you feel better, babe. Yeah, I feel better, but you know you're leaving work early, right?"

"Hmmm...well I guess I am now."

"Oh, no guessing. As soon as my meeting is done, I need to see you at my house!"

"Oh yes, ma'am!"

(Fixing her hair and skirt). "Ok, how do I look?"

"You look great, baby."

"All right then, I'm off to my meeting." (She gives Wayne a quick kiss and leaves the office).

(Wayne checks himself in the mirror and leaves the office). "Hello, Tarsha, thanks for everything. I'll see you later."

"See you...wait a minute, Mr. Tolbert."

"Yes?"

"You may want to wear some shoes if you're going outside."

(Wayne embarrassingly turns around and goes to Felicia's office for his shoes. He quickly speeds by Tarsha's desk after retrieving his shoes on his way out of the building without making eye contact). "Good bye, Tarsha."

"Bye, Mr. Tolbert." (So that's the reason Felicia was so relaxed and happy when she left for her meeting Um hum. He, he, he.)

Chapter 8

Phat Tuesday

"Hey Desiree, how are things going?"
"Oh just fine, Asia! I am just blessed, girl."

"How is the hubby doing?"

"Oh, he's just fine...oh, oh! He's preaching at his new church Sunday."

"That sounds wonderful."

"You should come out and join us this coming Sunday."

"Oh wow, that sounds lovely, but I will have to take a rain check this go-round" (Thank goodness!) "I'll be out of town visiting my in-laws."

"Oh. I understand. You're going to miss out, but there will be other sermons. I'm so excited about his first sermon there...I mean, I just can't wait!"

(Yeah, I bet you can't wait. Everyone knows you're miserable at home and pretending to be happy. To each their own). "Well, I'm sure it will be wonderful."

"Yes it will."

"So are you staying down for lunch?"

"Well...I usually read my Bible during lunch so..."

(Asia interrupts) "Come on, girl! Have lunch with us!"

"Well, I don't..."

"Come on. I..."

(Coercing voice) "Come on, get your lunch and meet us in the back. We'll be to the right at the round table."

"Ok, Asia, I'll be back there shortly."

"Great!" (With a concerned look) "Wait! Wait! How many folks are back there?"

"Well with you, it'll be four. All girls! Why?"

"Well, I thought there might be men and..."

(Asia interrupts) "Oh please! You know Brenda and Lacy. And if there were men, they aren't going to bite you, especially at work."

"Well...ok, I just don't want them trying to get between me and my husband."

(Well somebody needs to and maybe your ass wouldn't be so uptight). "Yes, yes. You will be just fine. See you in a minute."

(Desiree gets a salad and heads back to where the girls are sitting. She's holding her tray and looking around for the girls with a confused look on her face).

(Asia put up her hand to wave Desiree over) "Desiree! Desiree! Over here..."

(Desiree sees Asia and walks over to the table) "Good afternoon, ladies!"

(In unison) "Hi, Desi!"

"Glad you could join us."

(Desiree sits her tray down and takes a seat). "Please, ladies! I haven't been called that since I got married."

"What! What is wrong with..."

(Asia interrupts Brenda while rolling her eyes to the other girls except Desiree). "Brenda, you know she asked us to call her Desiree after she got married."

"Oh...ok. I truly forgot. I'm so sorry, Desiree."

"Oh, girl, no harm done. My husband feels like that saying my name that way is not lady like."

(Brenda with a stunned look). "Not lady like! Are you serious?"

"Yes, Brenda."

"Come on! Shortening your name is not lady like! Oh wow, that's the first time I heard some crazy shit like that!"

(Asia interrupts) "Brenda...Brenda...let's drop it."

"But..."

"Drop it!"

(Desiree looks surprised as she looks around at the other women. There is a deafening silence at the table. Only the clanging of forks to dishware can be heard with other company associates having lunch in the background. To break the mood, Asia offers up an invitation for the girls to visit Mardi Gras in New Orleans).

"Oooooh, ooooh! You know we got to make reservations soon for Mardi Gras!"

"Yeah, well you know Lacy and I are in! Oh my goodness, it's going to be so much fun!"

(Asia turns to Desiree) "How about you, Desiree? Are you interested in going?"

"Well...I don't know. I have heard so much bad stuff about it. Like women taking their tops off and showing their breasts!" (With her nose turned up) "That is totally disgusting! Showing my body to complete strangers, are you kidding me! And the crazy parties! Oh my God, Asia!"

"Wow! Desiree you're not serious are you?"

"Oh, yes I am. The debauchery! My husband would never approve of that."

"Ha, ha, ha! Oh he wouldn't approve of seeing all that tits and ass?"

"No, he wouldn't. He doesn't even like me saying 'tits' and 'ass'. He refers to it as 'breasts' and 'behind.'"

(Asia mocks Desiree) "*Breasts and behind!* Ha, ha, ha! I'm just playing girl. You need to loosen up a bit. You really should come."

"But my husband..."

"Doesn't have to know! And for the most part, what are you doing wrong by having a little fun?"

(Desiree says to herself. What is wrong with having a little fun? I don't do anything for myself. All I do is march to the beat of what John says. Fuck it! I'm going).

"Oh, and the parades..."

"I'm going."

"What!"

"I'm going! I am tired of pretending to be someone else. Yes, I'm married to a preacher, but shit! I'm not fucking dead! I'm going to take some time for me. Hell! Day in and day out, all I do is work on pleasing Pastor Hammond! By not saying this, or not saying that! Like, I'm some fucking puppet!"

"Ok, girl, ok! We hear you. We here you loud and clear!"

"Ha, ha, ha!"

"Now that is the Desi I know!"

"Ha, ha, ha! You're fucking right! This is Desi up in this bitch! So when do I need to make my reservation?"

"Well, you have until the end of the week."

"Shit! I'm making it as soon as I get back to my desk! Send me the information, girl, I'm ready!"

"All right, girl! That's the way to let your hair down! Oh my goodness! It is going to be so much fun!"

"Yes it is."

"So...do you'll think I'll be able to get some beads?"

(In unison) "What!"

(Asia looks Desiree up and down). "Bitch please! With those curves and that fat, rotund ass! Ha, ha, ha! You'll get so many damn beads, you will be sick of them!"

"But...but I didn't think no one would pay attention to me. My husband always says that men don't want ladies that show off her curves. And women that dress that way..."

"Hold the fuck up, girl! Excuse me for interrupting, but your husband must have some strange male friends. Let me tell you...and I'm not gay, but any real, red-blooded American man is going to be all over you girl! You got a nice figure. Like Betty Wright said, 'Use what we got, to get what we want!'"

"I second that, Brenda!"

"I third! Shit girl, we're all going to be getting showered in beads."

"You got that right! So, girl, don't worry about that. That will be the least of your worries."

"Thanks, Asia. I really appreciate you guys. I feel so much better all ready. I've been living a lie much too long. It's like I fell in love with what it meant to be married to the great Pastor Hammond, but I lost myself in the process. Like, before I got married, I used to get it on! I mean get it on! I love it when somebody talks dirty to me, oh my God! But not with Pastor Hammond. He says it's not proper to say 'dick!' It's 'penis!'"

(The girls are looking at Desiree amazed with eyes stretched).

"And 'pussy!' Oh, that's 'vagina!'"

(In a long voice) "Damn...Girl!"

"Well, girl, you know you can be yourself around us."

"I know that for sure. But you just don't know what it's like! Don't you guys ever have fantasies you want to fulfill?"

"Oh yes, girl."

"Well, I can't even mention anything outside of missionary position."

"Oh hell no! You got to be kidding!"

"I wish I was. Oh, and don't think about sucking his dick and having him explode in my mou–...th." (Desiree embarrassed puts her hand up to her mouth). "Oh, I mean...I'm sorry, girls. I got a little carried away."

(The girls look at Desiree in shock. Asia jumps in to comfort Desiree). "Oh, girl please! No harm done. We all have things we planned on doing with our husbands. For one reason or another, it just doesn't happen that way."

(Brenda joins in). "Yeah, girl, we all like different things. Ain't that right, Lacy?"

"Oh, don't bring me in this. I just say, to each it's own."

"Oh really! What about the time we went to the Carribean festival and you..."

(Lacy puts her hand over Brenda's mouth). "...di–d th...at g–uy."

"Brenda! Hush it!" (Lacy removes her hand).

"Ok, girl."

"I'm just saying."

"Yes, I know."

"Ok. Ok. Desiree, really, it's fine to do what you like. You own your happiness, so stop letting others define it."

"You know, you guys are right. I'm going to do what I need to do to be happy. And I am going to start with Mardi Gras baby!"

"That's right, girl."

"Now you talking."

(buzz, buzz) "Oh shoot! I almost forgot. I got my performance review in 15 minutes. Well, ladies, I have to run. Thank you guys again and you, Asia for inviting me to lunch."

"Oh no problem, girl. I will send you the information for the trip as soon as I get back to my desk."

"Oh, please believe, don't think I wasn't going to remind you!"

"He, he, he."

"Bye y'all."

"Bye, sistah Hammond!"

"Ha, ha, ha!"

(After several weeks of anticipation, Asia pulls up in to Desiree's driveway to pick her up for their trip to New Orleans). "Bomp!" "Bomp!"

(Desiree peaks out from the curtain. She motions to the girls through the window with one index finger up).

"Looks like she's saying one minute. She needs to get a move on." (Anxiously) "I would like to get on the road so we can get there and get some rest."

"Get rest? Girl, you know my best guy friend EJ lives there. He said that for Mardi Gras, no one sleeps!"

"What! Brenda you can't be serious?"

"Oh yes, I don't know, but that is what he said."

"Well, damn! As the saying goes, when in Rome..."

(In unison) "Do as the Romans do!"

"Oh, and before anyone asks, he has a girlfriend."

"Ha, ha, ha!"

"Bomp!" "Bomp!"

"Come on Desi! She's probably getting all her instructions from Pastor Hammond."

"Ha, ha, ha!"

"Ooooooh Lacy, you wrong for that, girl!"

"Well, you know, it's..."

(Desiree knocks on the car window) "Knock!" "Knock!" "Knock!"

"Pop the trunk, Asia!"

"Ok, ok, let me find it. This rental car has gadgets all over the place."

"Hurry up, girl! Before you know who changes his mind."

"Ha, ha, ha!"

"Oh, there it is."

(Desiree places her luggage in the trunk and gets into the backseat of the car with Brenda). "Why were you guys laughing?"

"Lacy mentioned you were getting your instructions from the Reverend-Doctor Pastor Hammond..."

"Ha, ha, ha!"

"That ain't funny. But unfortunately it's true. And the nerve, he was trying to tell me what to wear. He wanted to make sure no man would even look at me let alone talk to me."

"So what did you do?"

"You know I put one bogus outfit in the suitcase and my bad shit underneath. Hell, he'll be fine. I'm going to enjoy myself. As my uncle Nuke use to say, 'take my shoes off!'"

"Well, girl, hopefully you will be taking off more than that."

(Desiree looks over at Brenda) "Excuse me! I'm going to have fun, but I don't really know if I can be taking things off. I'm not acting above anyone, but that is a little too much."

"Well, girl, whatever you decide to do is fine. It's all up to you. As the saying goes, 'What happens in the N-O, stays in the N-O!'"

"I know that's that right."

(Asia backs out of the driveway) "All right, ladies, we are out of here!"

(Five and one half hours later, Desiree wakes up from falling asleep during the ride). (Groggy) "What time is it?"

"Eight thirty."

"Oh my, we shouldn't be far away."

"Yep, about 30 minutes out."

"Oh really, that is close. Man, I must have slept all the way."

"Hmmm...you think?"

"Ha, ha, ha!"

"You should have woken me, girl. I would have helped you drive."

"Oh please, not a problem at all. You know how I roll. Six hours driving is nothing to me."

(Brenda and Lacy wake up) "Good to see you getting up, Brenda. We aren't that far from your friend's house."

(Stretching) "Ummm...that was a good nap."

"Yeah all of you should be well rested."

"Oh, Asia, you should..."

"You should have woke me up! Yeah right. All three of you were slobbering like crazy."

"Ha, ha, ha!"

"Anyway girl, what exit do I take to get to your friend's house?"

"Exit 263, Old Spanish Trail."

"Oh good then, we have only about 10 miles to go."

"What! What! Oh shit! It's about to be on, ladies!"

(Asia takes Exit 263 and follows Brenda's lead to her friend house. As she pulls in to the driveway, they notice no cars around but the garage door is open.) "Hmmm...that's odd. EJ knew I was coming. I don't see his car anywhere."

"Maybe his girlfriend is in."

"Maybe. Well let's go find out."

(Everyone gets out of the car to enter the house through the garage. Brenda knocks on the door to the house from the garage). Knock, knock!

(A deep male voice comes from inside the house.) "Yo! Yo! Hold on to your horses! I'm coming!" (With a look of surprise and holding the door open). "Well, well! Oh my! EJ didn't tell me you girls were holding it down like this. Mmmmm, mmm!" (As they walk past him into the house.)

"Well thank you, mmmm? You are? And where is EJ?"

"Oh, oh sorry about that babeh! My name is Cory!"

"Hi, Cory."

"I'm sorry about dat! EJ had to pick up some more food for the cook out tomorrow. He'll be back in a few. So, let me be the first to welcome you ladies to the N-Oooooooooo! Nawlins baby! The big easy!"

"Thank you, Cory, we are so glad to be here! I can't tell you how excited we are about Mardi Gras! We are ready to get our party on!"

"Party on!..."

"What! Mardi Gras ain't no party, babeh! Ya heard! Mardi Gras is an experience!"

"Well all right then, tell us what's up. What are we about to experience?"

(Looking at Desiree after she asks her question). "And what's your name, baby girl?"

"Desiree."

"Well, let me tell you this, by the time you leave you will know what the 'Gras' is all about."

"Oh shit!"

"Shit, girl! We're losing valuable time. Let me get you ladies started off right!" (Cory continues to shout back at the girls as he goes into the garage). "Get you right before we head out! Get you some of this 190 octane, babeh! That's a daiquiri for your ass!" (Cory steps back into the room with four cups of daiquiri with straws in them). "Here you go, rookies."

"Ha, ha, ha!"

"Rookies?"

"What's up with that?"

"Well, this is your first Mardi Gras, right?"

"Yep. But..."

"Drink up, Rooks! You wanna do Mardi Gras, then..."

"Wait a minute, what is in this?"

"Awe...babeh! Dat ain't nuttin but a little get-up-and-go juice."

"Alcohol! Yeah, but it is really, really smooth."

"Are you kidding me! Its 9:30 in the morning!"

"Ha! Ha! Welcome to the Gras babeh! That's how we do it in the N-O! Actually, we need to catch up. We getting started a little late!"

"Well, I never..."

"Girl, what did we talk about before we left home?"

"Arrrgh! Ok. Ok. I can do this!"

"Oh don't worry, babeh!"

"We got you. EJ told me to get you guys started right! So that's what's up!"

"Mmmmm. This ain't that bad even though this is way early for me." (Desiree takes a few long sips).

"Whoa! Whoa! Slow down, shawty! It's smooth, but it can be a little sneaky. You don't want to get a brain freeze!"

"Ha, ha, ha!"

"Whew! Damn! You're right." (Holding her hand to her head). "This shit got some kick to it!"

(Loud car stereo is playing the background as it pulls into the garage).

(Asia frowns and turns toward Brenda) "Oh my goodness! Who in the world is playing their stereo that loud!"

"Let's take a wild guess! That would be EJ."

"Yep! That's your boy!"

"I see, some people never change."

"That is the one thing that you can always say, he doesn't change for nobody! Ha, ha, ha! You know that fool ain't gone never change."

(Desiree jumps in). "Hmmm, looks like I need to take some tips from him."

"You got that right."

"Shut up, girl! You didn't have to agree!"

"Ha, ha, ha!"

(Car door shuts and door to garage door opens.) "Woo! Woo! Woo! Woo! What's up, babeh's!"

(Brenda gets up from the couch to greet EJ) "Hey, baby girl! What's up with ya!"

"Just ready to tear it up at Mardi Gras!"

"Oh yeah, me and my boy Cory gonna show you'll the real Gras!" (Brenda leans in to hug EJ). "Mmmh! Damn girl, good to see you again!"

"You too, EJ."

"If I didn't have a girlfriend, I would…"

(Brenda lightly hits EJ in the chest). "Boy! Stop playin! Don't have your girlfriend jumping on me!"

"Ha, ha!"

"You crazy, girl. I got this!" (EJ looks around to make sure his girlfriend is not in sight).

"Yeah, you knows how I do it."

"Yeah right, that's why yo ass got hemmed up with that broad a few years ago."

"Oh, oh. That was different!"

"Whatever, Negro!"

"Ok, ok. Anyway, you girls ready to hit the town and do the Gras like it's supposed to be done."

"What! We just got here."

"What's that suppose to mean? You'll need to be ready to roll in 20 minutes."

"Damn, that's short! I got to…"

"You got to be ready in 20. Wasting daylight. Hey, you need any help getting your things out the car?"

"No we can handle it."

"All right, let me go change to some shorts and prep our portable drinks."

"Portable drinks?"

"Yes, portable."

"What are those?"

"Well, it's just used Powerade bottles that I have washed out and sterilized to fill with my secret drink mix."

"Mmmm…"

"Yes, so it looks like you're drinking Powerade."

"Damn! Yo ass think of everything!"

"Ha, ha, ha! See you'll in 20 minutes."

(The group stands by watching the first Mardi Gras parade of the day). "Desi! Desi! Here comes the Zulu float! Move up front! You got to get one of the coconuts!"

"What? What? Why would I want a coconut?"

"Girl! Everybody wants a coconut; they're the ultimate prize possession from Mardi Gras."

"Ok then, girl, I'm coming. I'm a little slow with all these beads I have. These things are getting heavy!"

"He, he, he! Well, you need to get rid of some of those small beads and save some room for some of the bigger ones."

"What big ones? These are all I've seen. Where do I get some?"

"Oh, girl, I keep forgetting you haven't done this before. You don't get the big beads unless you earrrrnnn themmmm!"

"Earn them? What do you mean?"

"I mean, earn them. Girl!"

"Be more specific!"

"Ok, ok. You got to show something, baby!"

(Desiree in shock). "Show something!"

(EJ, Cory, Asia, Lacy in unison), "Yes, show something! Tits or ass girl!"

"Oh my goodness! I....umm. Uh...I don't know! In front of all these..."

(Interrupted by her friends chanting). "Show your tits!" "Show your tits!" "Show your tits!" "Show your tits!" (Other bystanders join in to urge Desiree to show her breasts).

"Show your tits!"

"Show your tits!"

"Come on, girl! Show'em!"

(Desiree can't believe that her friends and the crowd are asking her to bare her tits in front of them. She reaches down and pretend to pull up her shirt. The crowd gets louder in anticipation.) "Show those tits! Show those tits!"

(Fuck it! It's all in fun).

(A loud scream of the crowd as Desiree pulls up her shirt) "Rahhhhhhhh!!!"

"Here! You see them!" (Propping her breasts up with each hand).

"Whew! Damn those shits are nice!"

"Damn, B! I didn't know your girl was stacked like that! Mmmh!"

(As Desiree pulls her shirt down, a tall attractive gentleman places a large necklace of beads around her neck). "Oh wow! Thank you. These are really nice!" (The gentleman smiles and nods without saying a word and backs into the crowd).

(Brenda, Lacy and Asia peer at Desiree with a shocked and surprised look) "Ooooh, girl! Who was that?"

"I wish I knew. I thanked him for the beads and he didn't say a word. And before I could say anything else, he backed away into the crowd. Damn! I wanted to at least know his name!"

"Dang, girl! Your tits left him speechless! But you all ready knew that, huh?"

"Ha, ha, ha!"

"Well, don't worry about finding out his name. He'll be back. With beads like that, he must have really liked what he saw!"

"You think so?"

"Hell yes!" (Desiree staring off into the distance—Damn, I hope that niggah comes back. Shit! That mutha-fucka looked good! Ummh! I haven't felt that good in a while!)

"He will be back. You don't give out beads like that and not have any interest."

"What will you do if he comes back?...Desi?" (Asia pushes on Desiree's shoulder) "Desi?"

"Hunh?"

"Did you hear what I said?"

"Umm...no, I'm sorry."

"I said, what will you do if he comes back?"

"Oh my God! Oh wow! Well, I wouldn't do anything. I am a married woman. I could never..."

"Girl, I didn't ask all that. But I see where your mind is going."

"What! No, I am just saying, girl."

"I could never. Umm...never mind. He's gone anyway. I just wanted to know his name. I can even remember what he was wearing. Oh well...it did feel good to have that kind of attention though."

(Asia in disbelief) "Oh yeah. Un hunh. Just wanted to know his name... Righhhht!!!"

"Stop it, girl."

"Ok, ok. He was interesting."

"Now that's more like it."

"Shit, girl, you are human!"

"Yeah, you're right. Hell, hope we'll run into him again."

(The other friends in the group begin to walk off). "Hey guys! Where are you going?"

"We are headed up to Club Opal."

"Hey, what about my coconut?"

"Come on, girl."

"I think you did pretty good with those beads!"

(Giddy) "Yes, they are nice."

"All right then."

"Wait up, we're coming." (Asia and Desiree walk fast to catch up to the rest of the group).

"Oh my goodness! That line is wrapping around the building! I hope it's worth the wait."

"Ha! Ha! Girl, please! We are not waiting in that line. Didn't we tell you we got y'all? Well, believe dat! We going VIP girl." (Cory leads everybody up to the front of the line to the VIP entrance).

"Hey, Cory, what's up, baby boy!"

"You got it, Remmy!"

"These your peeps?"

"Yeah they're friends of EJ."

"Oh what up, EJ! I didn't see you back there."

"No problem, playa! It's all good."

"Hello ladies."

"Damn, you looking really nice tonight!" (Remmy grabs the rope to let them through). "This way, ladies."

(Asia and Brenda walk through first with Lacy followed by Desiree in the rear). "Whoa! Whoa! Who are you, baby girl? You're last but certainly not least.

"Desiree. Desi for short".

(Remmy talks to Desiree but is focused on her ass). "Nice, nice. You look really nice, baby." (Damn, look at that ass! Fuck, that shit is plump!) Oh and the beads! Dang! Somebody must really like you. Beads like that are not easy to come by."

"So I've been told."

"Well, can't say I don't blame the guy. Ummh!"

"Ha! Ha!"

"Oh stop it!"

"No, I'm serious."

"Why thank you."

"I'm sorry. Not trying to hold you up. Go ahead and have a good time."

"Ok then, see you later."

"I sure hope the hell you do."

(Desiree goes into the club. She goes over to her friends).

"Come on, Desi! Let's get on the floor. That's my song!"

"Choppa style, chop-chop,Choppa style!" "We won't chop-chop!"

"Damn, girl that's my shit."

(Desiree and Brenda dance to several songs).

"Hey, girl, let's get something to drink."

"Ok, B, what do you want?"

"Crown and Seven."

"All right then, I'll be right back." (Desiree heads for the bar. She coincidentally bumps into the gentleman that gave her the beads).

"Oh excuse me, miss."

"I'm sorry, I wasn't looking were I was going."

"Oh no problem, miss." (Desire continues to the bar).

(Wait a minute. Was that him? He look kind of familiar, but I don't know. He left so fast).

"Hello."

"Yeah, baby?"

"Let me get a Crown and Seven and an amaretto sour."

"Ok, baby, coming up!"

(Desiree turns around to get another look at the guy she bumped into and saw him sitting at bar table across the room looking straight at her. She turns away and looks down). "Oh shit! That is him!" (He has got his eyes locked right in on me. He's probably been watching me all night. Desiree nervously turns completely away from him). "Oh my God!" (They said he would be back. What are you going to do if he comes back? Shoot, I don't know what to do).

"Here are your drinks ma'am."

"How much do I owe you?"

"Oh, those are all ready paid for."

"Who? What? Oh, never mind. Thank you!"

"Nice beads!"

"Thanks."

"Hold up one minute."

"Do you remember who gave you these beads?" (Nervously) "Somewhat."

"What! What!"

"Is there something wrong?"

"No, no. It's just that..."

"What! Oh, you really don't know. No one has told you."

"Told me what?"

"Ok, take a look at all your beads. They are all pretty similar except one."

"Hmmm. I really didn't notice anything."

"Well, you wouldn't since you probably never heard of it."

"But I see it clearly."

(The bartender points to the special bead). "See, this one right there. It has a pink cherry in the center."

"Oh my, I see it! I would have never noticed it." (Very excited) "So what does it mean?"

"Well, it's usually given to a female that a guy is really, really, really into. It's only used during Mardi Gras for someone that...um...I hate to say..."

"What? What?"

"He wants to fuck you!"

(Desiree places both hands up to her mouth). "Oh damn!" (Desiree is nervously excited). "Oh my God! I can hardly breathe. Oh shit!"

"Ma'am? Ma'am? Are you ok?"

(Desiree takes a deep breath) "Whew...yes, yes. I'm ok. That was just a little surprising is all. Ok. I think I'm good now." (Damn, this Mardi Gras shit is wilder than I thought. I don't know what to think. Should I? What the hell am I saying! I'm married. What will John say? What will the girls say?)

"Ma'am?" (The bartender waves his hand in front of Desiree).

(I...I...damn it! Fuck what everybody else thinks! I got to live my life! I'm going for it!)

(Desiree turns to walk across the run to meet her admirer).

"Ma'am? Don't forget your drinks."

"Oh shit! I'm sorry. Thanks." (Desiree takes the drinks back over to where Brenda and the group are standing. Brenda notices a peculiar look on Desiree's face).

"Desiree, are you ok?"

"Yes, why would you say that?"

"Well, you seem to be glowing or something. What happened over at the bar?"

"Oh, um nothing."

"Yeah right!"

"Seriously, nothing happened."

"Well whatever it is, it's got you looking pretty happy. So, do your thang girl. Like we said before leaving home..."

(In unison) "What happens in the N-O stays in the N-O!"

"Ha, ha, ha!"

"Damn! That Crown and Seven was really good! Desiree? Do you want another drink?"

"Oh no girl, I'm good." (Desiree contemplates a way to get to her admirer). "Actually, I think I'm going to get some air. This smoke is killing me!"

"That sounds like a good idea."

"Hey, you want me to come with you?"

"No! Uh... I mean, after you get your drink."

"Ok, girl. I'll be right back."

(Ok girl. You can do this. Take a deep breath. Let's go). "Asia, tell Brenda I will be back. I'm going to the ladies room."

"Ok, girl, no problem."

(Brenda comes back with her drink). "Hey Asia, where's Desiree?"

"Oh she went to the bathroom after you left."

"Oh really? That's a long time to be in the bathroom."

"You think? (Brenda's eyes get wide). "That trick! She done went after that guy!"

"Don't hate on her, girl, I'm proud of her. She needs to let loose."

"Shit! You're right! I'm not hating, I am just mad it's not me. The Negro was fine!"

"Unh hunh!"

"Yes indeed!" (Asia looks over Brenda's shoulder and sees Desiree standing by the gentleman that gave her the beads). "Hey B, isn't that her over there?"

"Yep! She's with that guy! Looks like they are about to leave! Go Desi! Do your thang, girl!"

"So you finally came over huh!"

"Yep!" (Taking a deep breath). "I'm here."

"Glad you finally came over."

(Nervously) "Yes, I'm here."

"Ha! Ha! Are those the only words you know?"

'No, just a little nervous."

"Oh, don't be nervous, it's nothing to be nervous about."

(Taking a deep breath). "Ok. Ok."

(Extending his hand). "Oh sorry, my name is Norie."

"Hi, Norie, nice to meet you. I'm Desiree, Desi for short."

"Very nice to meet you as well." (Oh my goodness, he smells so good! And that smile, shit! Those pretty white teeth).

"So, Desi, what took you so long to come over after I gave you the beads? Didn't you know what they meant?"

"No! I didn't have a clue. This is my first Mardi Gras ever! I nearly lost my mind when the bartender told me what the beads meant."

"Oh really? Ha, ha, ha!"

"But after thinking about it...fuck it! I'm at Mardi Gras!"

"Oh wow! I really thought you knew after you showed your breasts to the crowd. Unnh! Those breasts are delicious!"

"Thank you, I guess."

"You guess. Woman! Yo ass is fine! Then looking down at that big phat ass! I was like Damn!"

"Thank you, Norie. I just never hear that at home."

"What! You got to be kidding!"

"Nope. Not at all."

"Well, any man..."

"No more talking." (Desiree grabs Norie's hand and pulls him out of the club). "Come on! Let's do this shit! I hope you got condoms."

"Hell yes! Lead the way, babe." (Desiree and Norie exit the club. Asia and Brenda notice her leaving).

"Oh shit! Girl is going somewhere. Damn, Desi do your thang, girl, do your thang!"

(Damn, I can't believe I am doing this! I am so nervous! Shit, my pussy is so wet! I'm about to cum just thinking about it. A new dick in this pussy, oh my God!)

"Hey, let's go down there behind that dumpster."

"You lead the way. I have no idea where I'm going."

(Breathing hard) "All right, let's do this shit!" (Norie grabs Desiree and begins to kiss her). "Mmmm!" (Desiree feels Norie's dick bulging in his pants. Desiree grabs his dick and strokes it gently through his pants).

"Umm...that shit is big!"

"Oh damn, girl. That shit feels good!" (Norie starts to reach under Desiree's skirt but gets interrupted by a car passing by the dumpster). "Oh shit! We got to move somewhere else. Too much traffic moving through here. Let's move further into the quarter."

"Okay, daddy, lead the way."

"Oh...I have an idea. A lot of the houses in the quarter have alleys beside them. Let's try that one over there." (Norie walks over to the gate). "Damn, the gate is locked! I'll check the next one. This one is locked too."

"This is crazy!"

"It shouldn't be this hard to find a place to fuck in public!"

"Ha, ha, ha!"

"All these gates are locked. Fuck! I want your ass so bad! Think, Norie, think!" (Holding his hand on his head). "Hmmmm...I got it! Let's go down to the dog park."

"A dog park?"

"He, he, he. It's not what you think. It shouldn't be anybody walking their dog this time of night."

"There it is! We can go behind those trees." (Norie holds the gate open for Desiree and they head for the trees). "Awe shit, baby! I'm about to get up all in that pussy. Turn that ass around."

(Desiree bends over and places her hands on downed tree limb. Norie flips up Desiree's skirt) "Now what are you going to do with this?"

"Mmm! Unnh! Damn that ass is beautiful!" (Norie puts the unopened condom in his mouth and drops his pants).

"Wait! Wait a minute! Let me taste that dick first before you put that condom on." (Norie puts the condom in his hand as Desiree turns around to suck his dick) "Oh yeah! Somebody is ready!"

Kiss! Lick!

Slurp!

"Oh damn, girl! Suck that dick!"

Slurp!

"Oh shit yeah! Nice and slow. Oh yes, nice and slow."

Slurp!

"Mmmm...this dick tastes so good. Mmmm...mmmm...mmm.. Tasty pre-cum!"

Slurp! Slurp!

"Awe shit! Whew girl! You better stop before I explode in your mouth!"

"Ummm...that would be tasty, but I need to feel that dick! Hand me the condom." (Desiree takes the condom out the wrapper and places it on Norie's dick). "Now hit this ass!"

"Oh fuck yeah! Turn all that ass around!" (Desiree places her hand on the tree limb with her skirt flipped up. Norie flips his shirt back over his head and places his hands on the side of Desiree's hips). "Damn girl! I can't believe how the moonlight bounces off your ass!" (Norie puts the head of his dick slightly in Desiree's pussy).

"Ummm! Umm! Yeah, baby! Ummm..."

"Oh you like that huh?"

"Yes, baby, I can feel that shit. Push that dick all up in there. Ummm!" (Norie continues to tease Desiree with short strokes). "Come on, niggah! Get on this ass! You're driving me crazy!"

"Oh you think you ready to handle this dick!"

"Hell yes! Fuck me, niggah! Fuck this ass! Umm!" (Norie slides his dick all the way inside Desiree and continues to hold and press his dick inside her). "Unnnnnnnnnnnnnnnnnnnh! Damn, niggah! You in my fuckin stomach! Oh shit that feels good!"

"So you like that huh?"

"Oh yes, daddy!"

"Damn, this pussy is good!"

"Beat this pussy up, baby! Beat it up!" (Norie grabs Desiree's hair with one hand and begins to rapidly pound her pussy)

Plop!

"Unh!"

Plop!

"Unh!"

Plop!

"Oh God! I'm about to cum!"

"Go ahead baby! Let that shit go! Let it go, Desi! Unh! Unh! Unh! Ooooooooooh fuckkkkk!!!" (Breathing heavy) "D-amn! That...shit...felt good!"

"Oh you like that dick huh?"

"Oh yeah."

"Good! Well, you not done yet baby."

(Desiree wimpers). "Ooooohhhh Gooodnessss" (Norie continues to fuck Desiree rapidly).

Plop!

"Unh!"

Plop!

(The gate to the dog park swings open). Squeeeeeak! "Roof! Roof! Roof! Roof!"

(Norie stops mid stroke and whispers to Desiree). "Oh shit! There's someone in the park. Damn! I didn't think no one would come this time of night."

(Nervously). "What do we do?"

"Let's get ourselves together and hope they leave without seeing us." (Norie pulls his pants up as Desiree stands up and fixes her clothes).

"Roof! Roof!"

"Honey? Something has him excited."

"Looks like he is going for those trees over there."

"Probably a rabbit or something." (The dog goes directly to where Norie and Desiree are standing behind the trees).

(Desiree in a light whisper). "Shoo dog. Shoo!"

"Baby, he has been in the bushes for a while. Go see what he's barking at."

"Ok. Here, boy." (Whistle). "Here boy." (Whistle). "Oh honey, found him!" (Nonchalant) "It's just two people having sex."

(Norie and Desiree remain frozen until the man calls his dog).

"Come on, boy." (The dog runs off and the couple leaves the dog park).

"Shit! We need to get out of here."

"Oh baby, they are gone."

"Yeah, but what if they are going to get the police or something."

"Nahhhh! I don't think so, let's get back at it."

"I'm sorry, I just don't feel comfortable. Let's go back to the club, please."

"Ok, baby, better to be safe than sorry." (Norie and Desiree pull themselves together and scurry back to the club).

"How do I look?"

"Push the side of your hair down."

"Ok, looks good to me."

"Are you going back in the club?"

"No, I am going to head out."

"All right, I'm going back in to find my friends. Here, take my number down."

"Hold on let me put your name in. Ok go ahead."

"404 227-1234."

"Thank you."

"Let's get together tomorrow."

"We got some unfinished business to take care of."

"I definitely like the sound of that. Ok, Desi."

Kiss!

"Have a great time."

"Ok, Norie, call me tomorrow."

"You can count on it."

(Desiree goes back into the club and walks over to her group of friends. Brenda steps out to greet her). "Hey, Desi. Glad to see you are back from the bathroom."

(Friends laugh) "Ha, ha, ha!"

"Oh yeah, I just dipped outside."

"Oh really! So why do you look like you have JBF hair! It must have been very windy outside."

"What? What is JBF hair?"

"Ha, ha, ha!"

"Oh wow, you don't know what that is!"

"No, I don't. "

"Just Been Fucked!" (Desiree blushes with embarrassment).

"Well...umm...in that case, it was very windy outside."

"Ha, ha, ha!"

(Damn! My ass is so busted. Oh well, they will never know. To the grave baby, to the grave).

Chapter 9

A Christmas In Carol

"Good morning, Carol!"

"Oh, hi, baby! I mean, Jace."

"I don't think anybody heard you."

"Whew! That's good. So what are you having for breakfast, miss lady?"

"Well, I think I'll have my usual egg-white omelette with all vegetables."

"Well excuse me miss healthy-smealthy, I am having a pancake, fried egg and a sausage link."

"Ha, ha, ha!"

"Ok, ok you don't have to rub it in, Jace."

"No, I'm not doing that. I just need a few more calories to burn when I work out."

"Somebody keep saying you getting to lean. I'm not going to say any names."

"Ok, ok. You're right. So we sitting at our usual table?"

"Most certainly."

"I'll meet you back by the window then."

"Ok, Carol, see you in a few."

"Hi, Mrs. Linton!"

"Morning, Jace. I see you got your usual breakfast."

"Ha, ha, ha. So you know what I'm having for breakfast as well..."

"Well, I ring you up every day."

"True, True..."

"Where's your apple?"

"Oops, your right, I did forget that. Let me get it. Sorry folks, I just needed one more thing."

"No problem."

"Thank you again, Mrs. Linton."

"No problem, Jace. (Walks off to find a seat with Carol).

(Sits his tray down at the table with Carol) "Oh! Jace, before you sit down, could you get me another fork. I accidentally dropped mine as you were walking up."

"Ok. Be right back." (Jace goes to get Carol a fork). "Here you go."

"Thanks so much!" (Jace sits down).

"So what is your schedule like today?"

"Well, I got a couple of meetings this morning and me and a few of the girls were going to that new bistro on Cambridge Street."

"Oh good."

"I went there last week. Nice atmosphere and the food was delicious."

"Oh wow, now I'm really excited! (Excited) "Oooh! Ooooh! You know what I wanted to talk about this morning."

"What?"

"Did you hear Michael Baisden talking about fulfilling fantasies?"

"No...but I have a feeling I know where this is going."

"Ok...where is it going?"

"You must be ready to fulfill my fantasy of having a threesome with you and your mom..."

"What!! You can't be serious."

Well...no, Carol I was only playing. Your mom does look good, but you're my number one sweety!"

"Awee...so sweet."

"Ok...continue."

"All right. So, I'm listening to the radio show and this girl mentions how her and her girlfriend fulfilled her man's fantasy by making out with each other and then both of them sucked and fucked him."

"Shit! That's kinda hot! I wouldn't mind doing that."

"Oh really! All you have to do is ask baby, and I will make it happen."

"Damn! Well...shit, ok...make it happen."

"No problem."

"Wait a minute! You agreed to that too easy."

"No, baby. I'm just comfortable that you're my man and I am fully secure."

"Ok. I see then. Hmm...so let me brace myself. What fantasy do you want me to fulfill?"

"Well...it's way different, but I got the idea by putting a few things together from listening to the show."

"Is that right! He, he, he."

"What you laughing for, spit it out."

"Ok...ok...here it goes. I want to be fucked by three guys, including you, one after the other."

"Oh my damn! Wow...that is way different."

"Is it too much, baby?"

(Shaking his head). "No...no...it's just the first time I heard it. Wow!"

"Well, here are the particulars. I can't know the other two guys and they must wear condoms of course. You have to be present the whole time and they need to just fuck, cum and leave. It should be dark enough so I can't see their faces."

"Wow...ok...so you don't want to know them at all?"

"Yep... Not at all. And they can't talk while fucking me either."

(Jace Gulps). "All righty then... I'll see what I can do."

"Oh, two more things..."

"Damn! Ok now! What the fuck!"

"No it's not bad, I don't want to know when it's going to happen and the best part, you must start off fucking me and of course end by fucking me and cumming all over me!"

"Are you done? Finally a good part for me. He, he, he."

"Yes..."

"You sure?"

"Yes, baby. He, he, he."

"Ok now, it might take a little bit to get this together."

"Yeah, I know...there's no big rush. Even though I asked for it, I'm a little nervous, but all excited at the same time."

(Oh, you better be ready tonight! Perfect timing. My boys Penn and Laken just happen to be coming to town tonight).

"Jace? Jace?"

"Yes?"

"What were you thinking about?"

"How challenging your fantasy is. But I like challenges."

"Ok...but really honey, if it's too much, I completely understand."

"No, no. It's fine. We have strong relationship and our openness and spontaneity makes it so much stronger."

"That's why I love you so much."

"I love you too, baby."

"Buzz!" "Buzz!" (Carol looks down at her Black Berry). "Ok, baby, I got to go to my first meeting. I'll see you after work."

"Ok...sweety. Oh...oh, Carol, don't forget Mica's party tonight."

"Oh you're right. Thanks for reminding me. I'll leave the Bistro in time to get ready before we go."

"Let's head over there around 10."

"Ok, baby...see you later."

(Jace's phone rings) "Ring, Ring!"

"Jace Caldwell."

(Disguised girl voice) "Is my baby's daddy! Ha, ha, ha!"

"What's up, playa... p-laya! This has to be Penn."

"Yep! Yep!"

"What's going on, dawg!"

"Nothin much man. Me and Lakin just got in."

"Cool, cool..."

"So what's the haps for tonight?"

"Oh! You remember Mica Francis from back in the day right?"

"Let me see...Oh! Oh! Oh shit! You mean honey with the phat table ass?"

"Yeah, buddy! Well she's having a set tonight."

"Cool, cool."

"We rollin to that for sho!"

"Hey, Lakin says what's up."

"What up, playa!"

"Tell him old girl Valerie is supposed to be there as well."

"What!"

"Yessur!"

"Jace, this is going to be some night!"

"Oh hell yeah, and that's not the half!"

"What! There's more."

"Yes, Surr!"

"Ok then, what you got in mind, dawg!"

"Well..."

"Oh, dawg, before you say that, do we get to meet your girl?".

"Oh of course" (In more ways than one).

"Cool then, so what's up!"

"Well, this chick that I've been banging on the side asked me to fulfill her fantasy."

"Oh shit! Calm down dog!"

"Ha, ha, ha!"

"So she asks me to get two guys that she doesn't know to fuck her right after I start fucking her."

"What the fuck!" (Penn drops the phone).

"Penn? Penn?"

"Yeah, playa. You got to be..."

"Chill man, chill. Let me finish."

"Ok, ok."

"She also doesn't want to see their faces, just fuck her, nut and leave. Of course, you have to wear a hat."

"For sho! Damn dawg! I'm on my way over to the party right now. Ha, ha, ha! Lakin you down?"

(Lakin in the background) "Niggah! You ain't said nothing but a word. That is some bomb ass shit!"

"I told y'all niggah's you ain't heard nothing yet."

"Jace, you is da fuckin man! Ha, ha, ha! So, I suppose that means you're down."

"Do monkey's fly?"

"Ok, we straight. I'll set it all up then. I will send directions to the party to your phones. Just pretend like you don't know me until after everything goes down so she won't know what's up."

"Cool. No problem, pimp daddy! This will be one for the record books!"

"Aight then. I'll holla at y'all lata."

"Ok, Jace we'll see you later on then."

"Peace!" (Jace hangs up the phone and continues with his work day).

(Jace pulls up to his house and notices a bicycle in his driveway). "Beep!" "Beep!"

"Hey, Freddie."

(Freddie runs over to Jace's car) "Yes, Mr. Jace?"

"Do you mind moving your bike out the driveway?"

"Oh no problem, sir. I'm sorry."

"Oh no big deal, I just didn't want to run over it."

"Thanks."

"You're welcome."

"Have a good one." (Jace presses the garage door opener). "Oh Good, Carol isn't home yet? Good. Let me get everything together. She doesn't have a clue what's going down tonight. Humph. Challenge me to deliver on a fantasy! Ok, whoa, whoa! What am I saying! I'm about to let my boys fuck my girl! Damn! Well, that's what she wanted and I know she'd do anything for me. Well, she did give me an out. Man up niggah."

(Jace hears the garage door re-opening). Awe man, she's all ready here."

"Jace! Where are you, dear?"

"Hey, baby, I'm in here."

"Oh, there you are. How was the rest of you day?"

"Well things went pretty well. I finished up the Lofton account and was able to get halfway through the Aries account."

"Damn, boy! You were really hustling today!"

"Yep! How about you, darling?"

"Well, I kind of got dragged down on my account so I'll have to really hustle next week."

"Well, you always get it done and it's oh-so excellent!"

"Shut up, Jace!"

"Well it is. Your VP always says, oh Carol's work is so good, I want to eat Carol's shit."

"Stop it!"

"Ha, ha, ha! You know I'm not lying."

"But anyway baby, let's forget about work. We got a party to hit tonight!"

"Yes, yes, you're right."

"And I also know the last time we were at Mica's house..."

"Oh shit! I almost forgot! We went into the study and you fucked me on top of that big cherry oak desk she has..."

"And you fucked me in the ass for the first time. Whew! Niggah! I've been hooked ever since."

"Oh, so you do remember...he, he, he."

"How could I forget? That was some intense shit! Wait a minute, why did you bring that up? You up to something, Niggah!"

"Up to what? (Oh hell, how does she know?)

"You want to fuck me in the study again don't you?"

(Oh good, she don't know). "Baby, I want to fuck you anywhere!"

"Awee...Mama pussy good to Jace."

"Yes mommah! Wanh! Wanh!"

"Ha, ha, ha! You're so crazy."

"But yes, I want to hit that ass at the party. Actually, I want to hit it right now! But I'll be patient, my dear."

"Ooooh, daddy, momma gonna give daddy what he wants. Hmmn...mmmnh!"

"I'll be patient. Oh yeah, wear that sexy sundress that gets caught in your ass cheeks that I like."

"Why? What for?"

"Easy access baby!"

"What are you saying I'm easy?"

"Nope, it just makes me so hot when you wear dresses like that. And I know how much you don't like to wear underwear. Perfect combination! Whew! I can just jump right into the pussy."

"Well...ok... I was just playing, I know what daddy likes."

"Cool...cool. Well, I'm going to get a nap before the party."

"I think I'll join you. I want to make sure I'm full of energy."

(Good idea, you are going to need it).

"What are you smiling about?"

"Awe...nothing.

"You up to something."

"He, he, he. I'm going to get some rest. Could you set the alarm for 8:00?

"Ok, baby, sleep tight. Be in there in about 5 minutes."

(After their nap and showers, Jace stands at the bottom of the stairs) "Baby! Are you ready?"

"Just a minute Jace."

"Ok, Ok." (My God she takes forever no matter how much time...)

"Hey you! I know what you're thinking. What's taking her so long?"

"Oh no, baby..."

"Zip it! Don't even start. You know I got to look the best for my man. Ok, I'm ready."

(Carol comes downstairs). "Damn baby! Shit! Damn your ass is hot!"

"See, that's why..."

"Unnh! I love that fragrance, you smell so damn good!"

"Thank you so much."

"Well you ready?"

"Yes. Let's roll."

(Jace and Carol arrive at the party). "Ding!" "Dong!"

(Mica opens the door and shouts to the party) "Hey! Hey, everybody, its Carol and Jace!"

"Hi, Mica. You didn't have to announce us like a wedding party."

"Ha, ha, ha. You know I have to set it out for America's favorite couple."

"Girl, whatever!"

"Come on in..." (Mica and Carol hug then Mica hugs Jace).

"Hey, Mica, where do you want this wine?"

"Oh, hmm...wow, my favorite Pinot Noir, Eastlan Vineyards. Oh just put it in the kitchen."

"Cool. I will let you girls do your thang. I'll be in the den at the domino's table."

"How do you know she has domino's?"

"What! Mica with no domino's, you know better than that."

"True, true, that is her favorite game. Ok baby" (Jace kisses Carol) Kiss! Muah!

"You know where I'll be."

"Alright, baby, I'll catch up with you soon."

(Jace enters the den). "Yo Yo, what up, frat!"

"Oh shit! You boys are all ready here!"

"Dude, we just hit Valerie up and popped the address in the GPS."

"I should have known Penn is Mr. Gadget. I know he has the GPS."

"Awe, bruh how are you going to call me out like that?"

"Oh it's not true?"

"Yeah, but you didn't..."

"Bruh, come on, there's nothing wrong with being inspector gadget."

"Ha, ha, ha! So who got next game?"

"Oh, you got next game."

"We got you down, dawg. Only one more round and I will have skunked these punk ass bitches again! Hey, you're more than welcome to get your ass beat too."

"Ha, ha, ha! Lakin, you always talking all kinds of shit!"

"Uh huh, and I back that shit up to."

"Right. Right."

"We'll see about that. Domino niggah!! Told y'all assess!"

"Damn! How y'all let this niggah win again."

"Playa? I am the king of Domino's."

"Whateva man, I'm in. Lakin put me up."

"Here you go, dawg. Don't even look at your bones man, you going down just like the rest."

"Well, we will see about that."

"Show you right!"

"Ha, ha, ha!"

"Damn, every play I make, this fool is scoring."

"What did I tell you, boy! Shit! Domino baby!"

"Damn it! This is your game. Got to give it to you."

"Oh damn, sorry fella's I got to go check on my girl." (Jace winks and smiles at Lakin and Penn and puts up a hand to say 10 minutes).

"Yessur! Goes and checks on your girl, dawg, right away! He, he, he." (Jace goes into the living room where the ladies are sitting).

"Hey, Carol, how's it going?"

"I'm just catching up with Mica and the girls. You need something?"

"Oh no, just making sure you were doing ok."

(All the girls). "Aweee!!!"

"He is just so sweet, so precious...he, he, he."

(Jace blushes). "Ok, I'll be leaving now. You ladies enjoy yourself."

"Oh...don't go, it's all right precious...he, he."

"Leave my baby alone."

"Bye, bye, baby." (Jace heads to Mica's study).

(Jace looks around the study). "Ok let's see, if I start over here by the desk, then move her over here to the chase, that should be perfect.

Yeah...um hum. It is farther from the door. Cool...Let me text Penn and Lakin. It's about to be on!!!"

(Penn receives a text message) (Reading text message)

(Penn, take a right out of the den, down the hall, last door on left.)

"Whoa! Ho! Sorry fellas, got to roll for a minute."

"What! In the middle of the game."

"Yeah, Lakin and I will be back in a few. Hold it down for us, fellas." (Motions to Lakin and they proceed to the study).

(Jace waves Penn and Lakin to the study) "Come on in, fellas. Well, it's show time!"

"Bruh...damn! I can't believe this is about to go down!"

"Yeah...Man, this kind of shit only happens in the movies! Jace ! You da mutha fucking man."

"Ha, ha! Keep it down fellas. The women aren't too far away. First things first: here are your condoms. You guys can stand behind this corner away from the chase. It will be pretty dark so she won't be able to see. You guys can go ahead and strip down to your underwear so you will be ready when I give you the signal."

"What's the signal?"

"When I move over to the chase, I'll slap her on the ass two times, and then it's batter up!"

"Ha ha...as long as you keep it down, the background music will cover up any other sounds, like heavy breathing!"

"Shit man you're right, my heart bout to jump out my chest!"

"Ha ha...alight, alright, bring it down so I can call her."

(Carol's phone is ringing) "Hey, Jace!"

"Hey, Carol. How is it going, are you busy?"

"No, not at all, just catchin' up with the girls. Oh...hey wait a minute, where are you? Is that music I hear in the background?"

"What music? I don't hear..."

"Quit playing, Jace. Oh God! Oh god, I know exactly where you are! Don't say another word, I'll be there shortly."

"Ladies, I need to step away for a few minutes."

"Oh no, where you going?"

"Don't leave right now."

"I will be back, ladies, don't worry. I got some business to take care of. Back before you know..."

"Yeah right."

"No seriously, I'll be right back. He, he, he."

"Come in, baby."

"You're very attentive aren't you?"

"I know, my baby."

"Oh you do."

Kiss!

"Well you know..." Kiss! "That daddy been..." Kiss! "Waiting all night to get all up in this..." Kiss!

"I know, baby, I have been soaked ever since you came to check on me."

(Penn in anticipation). (Damn, my heart is beating a thousand times a minute!)

"Oh yeah, let me see how wet you are." (Jace slides his finger in Carol's pussy). "Mmmm..."

Lick! Slurp!

"Finger-licking good! Oh yes, you are so wet and that pussy tastes so good."

"Damn! Jace, please fuck me! I need to feel your dick all up in me."

"Is that what mommy wants?"

"Yes, daddy! Please!"

"Not just yet baby. Turn around. Put your hands flat on the desk." (Slowly pulls her dress up). "Mmmm...look at that juicy ass and the phat pussy. Damn!"

(Begging) "Come on, Jace, put your dick in!"

"Not yet, baby." (Jace bends down and starts to eat her pussy from behind).

"Ummmh! Oh baby!!! Ummmh...that feels so good. Damn, I'm about to explode. Suck that pussy, niggah, suck it!"

(Jace stands up and slaps her on the ass).

Plap!

"Now turn your ass around! Get up on that desk. Lay back."

"Yes, daddy!" (Carol unbuttons and removes his shirt and takes off his pants).

"Do you see how hard daddy is..."

"Yes I do. Take off your boxers baby...ooooh... I want it!"

(Jace slides of his boxers). "Spread those legs wider, girl."

(Jace grabs his dick and bounces it on Carol's clit). "Oh shit! You got your dick on my clit! Damn, slide I need to feel that dick! Unnnnh! Oh, that's it!"

"Not all of it yet, baby."

"You driving me crazy!!!"

"Ok, baby...now we ready. Let me feel all this pussy." (Jace slowly slides his dick in all the way). "Oooohhh shit!!! Unnnh!! Unnh! Hit that shit baby! Fuck! I'm about to cum all ready. Unh!"

"Bring it, baby! Let it go!"

"Damn, I'm cumming! Shit this dick feels good...unnnnh! Unnnh!"

"That's right girl, paint my dick with all that cum!"

"Unnnh!!! Unh!!!"

"Look at it! Look at that dick part those pussy lips! Oh my God, I love watching you go in and out of me. Oh mommy likes how daddy fucks her! Oh my God yes!"

(Jace slides his dick out) (She should be ready now).

"What!!! What!! Where you going baby! What the fuck! You got me all..."

"Come over here, baby. I want you over on the chase baby. I need some of that phat round ass!"

(Lakin is ready to get a piece of Carol after listening to them make out). (Damn, that shit sounds good. I can't wait to get up in that! I want to jump in so bad. Damn!)

"That's right baby, toot that ass up! I'm loving that." (Jace grabs her at the top of her hips and thrusts forward).

"Unnh!!! Unnhh!!! Oh baby, oh shit! You handling this ass!! Fuck me mutha fucka! Rrrrrgh!!!! Unnh! Damn, I'm about to cum again...oh shit!! Ohhhhhhh shittt!!! Damn!" (Breathing hard) "Fuck, that shit was good. Oh my God! Please do it again baby, please!"

"Oh! Oh! You want some more!"

"Yes, baby!"

"You sure you want some more!"

"Oh yes, baby, oh yes!"

"You really think you can handle some more!"

"Shit yes, baby!"

"Ok then, I got something for your ass!"

"Wait...wait...what do you mean?"

"You'll see...you'll see." (Jace moves onto the chase in front of Carol).

"Oh...oh, I got it! Daddy wants mommy to suck that dick."

"Yeah...ummmmm...yes, Carol, that's it. Suck it baby...that's what I like." (Jace reaches up and slaps Carol on the ass three times so that Penn or Lakin will come over. Carol continues to suck Jace).

Slurrpp!!! Slurrpp!!

"Ummmm...unh! Suck it baby!"

"Oh this dick tastes so damn goooooooooooooooooooood!!!" (Carol exclaims as Lakin slides his dick in. Jace grabs Carol's arms so that she won't move away). "Oh! Shit! Damn, baby! Unnnh!"

"I told you I had something for that ass!"

"Oh my God!"

"Just enjoy it, baby, just enjoy it!"

(Oh God, I didn't know this shit was really going to happen. Damn...Fuck...)

"Unh!" (Rapid strokes).

"Unh! Unh! Unh! Unh! Unh! Get that ass boy, get that shit!"

"Oh damn! Oh damn! Unnnnnnnnnnnnnnnnnnh! (Carol grunts hard as Lakin cums). "Arrrrgh! Unh!" (Lakin pulls out and moves out the way for Penn. Jace slaps Carol on the ass again 3 times).

Slap! Slap! Slap!

"Oh shit, there's more."

"Oh yeah baby! You know what you asked for!"

"I didn't think...Unh!!!"

(Slow hard thrust) "Unhh!! Unh!!!! Oh my goodness! Oh my pussy! Unh!!! Oh my... Unh! Unh!" (Faster stroke) "Unh! Unh! Damn! Unh! Unh! Unh! Unh! Oh shit! Mutha-Fucka!"

"Get it baby, get that dick!"

"Oh! Oh! Oh!!!" (Penn speeds up). "Oh God! Oh God! Oh God! Unh...unh...unh!!! Oh baby!!! Ohhhhhhhh!" (Penn cums). "Oh shit, niggah!" (Carol gasping for air). "He, he, he. Oh good..."

"Ha, ha, ha! Oh you not done yet." (Jace slaps Carol on the ass three times).

"Oh no way, niggah! You got to be kidding!"

"Oh no, I'm not kidding baby! You asked me to hook you up and that's what I am doing!"

"But damn, baby! Oh my God! I didn't want to...I mean, damn..."

"Oh you can handle it baby, it's just me coming to finish you off."

"Oh, thank goodness!"

"Now turn that juicy ass around!" (Carol turns and starts to back up to Jace). "Bring it down slow baby. Sit down on this dick and ride my ass home!"

"Oh my pleasure, daddy!"

"Not so fast, baby, I want you to ease down on my dick with that pretty round ass!"

"Ok, baby...yeah that's it. Ride it slow. Yes, baby. Up and down."

"Oh, Jace! I can feel you throbbing inside my pussy!!!"

"Oh yeah, I know you do!! I'm doing everything I can to keep from exploding!!!"

"Oh shit, baby, oh shit, baby!! Yes, niggah! Unh!...unh! Unh!!! I'm about to cum, baby!"

"I'm cumming with you baby! OHHHHHH! Shit!!! Unnnnnnnn! Oh my God!" (Jace gasping for air as they both cum together).

"Shit, mutha-fucka! That was so damn good!"

"Oh my God! Oh my God! Damn!!! Whew!!! Girl, that shit was good!!!"

"That was some real hot shit!"

"Fuck, I think I was more turned on than you, just watching your ass getting fucked. That shit blew my mind! I think it turned me on more than you."

"Oh really?"

"Yes really, that's why I came so hard in you!"

"True, but you know that you're the only one that can take me to a higher level like that."

"Ha, ha, ha!"

"Great answer, baby, great answer!"

"I love you sooooo much, Jace!"

"I love you too, Carol. Hey, let's get back to the party before they report us missing."

"Ha, ha, ha." Jace waves Penn and Lakin to come out as him and Carol leave the room.

Chapter 10

Above 10,000 Feet

"Do you have any other questions concerning your performance rating?"

"Hmmm...well, I would like to know what things I can do differently going into next year to increase my rating from satisfactory to excellent."

"Funny you should ask that. I took a look at all the assessment areas and you are on track there. What I believe is the biggest gap for you, Felix, is exposure to senior management. If you haven't learned all ready, most of the time it's not what you know—it's *who* you know."

"Yes, I am starting to figure that out."

"Well, I have an opportunity to give you a head start on gaining more exposure going into next year. Our Senior Vice President of Engineering is traveling to Switzerland to visit a new contract manufacturer that will be making aseptic bags for our juice lines. Jillian wanted me to assign an engineer that can provide an in depth technical assessment of their process and systems. I think this is a perfect and exciting opportunity for you in many ways. First of all, you will have to suffer and ride the corporate jet."

"Ha, ha, ha!"

(Felix puts a big smile on his face while listening to his boss).

"Secondly, you will have the opportunity to discuss your career and get to know her better. So, how does that sound?"

"That sounds great! I'm really excited! This will be my first trip to Europe, and on a corporate jet."

"Wow! Good, I'm glad you're looking forward to it."

"Ok, any more questions?"

"Nope, I think that's it."

"All right then, check with Becky on the way out and have her make your arrangements to match Jillian's Itinerary."

"Ok, will do, Scott."

"Thanks a lot. I will see you this afternoon at the department meeting."

"See you then.

"Bye." (Felix turns and leaves Scott's Office. He immediately stops by Becky's desk to make travel arrangements).

(Smiling as he approaches Becky's desk). "Hi, Becky, I need help making..."

"I all ready got you covered."

"Really?"

"Yes, of course. You know better than that. You should be asking what I don't know. What gets by me here?"

"I know, I know."

"Ha, ha, ha!"

"Check your email when you get back to your desk. I've all ready matched your itinerary to Jillian's and provided maps to the Corporate jet hangar. Just show your employee badge for parking and of course, don't forget you passport."

"Ok, got it."

"Oh and most importantly, dress business casual, not casual—as if you were going to the plant. You will be on the jet with some high level company officers. I believe each division has the Senior Vice President traveling to Europe to meet with this contract manufacturer. They're a really big company and this is really important to our company's continued growth".

"Oh wow! I wasn't aware of all of that!"

"Ha, ha, ha! Honey! What did I tell you? Doesn't much get past me here at Kinney & Ellerbee."

"I see that! I'm excited and nervous! I'm just a young engineer starting out at K & E and...what do I...I mean all these people are several levels above me..."

"Wait a minute, Felix. Hold your horses. One thing I want you to remember here is that these folks are people too! They put on clothes the same way you do. They laugh, they cry, they eat...uh...food!"

"Ha, ha, ha!"

"Hell! They do so much bullshit behind closed doors, it'd make your head spin! So my point is, don't be intimidated by them. Take advantage of this opportunity. Network and show them that you were rightly recommended for the assessment you are providing. Believe me, you wouldn't be going if you were not the right one for the job."

(Big sigh) "Woo! Thank you so much, Becky. I do feel much better. I'm going to get my stuff together and maximize this opportunity!"

"Now we're talking!"

"Oh! Oh! I know what I wanted to ask you Becky. Have you ever flown on the corporate jet?"

"Yes. I did fly on it once. You are really in for treat! First class on a commercial jet is like two levels below Coach Class compared to the corporate jet! Think about having your own personal recliner with enough space between seats to fit another entire recliner."

"You got to be kidding! Really!"

"Oh no, I'm not. And it reclines all the way out for sleeping and is wide as a twin bed."

"Ha, ha! Oh my goodness! That is hard to believe. Wow!"

"Oh! And the executive treatment! You will be pampered from the time you arrive at the hangar until you land in Europe."

"Ok then, what about food?"

"You can't get it any better. All meals are prepared by the Executive Chef on board. Breakfast, lunch and dinner depending on how long your flight is."

(With a wide smile) "Wow! I had no idea it was like that!"

"Oh yeah, it's like that. That's why you should take advantage of the opportunity. Remember, you are just as important here at K & E as anyone else."

"Thanks a lot, Becky. I can't wait to go now! I am so excited."

"No problem, Felix. Check the things I sent you and have a safe and enjoyable trip!"

"I will! Thanks again." (Walking away from Becky's desk) "See you later."

"Ok, Felix. Bye now!"

(Felix walks to the parking lot after reading emails and collecting a few items from his desk).

(Wow! I can't believe I am going on this trip! It's like the chance of a life time! Who would have ever thought a snotty nose kid from Eastlan Drive would have the chance to ride a corporate jet! What! Are you kidding me? When I didn't even ride a plane until after I graduated Basic Training in the Army! Man, this is unreal!)

(Car starting with radio in background) *"Don't stop believin!"*

"Oh shit! That's my jam!" (Following along with the song) *"Don't stop believin! Go ahead Journey! Street lights, people..."* (Now that's what I'm talking about. Never stop believing. Keep pushing).

(Felix merges onto the freeway for the commute home).

(Man, I still can't believe I'm going to Europe with my Senior Vice President! I've only met her twice since I have been at the company. Now I'll have several hours to get to know her better and discuss my career plans. I really hope she will become an advocate for me. Well, I'm going to try any way. Like Becky said, they are people just like you. Nothing to be intimated about. Ha, ha, ha! That's easy for her as to say! Oh well, what can you do, what can you do. Damn! I'm home all ready! That felt like the shortest commute I ever had. Hmmm...I guess I must be a little excited). (Stepping out of the car and closing the door shut).

"Clunk!"

(Standing by his door and checking both pockets for his keys). "Damn! Where are my keys?" (That's my cell phone. That's change.) "Dang! Where could..."

(From across the street). "Hey, Felix! Felix!" (Felix turns around).

"Oh hey, Graham! How are you doing today?"

"I'm doing fine. Just wanted to tell your car lights are still on!"

"Oh, thank you! Let me go turn them off right now. Thanks again."

"No problem!" (Felix checks the car and sees his keys in the seat). "Bingo! Damn, I was so in a rush to get out of the car that I forgot my keys and the lights. Good thing Graham saw that. All I need for tomorrow is a dead battery when I'm ready to get out of here for my trip! Whew! Thank you Lord!" (Felix turns off his lights, locks his car and goes inside the house. He sits all his watch, jewelry and wallet on his island). "Ok now."

(Time to pack and look over these directions to the hangar. I'm too excited to sleep! And best believe, I will be there early so they won't be waiting on me. Hells no! That would be fucked up to be waiting on the lowest man on the totem pole. Ha ha!)

(Felix pulls up at the guard shack to the corporate hangar). "Hello, Sir. How are we doing this lovely evening?"

(Feeling awkward) "Umm...good, sir! And you?" (Can't believe he called me "sir.")

"I am doing quite well today. Nice day for flying, huh?"

"Yes, it certainly appears to be, sir." (He called me sir. I am just a lowly engineer).

"Well, welcome to the K & E Corporate hangar."

"Thank you."

"Let me see your employee badge, driver's license, registration and proof of car insurance." (The guard looks at Felix's documents and scans in his badge).

"Beep!"

"You are all scanned in. Let me enter your driver's license and verify your registration and insurance. Here is your badge back, Mr. Jenkins."

"Wow! You have to enter and verify a lot of information."

"Yes, we do. It's necessary due to the clientele entering this gate. Everybody gets checked so don't feel singled out. We have very senior level people flying in and out of here. Our job is to ensure the safety and security of all that come in and out of here."

"That's really good to know."

"Yes, we take a lot of pride in keeping our company employees and leaders safe." (The guard hands back Felix's driver's license, insurance and registration).

"Thank you."

(The guard bends down to Felix's car window and points out directions). "Ok, Mr. Jenkins, take Corporate Drive, the road you are on now all the way past the main terminal building and make a left on K & E Way as soon as you past the building. The employee parking garage will be immediately on your left. A shuttle will bring you to the main terminal building. Clear as mud?"

"Yes, sir! Thank you again."

"No problem, Mr. Jenkins. Have a safe flight." (Felix drives off to the employee parking garage).

"Oh wow! Limousine entrance! 'All other vehicles enter here.' Geez! Look at those limos! K & E-1, K & E-2, a spot for K & E-3! Oh my goodness! This is really big time!" (Felix parks his car and pops his trunk. A shuttle bus immediately pulls up behind him. He steps out of the car and is greeted by the shuttle bus driver).

"Mr. Jenkins, will this be all the luggage for your trip?" (The bus driver is holding a suit case and his laptop bag).

"Yes, sir! Looks like you have it all."

"Ok, just make sure your lights are off, you have all items you need like cell phones and keys. Make sure to lock your vehicle."

"Thanks. I believe I got everything."

"All right then, have a seat on the bus wherever you like." (The driver loads the luggage and takes a seat and they begin the drive to the terminal) .

"Welcome to the K & E corporate hangar. If there is anything you need or questions you may have, feel free to ask. We want to make sure all your needs are met to ensure that your travel is as smooth as possible. Thank you."

"I am impressed all ready!"

"Good. Good. Here we go. Nice short ride. Here are two tags for you bags. If you need access to your laptop before the flight, you can hold on to it or bring the tag down to the bag claim station. Otherwise, your bags will be loaded into your personal compartment on the plane and be accessible when you board."

"What! You mean my bags will be taken to my seat?"

"Yes. We try to free you up as much as possible so that you are well relaxed for travel."

"Man! This is too good to be true."

"Ha, ha, ha!"

"Just a part of our service, Mr. Jenkins."

"Ok, thanks again."

"No problem. Go through those two glass doors and you will see the terminal waiting lounge to your right. Have a safe flight."

(Felix offers a tip) "Here you go, sir."

"Sorry, Mr. Jenkins, I am not allowed to take tips. Thank you anyway."

(Oh my, he can't take tips) "Ok sir, I appreciate your help."

"Good day, Mr. Jenkins. Bye."

(Felix walks into the terminal waiting lounge). "Hmmm...I'm the only one here. I guess I'm a little early."

(The bartender calls out from behind the bar) "Excuse me, sir! Would you like anything to drink while you wait?"

(Felix turns slightly). "Oh...there you are. I thought I was the only person in here.

"Oh no, we are always staffed during our flight times."

(Felix moves up to the bar and takes a seat) "Hmmm...I think I will start with a glass of water." (No telling how much a drink cost).

"Are you sure that's all you want? Everything is complimentary. Here is a list of beers and wines that we have. I can make about just any mixed drink you can think of."

"Oh really?" (I better get something light. Don't want to go too far with Jillian and other leaders coming). "Well in that case, could I get a glass of water and a glass of the William Woods Riesling?"

"Hmm...good choice. Coming right up." (Bartender fixes a glass of water and ice and pours a glass of Riesling). "Here you go."

"Thanks ma'am."

"You're welcome. Call me Teresa."

"Ok, Teresa. So how long have you been working out here?"

"Well, actually I have only been here two years. This is actually a second job for me. I teach school in the morning and do this in the evening. It's a great supplement to my income along with full employee benefits."

"Wow! That's sweet!"

"Plus, I make a lot of contacts that come through here. I know the full organization chart at the top from the CEO down. I hope it turns into an opportunity to be a trainer at the company."

"Sounds like a good plan...so how are they when they come?"

"What do you mean?"

"Well are they snobby? Or do they act artificial?"

"None of the above. They are actually really down to Earth."

"Hunh, that's what my administrator said. They are just people."

"Well, she's right."

"Ok then, since you know all of them, what about Jillian Sikes?"

"Oh you know Jillian?"

"Well, she's my Senior Vice President."

"Oh, you are very lucky then. She's probably the most down to Earth out of most of them."

"Well, down to Earth can mean a lot of things? Sooooo..."

"Well, she's very out spoken and very flirtatious."

"Isn't she married?"

"No she's the only single one out of the bunch."

"Oh my!"

"Yes, she's divorced and she just lives her life carefree. She really doesn't care if a person is married or single, if they make an adult decision, then that's on them, if you know what I mean."

"Oh, I follow you. I follow you real well. So, Teresa, why do you think she got divor..."

"Shh! Hey there, Jillian!"

(Felix takes a big swallow and freezes at the bar with both forearms on the bar padding and hands clinched).

"Hi, Teresa! How are things going this evening?"

"Pretty good. I can't really complain."

"Well, you all ready know what I'm drinking."

"Oh yes ma'am—Long Island Iced Tea."

"Yes indeed! You know what I like." (Jillian reaches the bar and sits next to Felix. She turns toward him to speak to him).

"Hello, sir."

"Hello Ms. Sikes." (She instantly realizes who he is).

"Oh, hi, Felix."

(Wow she remembered me).

"First of all, called me Jillian."

"Yes ma—um...Jillian."

(She rests her right hand on his left forearm). "Are you trying to say I'm old?"

"Oh no, Jillian. No way."

(Jillian starts to lightly rub Felix's forearm).

(Oh my goodness, I can't believe what's happening. I have no idea what to do).

"Just relax, Felix. I'm only kidding around with you. I am really glad to have you on this trip. I know we can benefit from your expertise during the assessment."

"No problem. I'm very excited about seeing the manufacturing facility and determining if it is up to K & E's standards."

(Bartender delivers Jillian's drink). "Hey, Jillian, here you go. One Long Island Ice Tea."

"Thanks so much, Teresa."

"You know you are welcome any time."

(Jillian lifts her hand from Felix's forearm).

(Whew, I am so glad she moved her hand. I didn't know what to do).

(Felix unclenches his hands and puts them in his lap).

(I didn't know whether to tell my boss to stop or keep going. My dick already got hard. Really surprised she's divorced. Bitch is fine as hell! Something about her is real sexy).

"And you were saying, Felix?"

"Oh, just saying I was excited about the assessment. Didn't want to get too much into work though."

"Well that's good to hear on both fronts. I like that." (Among other things). "We can definitely discuss work much later. We have a long flight together."

"That's true."

"You can sit near me on the jet so it will be easy to discuss work if needed."

"Ok, Jillian I look forward to it." (In a hurried voice, talk about career opportunities, talk about career opportunities). "Oh, one other thing" (Jillian turns her knee into Felix's knee and places her hand back on his left forearm).

(Oh shit) "I would liiiiiiiiiiiiiiike" (As Jillian lets her hand slide off Felix's forearm onto his dick as if it were coincidental contact) "Uh, um, some time to discuss career opportunities at K & E with you." (Oh my God! She's running her hand back in forth up my dick).

(Damn this dick is nice!) "Oh no problem." (Jillian squeezes Felix's dick while looking him straight in the eye as if nothing were going on). "There will be plenty of time for that. Just grab me anytime" (stronger dick squeeze) "when you're ready." (Jillian rereleases Felix's dick and picks up her drink for another sip).

"Uh...thank you so much, Jillian." (This cannot be happening. My Senior Vice President just grabbed and massaged my dick. What the hell! Not that I mind, but wow!)

"You're welcome Felix...hey, what time do you got?"

"Umm...6:35"

"Oh ok. Everyone else should be here in a minute. It doesn't take long to board since they take care of everything."

"Great, I can't wait!"

"Do me a favor. Watch my drink for a minute. I am going to go to the little girl's room."

"No problem, Jillian." (Jillian grabs her purse and heads for the ladies bathroom. Felix asks Teresa about what just happened).

(Whispering) "Did you see what she did?"

"Oh her flirting with you? Ha, ha, ha. I told you that. She's very carefree."

"Carefree? Carefree? That ain't the word. Oh my goodness! She had her hand on my," (whispering) "dick!"

"Oh wow! I have never seen or heard of her doing that, but...but I wouldn't put it past her."

"What do I do? Well, not really much you can do. If you are uncomfortable with it, then you need to let her know. Otherwise, you will definitely gain a very good advocate."

"Yeah, I guess you're right. Of course I don't mind, she happens to be very nice looking. I was just shocked how to the point she is."

"Shhh! Shhh! Here she comes."

(Jillian sits back down at the bar) "Here is your drink."

"Thanks, Felix. I just saw several of our folks pull into the garage. We should..."

(Intercom) "Ladies and gentleman, please make your way to gate 1A in 5 minutes to begin boarding. Please have your employee badge and passport available for boarding. Thank you."

"Right on time. Folks are so spoiled. There is no way they could board that close to departure in a commercial airport."

"That's for sure."

"Ha, ha, ha!"

(Felix finishes his wine) "Well, I'm going to run to the bathroom and I will see you on the jet, Jillian."

"See you shortly."

(Felix runs to the bathroom while Jillian proceeds to gate 1A and boards the plane. Felix speaks to Teresa as he passes by the bar on the way to the gate for boarding). "Thanks again for everything, Teresa."

"You're welcome. Hope to see you again on your next flight."

"Thanks."

"Have a safe flight."

(Across the room) "Ok, talk to you later."

"Passport and employee badge please?...Ok, Mr. Jenkins, have a safe flight."

"Thank you, sir." (Felix boards the plane and looks for Jillian. He is in shock how nice the jet is arranged. Jillian raises her hand and waves him all the way to the back of the plane).

"Back here, Felix." (Felix acknowledges her signal and walks back toward her. He speaks to other Senior Vice Presidents on the way back to her).

"Hello."

"Hi."

"How are you doing?"

"Just fine."

"Hello."

"Hi there, young man."

"Hello."

"Hi."

(Jillian pats the large leather recliner right next to her). "Have a seat."

"Thanks, Jillian. Oh my goodness, this recliner feels so comfortable!"

"Yes, they are quite nice. Hey, you looked a little lost up front."

"Oh no, I was just pinching myself. I can't believe a jet could be this nice."

"Oh yeah, I am forgetting, this is your first time traveling on the corporate jet."

"Yes."

"It is quite impressive huh?"

"Oh yes it is."

"Well, sit back and relax. The crew will do the rest. Did your administrator fill you in on service aboard the jet?"

"Oh yeah, she said it is top notch."

"How about specialty drinks?"

"No, she didn't mention that."

"Well, once we are above 10,000 feet, you can feel free to make your own drinks. There are recipe tabs by the bar to make your own drinks. That is really convenient since you can always personalize the drink" (nudging Felix). "You know what I mean?"

"Huh...huh...oh yes, I follow you loud and clear."

"Ha, ha, ha!"

(From the cockpit). "The boarding door has been closed. We are cleared for takeoff. Please fasten all seatbelts with seat backs upright and lap trays stowed. All right, here we go." (The plane taxi's to the run and takes off for Europe).

(Ten minutes into the flight). "From the cockpit, this is your captain speaking. We have just reached 10,000 feet. You are clear to use portable and onboard electronic devices. We are looking at approximately 10 hours of flying time into Geneva International Airport. Expecting a pretty smooth ride over, so sit back, relax and enjoy the ride. If there is anything you need to make your ride more comfortable, don't hesitate to ask any of our crew. We will be glad to assist you in any way. Thank you."

(Two hours into the flight, Jillian is reading a book. Felix wants to get a drink). "Excuse me, Jillian."

(Jillian lowers her book). "Yes, Felix?"

"I'm going to get a drink. You want anything?"

"Hmm...that is real nice of you. Well, let's see how good of a Long Island Iced Tea you can make."

"I should have known. I know that is your favorite from the terminal lounge."

"Great attention to detail. Keep that trait, Felix. Add that to your list of strengths for a successful career at K & E."

"Ok, I will keep that in mind. Be right back." (Felix goes to make the drinks while Jillian resumes reading).

(Jillian is pretty cool. I was a little nervous at first but she really seems like she would be a good advocate for me). "Ok. Let me see." (Flipping through drink recipes) "Gin sour, Hurricane, bingo...Long Island Ice Tea: ½ oz vodka, ½ oz gin, ½ oz rum, ½ oz triple sec, ½ oz tequila, 1 oz sour mix and top off with cola. Sounds pretty good. I think I'll have one myself." (Felix finishes making both drinks. He walks back to his seat to give Jillian her drink. Jillian looks up as he approaches and saves her spot in her book). "Here is your Long Island, Ms. Sikes."

"Oh thank you, Felix."

"I think you're going to like it."

"I'm sure I will." (Jillian takes a sip) "Mmmm...mmmm. This is excellent! Good job, baby. Damn, this is really good!"

(I don't think she realized she just called me baby). "Glad you like it."

"Shit. I love it! Come on, sit down next to me."

"Ok. Let's make a toast."

"A toast to what?"

"To a successful trip in Switzerland."

"Ok. To a successful trip in Switzerland." (They tap glasses and take a sip).

"Oh that is so good!" (Jillian leans over the arm rest and kisses Felix in the mouth).

Kiss!

"Mmm..."

Kiss! (Felix and Jillian look at each other in shock).

"I'm so sorry about that, Felix. I got carried away."

"Oh, it's ok, Jillian. Honest mistake."

"I have to be more careful when I drink these Long Island Iced Teas."

"Yeah you do. I'm just glad we are all the way in the back and it's relatively dark except for the reading light. Again, I really apologize."

"Let's just drop it."

"Ok."

"How about we talk what things I can do to have successful career at K & E?"

"All right that sounds good. Well Felix, there are three things that make up everyone's career at our company. It's best described using and acronym we call P.I.E."

"So what does that stand for?"

"The P represents performance, I stands for Image and E stands for Exposure. The key is the percentage of time you devote to each letter per say. P is pretty straight forward. I is how you look in the organization, and E is more the result of networking, that is, who you know. Take a guess on the percentages for each letter.

"Well, I would think performance would be 100% but I would say around P at 75%, I at 15% and E at 10%."

"Well your percentages are close but totally opposite of what you are thinking. Performance is only 10% of the equation. Image at 20% with Exposure at 70%.

"Wow! Really?"

"Yes, really! Exposure is the most important component. In plain words, spend your time getting to know folks and folks getting to know you. You will see over your career that some people will not seem qualified but will get promoted."

"Oh my!"

"Yep, but that's the way it is. So by coming on this trip. You are making a great first step in maximizing exposure."

"Thank you very much, Jillian. I had no idea."

"Well, that's part of my job. You do all the real work. But now you know that you can count on me to help you with your career. That is my primary goal for folks that fall in my organization."

"Thank you, Jillian. I really appreciate your insight."

"No problem, Felix."

(If you do what you are suppose to do, you won't have to worry about your career for a long time. You let me feel that rock hard dick and you're in. I got to have it. How can I get closer to him? Hmmm...I got it!)

"Hey. Enough talk about work; let's watch a movie."

"Ok, I'm game."

"What do you wanna see, Jillian?"

"How about Uptown Saturday Night?"

"Oh I love that movie. Cool, then Uptown it is. Let's set up your screen for the movie."

"My screen wasn't working earlier when I checked it."

"Ok, no problem."

"Do you mind if I fold this arm rest back?"

"No, not at all." (Felix selects the movie and leans back with his legs crossed and hands behind his head. Jillian takes her blanket and flips it out to cover both of them). "Ahhhhh...now we are ready." (Jillian leans onto Felix's side).

"Ok, pressing play."

"Wait, wait! Let me turn off the reading light." (Jillian reaches up to turn off the reading light. Her breasts touch Felix on the head. She moves them around slowly making her nipples hard.) "Ok got it." (Jillian presses up against Felix and they begin to watch the movie).

(An hour into the movie). "Ha, ha, ha! I love this part."

"Ha, ha, ha! Look at Richard Pryor's face."

(Jillian eventually drifts off to sleep as the movie comes to an end). "Jillian? Jillian?" (Jillian is knocked out lying on the side of her face in Felix's lap). "Well, I guess I'll turn this off. Looks like everyone is asleep." (Jillian moves her head slightly realizing she's in Felix's lap. She continues to pretend she's asleep) Jillian? (She's not waking up for nothing. Let her sleep). "All right, good night, Jillian."

(Jillian adjusts her head as if she's moving in her sleep. The side of her face is lying on top of Felix's dick. Felix is getting aroused by her slight movements).

(Whispering) "Mmmm..."

"Jillian?" (Damn my dick is getting hard! I have a Senior Vice President lying on my dick! Unfucking believable).

(Jillian with a sleepy voice but not lifting her head). "Ummm..."

"Jillian?"

"Ummm..." (Oh shit, I have this dick right where I want it).

(Jillian brings her hands up to loosen Felix's belt).

"What are you..."

"Shh! Shh!"

(Oh my God! This is not going to happen! This is not going to happen. Felix starts to breathe harder).

(Felix whispers) "Umm...oh shit!"

(Jillian lifts her head up and slides Felix's pants down). "Lay the chair back."

"Are you sure?"

"Lay the chair back. No talking." (Jillian dribbles spit on Felix's dick. She puts Felix's dick all the way in her mouth).

"Unnnnh....oh shit! That feels so good."

"Shhhh!" (Felix puts both of his hands over his mouth). "Ummmm..."

Slurp!

(Jillian puts the cover over her head).

Slurp!

"Unhh!"

"Suck it, Jill! Suck it, baby!"

Slurp!

"Come on, Felix! Put all that shit in my mouth! Come on!"

"Oh, Jillian! Shit, that feels good!"

(Rapidly sucking).

Slurp! Slurp! Slurp! Slurp!

"Oh damn!"

Slurp!

"Oh Damn! Bring that shit, Felix! Bust in my mouth! Come on, baby!"

Slurp!

"Oh shit, baby!"

Slurp! (Strong and slowly sucking). Slurrrrrrrrrrrrrrrrrrp!

"Unnnnnh!"

(Muffled under his hands). "I'm about to cum! It's all yours baby!"

Slurrrrrrrrrrrrrrrrrrrrrrrp!

"It's all yours! Oh shit! It's all yours! Unnnnnnnnnnnnnnnnnnnnnnh!!!"

(Slight gag) "Ugggggh!" (Jillian swallows all of Felix's cum). "Mmmmmm...shit, that tastes good! Damn that shit was sweet!"

(Breathing hard) "Oh God! Oh God! I can't believe what just happened."

(Jillian puts her finger up to Felix's mouth.) "Believe it, baby. Also know this: you will have a good career here...I so needed that! You did well."

(Breathing hard) "I did? You did all the work."

"Trust me. We didn't wake anyone did we?"

"True."

(Soft laugh) "He, he, he."

"Ok, I got to run to the ladies room."

"Alright."

"Be right back."

Chapter 11
Spin Cycle

"Mmmm...nice legs!" (Shane comments on India as she stands by the large cherry oak table in the main conference room. She's slightly bent over with both hands flat on the table looking over her presentation).

(Peeping around Shane as he enters the conference room door).

(Whispering) "Shane Brooks! Watch your mouth! You know we're at work."

"Yes, but you know you like it."

(India smiles and begins to turn around to continue reviewing her presentation). "But, what if..."

"Oh please! Don't give me that, India."

"He, he, he."

"You know what yo ass is doing wearing that short ass black skirt up in here today."

"Who me?" (As India gives him an innocent look).

"You know damn well..."

"Ok, ok. You got me." (India looks around and rushes to close the conference room door. She immediately turns to Shane and puts her arms around his neck) "Mmmm..."

Kiss!

(Shane reaches around India's waist and puts his hands on the back of her thighs right below her skirt. India begins to moan and breathe harder as he slowly moves up her thighs to squeeze her pantyless ass.) "Umm...girl. This ass..."

"Mmmm...ohhh...mmmm..." Kiss! "Oh shit, Shane! Stop, baby." (Shane reaches under her skirt and squeezes her ass harder). "Oh, baby...oh God! We got to stop..."

"We are..." (Shane spreads open his right hand and slides his index finger under her ass and into her pussy).

"Mmmmm! Damn, baby! Please, please!"

"Shit, girl, this pussy is so wet and juicy!"

"Oh, Shane, please! You're going to get us..."

"All right, all right..." (As Shane slides his finger out of her pussy pretending to stop).

(India sighs in relief) "Whew! You know that wasn't..."

"Ummmmmm!" (As Shane pushes his finger back in to her pussy, moving his finger in and out rapidly). "Umm! Umm! Umm! Umm!"

(Voices are approaching the conference room).

"Damn!" (Shane quickly backs away from India as she quickly straightens her clothes. Shane rushes to take a seat away from India. The conference room door opens).

"Hello, India."

"Hi, Ken."

"Sorry we are a few minutes late."

(No problem at all. Believe me, no problem at all). "Not a problem, Ken."

"Are you sure?"

"Yes...it just gave me more time to get ready."

"Ok then."

"Hi, Shane." (Shane is daydreaming about India). "Shane?"

"Uh...um. Yes, Ken?"

"How are you?"

"Oh, I'm fine." (Think of a lie quick). "I was just thinking to myself about some of the data I provided India in her presentation."

"Oh ok. I am sure it's all correct."

"Oh yes. I went over it with a fine-tooth comb."

"Great, great!"

"You and India work so well together. If I didn't know better, I would think you guys were married."

(Shane's eyes grow big as he looks on in shock). "Whoa! Whoa!"

"Ha, ha, ha! Come on, Shane, it's not that serious. I am only yanking your chain."

(Shane laughs with Ken). "Ha, ha, ha! Yes, that is funny. Funny you would say that. Ha, ha, ha!" (Ken walks on to take his usual seat on the right side near the front of the table).

(Shane sends an instant message to India while the team waits for their colleagues to show up)

"Ding!" (Reading message) "India, did you hear Ken talk about us being married?"

(India looks up and gives Shane a quick glance confirming her shock about Ken's comments).

(Reply message to Shane). "Buzz, buzz!" (Reading message) "I know! I know! And the fact they almost caught us, lol! So Close!"

"Ding!" (Reading message) "LOL! Why do you think I didn't shake his hand? Busted! Pussy juice!"

(Ken starts the meeting). "Ok, India. I think we got everyone here."

(India puts her Blackberry down). "Ok then, I'll get started. Ok. Today, my presentation covers the results of a 25-state consumer research study on the Cool Wave. The topics I would like to cover today are as follows: Background on the cool wave, Test parameters used in the study..."

(India completes her presentation and opens the floor for questions).

"Does anyone have any questions?" (Silence as colleagues look around at one another. Ken looks around for any questions).

"I think we asked them all during the presentation."

"Ok then. Since there are no further questions, I would like to thank you all for listening."

"Let's give India a big hand. (Clapping)

(The team begins exiting the conference room. Shane and India are about to exit the conference room).

"Great presentation, India!"

"Thank you, Shane." (Shane signals India back into the conference room just to the side of the door).

(Shane whispers). "What are you going to do India?"

(India pretends she doesn't know what Shane is referring to). "What am I going to do about what?"

"You know..."

"No...I don't know."

"About what happened before your presentation."

"Oh. Oh. That." (Whispering) "Um...I don't know, Shane. You know we shouldn't..."

"Yes, yes. I know." (Pleading) "But come on India! You know you felt something in there. Your pussy was so fucking wet... I mean...damn! I got to have some, baby. Damn!" (Peeping out the door to make sure no one is coming).

"Ok, Shane. Yes, I admit. That felt good. But we are at work."

"I get that Ind—"

"Let me finish! We are both married for God's sakes. And yes, I know we have played around before. But not at that level. You know we could have got caught?"

"Yes but..."

"And don't forget. We could lose our fucking jobs!" (Tapping his hand on India's forearm).

"Ok, ok. I can respect that. But I want to see you out of here."

(With a frightened look). "Out of here? Are you serious!"

"Yes, baby. I'm serious! Look. We have been walking around this for almost a year now. Kissing here, kissing there. Holding each other. Feeling each other..." (with a questioning look on his face). "Am I wrong?"

"No you're..."

(India is interrupted by an associate that has a meeting in the conference room). "Are you guys done? We have a meeting in here at 3?"

"Oh, oh yes. It's all yours. Thank you. Shane, let's go discuss what you are proposing later in the day."

"No problem, India." (India and Shane return to their offices).

(India sits at her desk wondering about what Shane asked her).

(Is Shane serious? He knows we just flirt with each other. Harmless...but, I guess our spouses wouldn't think it was so harmless. But damn, that shit turned me on! I haven't felt like that in a while. Terry never gives me attention like that. I mean, he would never do something this edgy Umm! That shit was exciting! I'm getting wet just thinking about it).

(With elbows propped and hands interlocked under her chin) "Arrrrgh!"

(Girl, what are you doing? You are married. You keep forgetting that...ok, ok. I will just have to avoid going anywhere with Shane. Yeah! That's the best way to do it. I know myself. In the past! In the right situation! That shit is on!)

(Phone ringing startles India) "Whoa!" (Answering the phone) Hello. India speaking.

"Hi, baby."

"Shane, you know we talked about this. We can't..."

"I know India. I apologize for what happened earlier. I just got carried away. I know we just flirt. And, I never meant to take it that far. But...Hell! You're fucking worth it!"

"Shane, it's fine."

"But...damn! You are so fucking sexy!" (Regaining his composure). "But again, I am sorry I did what I did and about asking you to get with me outside of work."

(India is unsure of which way she wants things to go). "Um...uh...I appreciate your apology, Shane. But, I will admit. I do like the attention that you give me. I did consider what you were saying, but I know...like you said, we got carried away. So...so, I say all of that...I know this sounds crazy. I want us to keep on flirting, but not go any further." (India cringes waiting for Shane's answer).

"Hmmm...well, I'm ok with that."

(Surprised). "Really?"

"Oh yes. Like I said, you're worth it. At least I can have some of you. And, you know...maybe in the future...I mean, I'm totally fine with it."

"In the future what?"

"Oh, it was nothing."

"Um hum. All right, Mr. Nothing."

"Ha, ha, ha!"

"Anyway, I also called you for something else."

"Yes, what?"

"I was wondering if you got my special invitation in your inbox?"

"Now wait a minute Shane, we just talked about..."

"No, it's not that. I'm talking about my 40th birthday party."

"Oh, oh. Ha, ha, ha. Sorry about that."

"I was just wondering if you received the invitation from my wife Vera."

"Oh. He, he, he. Let me check. Hmmm...Credit Union, Benefits...Oh! Here it is. Yep, got it right here."

"Great! I hope you'll be able to make it."

"What? Are you kidding? I wouldn't miss this for the world. Old man!"

"Ha, ha, ha."

"Uh huh. I got your old man!"

"Oh you do?"

"You heard me."

"Shane! You know you can't handle this!"

"Anyway, about the party..."

"Oh, you backing down? Just like I..."

"Go head with that girl. I...go head with that! Like I was saying, the party is this Friday at my house. Directions are on the back of the invitation."

"You know I don't..."

"Yeah, I know. I included landmarks."

"Ha, ha, ha."

"Hmmm...you know me so well. Terry is always giving me directions about going east 1.5 miles, turn right at the intersection, blah blah. He is so damn rigid! But, anyway. I will be there, babe. I mean, Terry, and I will be there. "

"That's awesome!"

"Who else is coming?

"Oh yeah. Well there'll be a lot of folks from the office and about 5 couples from our neighborhood."

"Wow, that should be a nice turn out."

"Yes, I am just excited that folks are coming, especially you."

"Awe..."

"No awe. You all ready know how I feel about you."

"Oh! How do you f...I'm just kidding. I'll see you there."

"Good. Well, you have my cell in case you guys get lost."

"Thanks for the invite, Shane."

"You're welcome."

"Talk later."

"Bye." (They both hang up the phone).

(Terry and India hear music as they approach Shane's residence for his party).

"*Thighs high, to the sky...*"

"That's my jam!"

(Following the beat) "*Doon, doon, doon, doon, doon!*"

"*I wanna grip your hips and move!*"

(Terry interrupts). "I don't see what you hear in that music. So many sexual overtones. It might as well be that rap mess. "Spuh! Spuh! Spuh! Spit!" (As Terry attempts to mock a rapper).

"What! You think that music is bad. Oh my goodness! Take the corn cob out your ass, honey!"

"Well, I'm just..."

"Well nothing. Let's enjoy the party. Loosen up a little."

"Well..."

"No, could you do that for me?"

(Terry concedes). "Yes, dear."

"Good. Now that's better" (as she turns around to face Terry). "Come here. Bend down some." (India reaches up to fix Terry's collar).

Kiss!

"Ok, that's better. Now let's go in here and have some fun."

(India presses the door bell) "Ding, Dong!"

(Singing under her breath). "*Thighs high, to the sky...*"

"Ding, Dong!" (Terry starts to rustle his jacket as he gets impatient waiting for the door to open). "Ding, Dong!"

(India turns around and looks at Terry).

"It's ok, baby, they're coming."

(Pretending to remain calm). "Ok, baby. I'm good."

(Door swings open) "Hi there, India!"

"Hello, Shane. Here is my husband Terry." (Shane put's his hand out. He shakes hands with Terry).

"Nice to meet you, Terry."

"Same to you, Shane. And last but not least, this lovely lady on my side is, Vera, my wife."

"Hi, everybody."

(Terry and India in unison). "Hi, Vera."

(India walks in and gives Vera a hug as Terry reaches around to shake hands with Shane).

"It's good to finally meet you."

(While placing her hands on Vera's forearms). "You too, India. I've heard so much about you. You and Shane must work together a lot."

(India glances quickly at Shane and responds to Vera). "Yeah, we do. But we are in separate departments so it's really not that much."

"Well, he just mentions you a lot when it comes to work."

(Terry jumps in). "I'm glad to meet you as well, Shane. India keeps saying how she can't get anything done without you."

"Well...it's really nothing, but thanks. Hey, enough talk about work. We got the music on in the family room and the game is on in the basement."

(Terry's eyes light up). "Oh that's right! The Patriots are in the AAA playoffs."

"Yep, their first game."

"Honey, you mind?"

"Like I can stop you. Go ahead baby; I know where to find you."

(Terry lightly hugs Vera). "Nice to meet you again, Vera."

"You too, Terry." (Terry points to a door inquiring about the basement location).

"That's the one."

"Thanks, Shane." (Shane calls out to Terry as he opens the basement door).

"Oh, Terry. There's a mini-bar in the corner. Help yourself."

"All right then." (Terry closes the door and walks down the stairs to the basement).

(Vera's next door neighbor calls from across the kitchen to tell Vera that the oven timer is going off). "Vera! The oven timer is going off."

"Ok, Deanne. I'll be right there! Excuse me, India, I've got to get the rest of the food together. We can talk later on. Really nice to meet you."

"Same to you, Vera." (Vera begins to turn and walk to the kitchen).

"Do you need a hand?"

"Oh no, you are a guest."

"You sure?"

"Yes, it's only a few things left. I appreciate you asking." (Vera turns and calls out to Deanne). "I'm coming, Deanne. Be right there."

(India turns to go and join the party. Shane reaches around her waist to pull her back), "Hey, hey. What about my birthday hug?"

(India is now facing Shane with her hands lightly pushing his chest away). "Oh goodness! I hope no one is looking."

(In a soft voice). "No one is looking, baby." (As he wraps her with both arms).

"Ok, but hurry up!"

"It's ok, India. No one is looking." (India relaxes her hands and puts them on Shane's back. Shane pulls her closer so that her soft breasts lie on his chest. Shane tilts his head and kisses India on her neck).

(Shane whispers). "See."

Kiss!

"I told you it would be ok."

(Low sigh). "Umm...yes. Oh damn. You're getting me wet talking like that!" (Shane squeezes India tighter).

"Ummm...girl. You feel so good!"

"Damn! I can feel your dick throbbing." (Shane looks over India's shoulder and sees the kitchen door pop open. He quickly pulls away from India and walks toward the kitchen). "Hey, where you going?"

"Oh, to get a drink. You want anything?"

"Sure. Get me a Vodka and Cranberry." (He, he, he. Bout to get us busted. It's good we stopped anyway before our asses get caught. Just keep playing with fire. Ok, I know better, but damn people keep putting us together. Even our freakin spouses! What am I saying? Shane just excites me. Why is that? I don't know).

(India flashes back to the time when Shane was fingering her pussy in the conference room). "Ummm!" (Shit! His finger felt so good! Damn! I can just imagine the dick. The mother fucker was so hard! I may have to...)

"Here is your drink India...India?"

"Oh, oh I'm sorry. I must have been daydreaming."

"Yeah, you were doing something. Look like you were in a trance. What were you thinking about?"

"Oh nothing."

"Hmmm...I bet. Anyway, here you go."

"Thanks, Shane." (They hold up their glasses to make a quick toast). "To a happy birthday, and many more!"

(Glasses touch and they take a drink). "Mmmm...this is really good for a Vodka and cranberry."

"Um hum."

"Oh you like?"

"Yes, I do."

"Well, there is a little extra ingredient in it."

"Oh, you got to tell me."

"Well, you know I can't do that."

"Why?"

"Cause I would have to kill you. And lord knows I don't want to do that."

"Ha, ha, ha."

"Fine! Oh, I will get it out of you one way or another."

"Yeah. You just keep trying."

(India and Shane have several drinks).

(Music playing) *"Slide to the left. Now slide to the right."*

"Oh come on, Shane. Let's get out there."

"Naw, I'm good. You go ahead."

"Well suit yourself."

"Yeah, I'll catch you on the next song."

"Ok then."

"Criss-Cross."

(India joins in with the crowd doing the Cha-Cha slide. Terry comes upstairs to get a drink).

"What's up, Terry? Are you enjoying yourself?"

"Yeah, the game is at the half, so I decided to get a drink and maybe a little food."

"Oh good, plenty of food and drink. Help yourself."

(Terry enters the kitchen. The next song comes on. India waves Shane onto the dance floor.) *"Freak show, baby, baby on the dance floor, it's a freak show. Yeah, ah Yeah"*

"Keep up now! Show me those moves, boy!"

"Oh, don't worry about me. I got this!" (Shane moves in closer and puts one hand on the side of India's hips and one in the air).

"All right now!" (The crowd starts to chant.)

"Go, Shane! Go, Shane! Go, Go, Go! (Terry comes out of kitchen and stands by Vera at the edge of the dance floor. Terry is unphased by Shane dancing so close up on his wife).

"Hi, Terry."

"Hi, Vera. The party is really nice."

"Why thank you. I just like to keep it simple. But I'm and glad you're having a good time."

"Thank you."

"So, why aren't you dancing, man?"

"Well, I really don't dance."

"What! At all?"

"Nope. I just don't get into things like that."

"That's amazing, since your wife looks like she dances quite often."

"Yeah, she does. She typically goes out with her girlfriends."

"Ok, that explains it."

"Well, your husband isn't too shabby himself."

"Right, right. We go dancing sometimes, but I feel you. I'm not so much into it either, but I go since he likes it."

(Shane looks around and sees Terry and his wife looking at them dancing. Shane tells India not to overreact and slowly backs off. He then waves them to come on to the dance floor).

"Come on! Come get some of this, baby!" (Shane turns toward Vera with his arms open, dancing and waving her onto the floor. Terry lets Vera know that he is going back to the basement and leaves).

"Oh no, honey. I'm fine. You keep dancing."

"Awe, baby. Come on!" (Vera waves her hands to have Shane stay on the dance floor).

(Talking over the music)

"It's fine, Shane! You guys seem like you're having fun! Go ahead! Enjoy yourselves!" (Shane turns around and goes back to continue dancing with India. He moves just close enough to India to tell her what Vera said).

"She didn't want to dance. She said that we were having such a good time. Just keep dancing."

"Really?"

"Yep."

"Did she say anything about us dancing close?"

"Not a single word."

"I know Terry didn't say anything. Plus, I know better not to even ask him to dance. He never dances with me. Not one time."

"What you are kidding me?"

"Not one time! And even more odd is that, I know he didn't have anything to say about us dancing together."

"You're right. He didn't. He actually just turned around and went back to the basement."

"Ha, ha, ha! No surprise. I know him like a book." (The song ends and Shane suggests they should both go check on their spouses).

"Hey. Why don't you go check on Terry?"

"Yeah, that's probably a good idea."

"Yeah, just make sure he is enjoying himself and not...well, not mad or anything. Ok then. But you better save me another dance."

"What? Baby, you can count on it!" (India heads to the basement as Shane goes to find Vera).

"Take a time-out! Take a time-out!" (As India comes down the stairs of the basement, she sees Terry sitting on the edge of his seat pleading with the coach on television to take a time out). "Thank you! Thank you!" (India comes up to his side and places her hand on his shoulder).

"Hey, baby. How's it going?" (Terry feels slightly annoyed since he is very much into the game).

"Oh hi, baby! We got a close one here."

"Oh good. Are you enjoying yourself?"

(Under his breath) "Yes, baby!"

"Cool. Wanted to make sure my man was all right."

(Hurriedly since the next play is about to start). "Yes, baby, I'm all right."

(Not realizing that Terry is slightly irritated, India plops down in his lap. Terry looks up at her watching the game rolling his eyes and then turns back to the game). "So, baby, why is that guy running while everybody else is being still?"

"Well, honey...wait! Let me tell you after this play! Ohh!!!" (Terry almost throws India off his lap). "He got them within field goal range! Whew! This is close!"

"Baby?"

(Restraining himself). "Yes, dear?"

"So, is the field goal line the yellow line they keep showing on the screen?"

(Quick answer) "No, baby." (Baby, please let me finish the game).

"So then what..." (India hears their wedding song). "Oh, baby! You hear that! It's our wedding song. Come on! Come dance with me."

"Baby, I'll come as soon as this game is over."

"The song will probably be off by then."

"Baby, we can have the DJ play it again and...hey, why don't you ask Shane to dance?"

(Ask Shane to dance! This is our special song. What the...what am I thinking? He doesn't care about a special song. This damn game is more important...)

"Ok, honey. Enjoy your game." (India get's up and walks off upset. Terry goes right back to the game).

"Oh wow. They got the lights turned down. Damn! Oh my goodness! I love this song." (Well, he did say dance with Shane).

(India scans the room for Shane).

"Oh there you are. Why aren't you and Vera out there?"

"She's in the den gossiping with Deanne."

"Gossiping?"

"Yes, gossiping. Deanne's mouth runs 100 miles an hour."

"Ha, ha, ha!"

"Come on then. Let's dance. She's not around."

"What about Terry?"

"Please. He told me go dance with you." (Blowing out air to signify that it's ok). "Pssst!"

"Ok then. I owe you a dance anyway." (Shane and India move out on to the dance floor).

"Here and now! I promise to love faithfully!"

"Ha, ha, ha!"

"How fitting."

"Um hum. Must be a message in there somewhere, huh?" (Shane places one hand in the small of India's back and pulls her closer. India exhales as she relaxes while enjoying the song).

"Ummm...damn, I love this song."

"Me too. It just feels so natural."

"Yes it does."

(India lays her head into Shane's chest. Shane brings his hand to the back of India's head and gently presses it against his chest. He whispers in India's ear). "Damn, girl. I haven't felt this way in a long time. It's like being in high school."

"I know. I know."

(Shane begins to rub his hand up and down India's back). "Mmmmm. Oh my goodness. That feels so good. Oh damn, baby, don't stop!"

(India grabs Shane's hand and pulls it down slowly to her skirt. She looks around and asks Shane about Vera and Terry). "Do you see Vera around?"

"No, she's still in the den."

"How do you know that?"

"If she comes from the Den, then she has to pass through and come out the kitchen. The lights are down low just in case she comes through. And you know Terry is still in the basement."

"Right."

"Ok then. So what..."

(Before Shane finishes asking India about her questions, she guides his hand under skirt and onto her pussy).

(Shane responds in a quiet and surprised voice). "Oh shit! You...damn, you're so wet!"

(India pushes two of his fingers in). "Ummmm! Oh yes! Rub that pussy, baby!"

"India! This pussy is so fucking hot! Damn it! I want you so bad!"

"We better stop before..."

"Fuck it! I am tired of playing around. Come on." (Shane grabs India by the arm and pulls her off the dance floor into laundry room that leads to the garage).

(Breathing nervously hard). "Lock the door!"

"Ok. I can barely see you, Shane." (As soon as India locks the door, Shane grabs her and begins to kiss her passionately).

(India is slightly startled at how strong Shane grabs her). "Woo!" Kiss!

"Mmmmm! Oh, baby! Mmmmm!!! (Breathing hard) Oh God yes! I want you, Shane. I want your dick! No more denying."

"Oh, baby! I've wanted you for so long!"

(Shane picks India up and places her on the washing machine). "Oooh! He, he. Damn this thang cold!"

"Shhhh!!!"

(Whispering) "Oh sorry. You...um...forgot I don't have any panties on."

"Oh damn! That's right. I'm sor..."

"Fuck that, get in this pussy! Hurry up! Before they come looking for us." (India spreads her legs open and starts to massage her clit and alternate with putting a finger in her pussy). "Ummmmm! Ahhhhhh! Come on, niggah!"

"Oh yeah, baby, I gotta have you!"

(Shane unbuckles his pants and lets them fall to the floor. India grabs his dick with her other hand). "Yeah. That's what I want. I want all that fat dick!"

(India places the finger that has been in her pussy in Shane's mouth).

Slurp!

"Mmmm!"

"That's what you want, ain't it? Lick all that pussy off!"

Slurp!

"Oh yes, baby. Damn that pussy tastes good."

(Sucking through his teeth) "Pssssh! Oh hell yeah. Let me taste all that pussy. Lean back slowly, baby."

(India grabs the bottom of her skirt and places it in her mouth. Shane places one hand on the bottom of each thigh and pushes India's knees back onto her breasts. He bends over and begins to lick and suck her pussy).

Lick...

"Mmmm!"

Slurp...

"Unnnh!!! Suck that pussy! That's it!" (Shane stiffens his tongue and begins to slide it in and out of India's pussy). "Unnnh! Unnh! Oh God! Oh God! Unnh! Unnh!" (Shane flattens is tongue out and begins to make long licks from right above India's ass to her clit).

Slurrrrrrrrrrrrrrrrrp!

"Ohhhhhhhhh fuck!"

(Breathing fast) "Oh shit, oh shit, oh shit! I'm cumming, I'm cummmmmmmmming!" (India jams more of her skirt in her mouth as her stomach muscles tighten).

(In a muffled voice). "Rrrrrrrrrrrrrrrrrh!" (Breathing fast and heavy) "Woo! Woo! Woo! Woo! Oh my God! Oh my God!"

"Don't call on God now. You ain't seen nothing yet baby!"

"Oh damn!"

(Shane places one leg over each shoulder) "Slide up, baby."

"Yeah…"

"Place that pussy right on the edge." (Shane walks up closer. His dick head is slightly parting India's pussy lips).

"Unnh! Oh, baby! Push it in! Please push it in!" (Shane grabs his dick with one hand and starts to circle it around India's clit). "Ummm…ummm…ummm…" (Pleading) "Shane!…Fuck me, please! Fuck me!"

(In a quiet voice) "Oh, don't worry, baby. I'm waiting for another song to come on."

"Oh fuck! Play some music, damnit!"

(Music begins playing) *"Give it to me baby!"*

(Shane thrusts his dick all the way in and up, lifting India up slightly from the washer).

"Unnnnnnnnnnnnnnnnnnnnnnnh! Sssssss! Damn, niggah!"

(Shane goes in and out slowly). "Unnnnnnnnnnnnnnnnnh! Sssssss!"

"Shit girl! Oh fuck! Unnnnnnnnnnnnnnnnnnnh! This pussy is so good!"

"Fuck it, niggah!" (Shane begins to fuck India faster. The washer begins to clank lightly against the wall). "Unnh!"

Clank!

"Unnh!"

Clank!

"Give me that pussy! Oh, baby! Oh, baby! I'm about to cum!"

"Come on, daddy! Come up in this pussy. This your pussy! Come on! Unnh!"

Clank!

"Unnh!"

Clank!

"Oh baby! I'm cummi… (The handle to the laundry room door jiggles. India and Shane stop. India's skirt falls from her mouth and onto Shane's dick as he continues to cum. Shane covers his mouth as they both hear voices outside the door).

"That's odd. Sounds as if the washer just finished its spin cycle. Not sure why Shane would be washing clothes during his party."

(Oh shit! It's Vera. Damn. Oh hell!)

"Hi, Terry. Was Shane in the basement?"

"No, I don't remember seeing him."

(Fuck! Terry is looking for me).

"Hmmm...I guess he must be outside. I'll go check."

"Ok, I will let him know you are looking for him if I see him. I'm headed back to the basement."

(Shane helps India down off the washer as soon as he hears Vera leave). "Ok, you go back through the door into the house. I'm going out the garage. Oh, here, a paper towel to wipe off."

(Shane and India both wipe off and exit through the door and garage respectively. Soon after the garage gets up, Shane hears Vera coming out the door. Shane approaches Vera before she reaches the garage). "Hey, baby! How are you doing?"

"Oh, I'm fine."

"Good. You need something?"

"No, but I was wondering why the door to the garage was locked and it sounded like the washing machine was on spin cycle."

"Oh, I'm sorry. That was me. Somehow, the lock got stuck and I kept bumping the washer trying to shake it loose."

"Oh ok. I thought that would be odd for you to be washing on your birthday."

"Ha, ha, ha! Baby, you know I don't like to wash that much."

"Right, right. I should have known." (Shane puts his arm around Vera and they walk back into the house together).

(To play as if she hadn't seen Shane, India approaches Shane and Vera to ask where Shane has been). "Hey birthday, boy! Where you been?"

"Oh, I was outside in the garage trying to get that stupid door unlocked."

"Oh, ok. I was wondering. Hadn't seen you in a while."

"Well, you know my Shane." (Vera pats him on his chest as she continues hugging his waist). "Always got to fix something. No matter what the occasion is."

(Vera takes her arm from around Shane. She needs to go to kitchen to light his cake).

"Well, hang on to him for a few minutes for me. I will be right back."

"Ok, no problem."

"Good. Oh, there's a white spot on the bottom of your skirt." (Shane's eyes get big as he sees that it's cum on India's skirt. India nervously tries to play it off).

"Oh my! Let me go wipe this off right away." (Think, think!) "It looks like ranch dressing. I'm always spilling something! Shoot! I'll be right back." (India goes to the bathroom).

(Oh shit! It's about to be some shit! Our ass is busted.)

(Vera turns to Shane. Shane immediately calms his face to keep Vera from connecting him with India). "Didn't you think that spot on her skirt looked a little thick for ranch dressing?"

"No, not really. She probably spilled some when eating some of the wings. She really likes wings."

"Oh really?"

"I mean she must really like wings." (Ok, that sounds much better.)

"Well, go check the date on that bottle. It just didn't look right."

"Ok, baby, will do, will do."

(Shane gives Vera a spank on the butt and sends her off to the kitchen).

"Off you go!"

"Ha, ha, ha! You're so silly."

Chapter 12

Conference Call in Progress

"Paging Wendy Campbell! Paging Wendy Campbell! You have a phone call on Line 2! You have a phone call on Line 2!"

(Wendy walks off the manufacturing floor to the nearest phone. She takes the phone off the hook and presses line 2. There is a lot of background noise from the running equipment as she answers the phone).

"Hello! This is Wendy!"

"Hey, baby. How is it going?"

(Wendy starts smiling). "Oh, hi, Daniel. I was just thinking about you."

"Oh you were?"

"Umm...yes!!! I was just thinking how long it's been since we've been together. I've been dreaming about touching you, kissing you and feeling you!"

"Shit, girl! Are you reading my mind?"

"Ha, ha, ha."

"I miss being behind that juicy ass and just pounding that pussy! Oh! Oh! And the way you..."

"Stop it! Daniel please stop! You are making me wet. I still have 2 hours left in my shift."

"Well, I..."

(In a cynical voice). "Oh no! Unlike some folks, Mr. Big Time manager, I have to work for a living".

"Oh come on, Wendy. You know I don't care anything about that."

"Ha, ha, ha. I know, I know...oh we know all right! That's quite obvious. You know that a manager shouldn't be involved with a technician. And further more..."

"Ok, ok. I get it, babe!"

"Ha, ha, ha. I'm just messing with you, baby. You know I love you, baby."

(Daniel smiles). "Um hum. Now that's better. That's my, baby."

"So, mister...when are we getting together?"

"How about as soon as you get off?"

"How are we going to do that? Don't you and your wife ride home together?"

"Nope. Not anymore. She has her on car now. Plus, she'll be leaving the plant early to pick up the kids."

"Hmmm...looks like somebody has things all planned out."

"You better believe it, baby. I need to feel you so bad. It's been weeks since you been on this new schedule. You know it's so much easier when you are on 2nd shift. But we have to work with what we got."

"Right, right."

"Ok then. I will see you at my place in about thirty minutes after I clock out."

"Don't keep me..."

"Wait, wait, Wendy. I can't make it to your place after work. I have to be home not too long after my wife gets home with the kids."

"So how..." (In a cautious voice).

"Well...um...I was thinking maybe we could meet in the back of the plant by the Silos for a quickie."

(Slightly shocked). "Whoa! Whoa! Whoa!" (Wendy places her other hand near the phone handle to hide her conversation). "You want to fuck on site? Are you serious?"

(Daniel swallows hard and then answers). "Well, I...I thought that it would..."

"You thought what?" (Wendy moves around the corner further away from the phone base stretching the phone cord to its limit). "Hmmm! I don't know, Daniel. I just don't know."

"We're already violating plant rules. I mean..."

"Oh my goodness! If we get caught! We won't only get..."

"Shit! I really miss you too, but..." (Daniel tries to calm Wendy down). "Wendy? Wendy? It's ok. We don't have to..."

"No, I didn't say that, Daniel. I just have to think about it. I'm scared and excited."

"But really, Wendy, I can wait if..."

"Fuck it! Let's do it!"

(Shocked). "Umm! Ok. Ok. Ok, let's meet back..."

(Daniel's other line rings) "Ring!" "Ring!"

"Hold on one second, Wendy. My other line is ringing." (Daniel places Wendy on hold).

"Daniel Ellerbee speaking."

"Hi, Danny." (What does my wife want?)

"Oh, hi, Grace..."

"How is your day going, babe?"

"Umm. Not that bad." (Rushing voice) "So, what can I do for you? I have a client on the other line."

"Oh, I'm sorry."

"Not a problem."

"Do you want me to get them off the line and..."

"No, no."

"I just need a big favor today."

"Ok, shoot."

"I need to stay over a couple hours at the plant for month end reports. So I need you to pick up the kids." (Fuck! Not today).

"Oh sure, honey. Not a problem."

"Thank you so much, Danny. I'll talk to you later. Bye."

"Bye, babe."

(Daniel takes Wendy off hold).

"Wendy?"

"Yes Daniel."

(Sounding disappointed) "That was my wife. She wants me to pick up the kids. We can't..."

"Don't even say it. It's alright, Daniel. This is what we signed up for."

"But I really..."

"Yes. But it's reality. My girlfriends always ask, 'How do you put up with all the sneaking around and being second to the wife?' I tell them first of all. This is my life. And most importantly, you make me happy. I've accepted that you're married. All I asked for was to not meet your wife. I have probably seen her at the plant for sure. But I don't know her from Adam. And I'm good with that. Second of all, you know everyone in her organization and you would know if I was reporting to her. Right?"

"Yes."

"So really, it's on them to accept me for me and the decisions I make."

"Wow, baby. That's an awesome perspective."

"Well, it's like I always say. You can't help where you find love."

"That's true, baby. It's like that old song, 'When love calls, you better answer.'"

"He, he, he. That is so fitting. Well put."

"Well, it's all true."

"So...I guess we will have to wait until you are back on 2nd shift."

"Oh no, no! I need some dick way before then! Tomorrow is my last day before changing over to 3rd shift. So, you need to figure out how this going down."

(Excited) "Ummh! Shit! I'll figure something out."

(Wendy turns back toward the line and notices that the line siren is blinking). "Hey. Gotta go! The line stopped."

"Ok, baby. I will figure something out."

"Ok. Love you."

"Love you too."

"Bye."

"Bye, babe." (Wendy and Daniel hang up the phone. Wendy goes back to the line while Daniel finishes up so he can leave and pick up the kids).

(As Wendy approaches the manufacturing line, a co-worker, Erin inquires about her whereabouts). "It's about time you get back here! Where have you been, girl?"

(Wendy shrugs her shoulders with a big smile on her face). "Talking to my sister."

"Please! I should have known. Don't even tell me. You've been talking to Mr. Manager haven't you?"

(Wendy smiles and turns to the line. Erin keeps talking to the back of Wendy's head).

"Haven't you?"

"Ok, ok. Yes! So what?"

(Erin shakes her head back and forth) "Un! Un! Un! I will never understand it. Why do you keep messing around with this married man? You know he isn't going to leave his wife, right? And all you get out of it..."

"Hold it right there! First of all, it is none of your fucking business what I do with my life! As of a matter of fact, I've gotten more out of my relationship with him then the time I was married as well when I was dating single men! The point of it all is" (bringing her voice down) "that I'm happy...just happy. Please realize that." (Looking eye to eye with Erin). "I am not asking him to leave his wife. He has young children, which is the one thing I respect the most. What man can be any good to me if he doesn't have anything to do with his children?"

"Hmmm...well, I never thought about it that way. I can see your point. And I'm glad you're happy. But..." (With a face of concern) "But what about the fact his wife works out here?"

"Well, it hasn't been an issue so far. We have been dating for over a year now. And besides, I don't know of her from Adam."

"Really?"

"Yes, really. I asked him to not even tell me her name."

(Erin looks back at Wendy with a surprised look) "What? Are you crazy! What if you guys run in to her?"

"Not a problem. That's the thing. We decided to never be seen together at work." (That may be changing soon.) "We decided to only talk on the phone."

"Ok. I feel better now knowing that..."

"Come on, girl! I may not be that smart, but I ain't stupid."

"Ha, ha, ha. Ok, girl. I apologize for prying in your business. I just want to make sure you don't get hurt." (Erin grabs Wendy's hand with two hands). "I'm really sorry."

"It's ok, girl. I know you got good intentions. And please believe, I am not going to do anything stupid."

(Relieved). "Ok, Wendy. I trust you."

"Thanks, Erin." (Wendy and Erin begin to focus on getting the line back running. Wendy starts to contemplate getting with Daniel at work as she works inside the line).

(Hmm...I don't know. This feels a little risky. I mean, we've never done anything at work. Not even lunch...and, add the fact that we are definitely in violation of codes of conduct. A manager and technician fraternizing, let alone he's married! Damn! I don't...But, but it's been a while since we've been together. I really want to feel his kiss, his touch and all 8 inches of his juicy fat dick!) "Unnh!"

"Yeah, Wendy?"

"Oh, nothing, Erin. I was just singing."

"Ok then."

(Alright, alright. Ok, let's be rational about this. One time can't hurt. I mean, it's not like we're going to do this all the time. Most likely never again...so one time should be ok? Yes, one time is ok. Ok then, its settled. Thanks, girl. I knew you wouldn't let me down).

"Wendy?...Wendy!"

"Oh, oh. Yes, Erin?"

"I need for you to take off your lock so we can restart the line."

"Oh sorry."

"I was just..."

"I know, I know. Don't tell me. Thinking about Mr. Manager."

(Wendy smiles big). "What? I was not!"

"Whatever, chick. I saw your face all lit up."

(Wendy blushing). "Girl..."

"What everrrrrrrrrrrrrrrrr!"

"No really, I..." (Wendy removes her lock)

"All clear!" (Erin starts the line. Wendy and Erin finish out there shift and go home for the day).

(Wendy reports to her interim manager's office to discuss a note left in her box overnight. Wendy is slightly nervous since she has no idea what the note concerns. The note said report to office AZ-23).

"Knock, knock!"

"Come in."

(In a shaky voice). "Good morning!"

"Good morning...umm...Wendy?"

"Yes, good morning ma'am."

"Oh, call me Grace."

(Taking a deep breath). "Ok, Grace."

"Oh, you can relax, Wendy. Can I get you anything?"

"Oh no, I'm fine."

"It's nice to finally meet you in person. I've heard so much about your work. I think the first day you came over from the bagging department, I was in Europe for about 2 weeks. Then I was at headquarters in Akron for 1 week."

"Wow! You keep a busy schedule."

"Yeah, it gets hectic sometimes, but I enjoy it."

"Well that's what counts. We spend too much time at work not to make it enjoyable."

"Um hum..."

"Enough about me, this meeting is for you. Let me first start by thanking you for coming over and helping us out on short notice. I have seen your weekly results and in a few short weeks, you have achieved huge efficiencies and savings!"

"You're welcome. I'm just here to get the job done."

"Well, I want you to know that we appreciate that."

"So...I wanted to gauge your interest in permanently moving to the supervisory position you are in now."

(Wendy's eyes light up). "Oh wow! I guess I need to talk to my..."

"Step ahead of you. I've talked to your boss and he says it is up to you. He has already identified a candidate to back-fill you if you accept. So again, it's all up to you."

(Wendy is speechless).

"And of course, there is a generous pay increase as well as becoming eligible for year-end bonuses."

(Wendy smiling). "Oh my goodness! I don't know what to say."

"He, he, he. Well hopefully after some thought, you will accept."

(I accept! I accept!) "I..."

"So...before you answer, take a few days to think it over."

(Excitedly). "Yes ma'am!"

"Please call me Grace."

"Yes, Grace, I will think it over tonight!"

"Good. Take your time. No real rush. But if you make a decision in the next week, we should have enough time to get everything processed through the payroll division."

"That sounds great! I am so excited. I really appreciate you considering me for this opportunity."

"You're welcome, Wendy. We just don't like to waste time when we see an employee that has the potential to take themselves and this company to higher heights."

(Big sigh) "Whew! This is going to be a great day!"

"Well, enjoy it. You deserve it, Wendy."

"Thanks again Grace."

"Thank you so much."

"See you later Wendy."

"Ok, see you soon." (Wendy leaves Grace's office to start her shift. Erin and other co-workers notice that she seems extremely happy).

"Ok, what's the happy face all about?"

"Awe...nothing."

"Yeah right. You are smiling ear to ear, girl."

"Well..." (Wendy is so excited that she can hardly get out her thoughts). "Ok! So, I check my inbox this morning. There's a note in there. It just says...um...see me at office AZ-23. I'm like AZ-23. Whose office is this? I mean...is this HR? Did I do something? Or what happened to my job? So I'm so nervous."

"Oh goodness!"

"That's what I was thinking! Anyway, I get in there. And I meet this nice manager. Um...Grace. So she says they like my work. And..."

"Spit it out, girl."

"They offered me a supervisory position."

(Wendy and the co-workers jump with excitement. Erin grabs her on the shoulders shaking her slightly) "Way to go girl! Congratulations! That is super news."

(Wendy breathing hard) "I know. I'm so excited."

"Well, you deserve it, girl. Do your thang!"

"Thanks everybody. Thanks. I couldn't have done it without you guys."

"Oh girl, we are just doing our jobs. You deserve it!"

(Wendy gets a little choked up). "I really...appreciate...you" (sniffle) "guys."

"Awe, girl come on now, don't go there. You gonna have all of us out here crying."

(Sniffle) "I know. I know. I'm sorry."

"It's all good girl. We know those are tears of joy."

(Shift whistle goes off). "Woo, woo! Woo, woo!"

"Alright, supervisor. Put our asses to work!"

"Ha, ha, ha. Go on with that girl." (Everybody leaves to do their jobs).

(Wendy receives a text message from Daniel right before lunch).

(Reading message) "Hey sweet thing! Can't wait to see you later. Love you."

(Awe...that is so sweet. I can't wait either baby. I can't wait to share the good news with you. This is turning out to be a really good day.)

(Wendy sends a reply message back to Daniel.)

"Buzz, Buzz!" (Hmmm... A message from Wendy).

"Can't wait to see you too baby. I got some wonderful news to share with you! Love you! Miss you!"

(That's my baby. I miss you too!...Damn! I can't wait to get all up in that ass! Un! That woman... Un! Whew that pussy is good! Shoot! Where we going to go? I don't know about the silos. May be too obvious. Hmmm...too risky. How about the back conference room?)

"...Arrrrgggh!" (None of the doors lock. And it's still daylight. Damn! Think man, think!)

(Placing his hand under his chin) "Got it!" (I'll have her come up to my office towards the end of her shift. And then I could put the conference call sign up in the window. That should work. I mean most people are gone around that time.) "Hmmm..." (Wait a minute. Jerry always stays late. Damn! Maybe he'll go home early. Nah... Fuck, I don't know. Hold on. Just tell Jerry that I have an important conference call and make sure no one disturbs me). "Ok. Got it." (Stop thinking about it. Just do it. All right, it's on).

(Daniel sends Wendy a message of their meeting later) "Buzz, Buzz!"

(Wendy reads Daniel's message).

(Ok baby. I have a plan. Come to my office towards the end of your shift for a personal conference call. Lol!)

(Wendy's heart starts to beat very fast). (Oh my goodness! He wants us to do it in his office. Wow! Um...wow. This is some crazy shit. I get a supervisor position and will be fired before I work one day. That's funny. No one would believe you. Ha, ha, ha.) (Long pause) (Well...I know Daniel has thought it out and God knows I am horny as shit!) (Large exhale) (Whewww! Fuck! Fuck! Fuck!).

"Buzz, Buzz!" (Hmm...another message: Candy!).

(Wendy's eyes get big) "Oh shit! His di...(Covering her mouth)..."his dick looks so damn tasty! Oh God! It's so fucking hard. I know that shit is full of cum! Oooooh! I want to put this phone up my pussy right now! It's on!...We is fucking today! No doubt).

(Wendy sends a message back to Daniel) "Buzz, Buzz!" (See you in a couple of hours. Ready to feel my candy?)

"Mmmm. I ready to feel you too, baby." (Daniel reaches under his desk and rubs his dick slowly through his pants.) "Unnnnnh... Unnnnnh... Damn!" (Sucking air through his teeth) "I can't wait to get up in that ass. I don't know what it is? It's just something about her. Umm!"

(Daniel checks the clock anxiously anticipating Wendy's arrival. His heart starts to beat faster) "Oh shit! It's 3:25!" (Let me go let Jerry know about the conference call).

(As Daniel walks to the back corner of the office floor, he scans the room for other co-workers).

(Hmmm...looks like Jerry is the only one up here. Looks like we will be ok).

(Daniel starts to calm down some as he reaches Jerry's office. Daniel stands at one side of the door entrance and leans his head into Jerry's office).

"Hey, Jerry!"

(Jerry turns around and places his index finger up denoting hold on for one minute).

(In a quiet voice) "Oh, sorry. I didn't see you were on the phone."

(Daniel leans off the door frame and stands outside the door as Jerry finishes talking).

"Ok, Bob. Let's reconnect next week. That should give us time to analyze the data and move forward with a recommendation."

(That sounds good Jerry).

"Have a good weekend."

(You too).

"Talk with you later. Bye."

(Jerry hangs up the phone). "Click!"

"Daniel?..."

(Daniel stands in the entrance of Jerry's door). "Hey, sorry about that, Jerry. I didn't see you on the phone. I..."

"No harm done. What can I do for you today?"

"Well, I just wanted to let you know that I have an extremely important conference call coming up in about 2 minutes. I just wanted someone to let any visitors know that I can't be disturbed."

"Oh, that's easy. I'll just listen for the door to the office to open and let them know you can't be disturbed."

(Daniel smiles and clasps his hands together). "Jerry, you are a life saver! I really appreciate it."

"No problem, my friend."

"Good. Gotta run."

"Ok. Talk later." (Daniel turns and goes back to his office).

(Ok now. Let me get this conference call sign up).

(Daniel looks back over his shoulder) (Ok, where is the tape? This thing will not just hold in this door window).

(Nervously looking on his desk and inside the desk drawers).

(Tape? Tape? Nope. No tape? Hmmm...tape! Found it).

(Daniel gets the conference call in progress sign taped to his door).

"Buzz!" "Buzz!" (Reading message) "I'm on my way baby!"

(Daniel starts breathing rapidly) "Oh God! Here we go." (Nervously typing a message back to Wendy) "Come.. on.. ba..by! I'm reaaaa..dy." (Daniel hits send on his phone. He closes the door gently to let it rest against the doorframe. He sits nervously at his desk fidgeting his hands, periodically looking back at the door waiting for Wendy to enter).

(Wendy is passing by the plant cafeteria on her way to Daniel's office. With her eyes focused forward, Wendy doesn't notice that her new boss is inside the cafeteria. Grace sees her and hurries to the door to speak with her. Grace is standing between the double doors to the cafeteria with one side propped open).

"Wendy! Hey Wendy!"

(Wendy finally hears her name and turns around. She turns to walk back toward Grace. She's nervous inside but trying not to show it). "Oh, hi, Grace."

"Hi Wendy."

"Umm...did you need something?" (Wendy's heart is racing inside).

"Oh, nothing major. I just wanted to let you know I talked with your old boss again and he really hopes you take the opportunity. He had a lot of good things to say about you."

"Oh wow. He did?"

"Yes. He says, if anyone deserves the opportunity, it's you."

"Wow. I'm just happy I was considered."

"Oh, you should be very proud of your accomplishments."

"Thank you, Grace. I really appreciate it."

"Good. Good for you."

"So where are you headed?"

(Oh damn. Well, I am going to fuck a married man in his office. No, can't say that). "Oh, I have to go to the bone yard room at the back of the plant to look for an old part for the Line 1 filler."

"Oh ok. I was just asking. I wasn't sure since you're going towards engineering. Unless you were headed there."

(That's exactly where I am going). "Oh no, just checking on some the part so we can get that old machine running."

"Ok. Well have a good day. Don't get stuck back there. That bone yard room is creepy."

(How interesting). "Ha, ha, ha. I will be careful."

"Ok."

"See you, Grace."

"Bye, Wendy."

(Wendy pushes open Daniel's door. She quickly enters and turns to lock the door. Daniel jumps up from his seat and pulls her close and begins kissing her).

Kiss!

"Mmmm!"

Kiss!

(Daniel breathing hard) "Ummm! Oh, baby!" Kiss! "I thought..." Kiss! "You would never..." Kiss! "Come!"

"Yeah. I would have been here..." Kiss! "But my new boss..." Kiss! "Stopped me on the way here."

(Daniel puts his hands around Wendy and grips her ass to pull her closer to him).

(In a high pitched voice) "Ummmmmm! Yeah, baby. Let me feel that soft ass."

(Wendy starts to feel Daniels hard dick against her stomach). "Unnh hunh...look who wants to come out and play."

(Daniel takes a deep breath through his teeth). "Ssssss...oh baby, he wants to come out so bad."

"How bad?"

"Oh, baby, come on now! You know how much I have missed you sucking this dick!"

"Oh really?"

"Yes baby, yes!" (Wendy begins to unbuckle Daniel's pants. Daniel starts to look up at the ceiling in anticipation of Wendy grabbing and sucking his dick).

"Oh, baby!" (Wendy places her hand in his underwear). "Oh shit, baby! That feels so good."

(Daniels pants and underwear fall to the floor. Wendy bends over and kisses the head of Daniels dick then she starts sucking it). "Un! Ummmmmmmmm!"

Slurp!

"Oh baby! Suck it please!"

Slurp! Slurp!

"Ummmm! Yeah baby! Just like that! Ummmm! Oh my goodness!"

(Wendy stands up to kiss Daniel again).

Kiss!

"Mmmm!" (Daniel begins to unbutton Wendy's uniform). "Mmm!" (Daniel reaches in after a few buttons and massages Wendy's breast through her bra). "Unn! Oh, Daniel! Unn! Sssss...ahhhh!" (Daniel pops one of her breast from under her bra).

"Oooooh yeah! Look at that juicy..." Kiss! "Perky, round titty!"

"Ohhhhh! That's my spot baby!" (Daniel finishes unbuttoning Wendy's shirt while sucking her titty. He grabs her shirt with both hands and pulls the shirt out of her pants).

"Oh damn baby! You ain't wasting no time!"

(Breathing hard). "Umm...I want you, baby!"

(Daniel continues sucking and begins to unbutton Wendy's pants). "Oh it's on now! Come on D! Give me that dick!" (Daniel pushes Wendy's pants down to the floor. He guides Wendy backward to his desk. Wendy's ass cushions her as she leans back on the edge of the desk with her hands behind her to support her from falling back. Her pussy is slightly spread apart. Daniel goes to his knees and begins to eat Wendy's pussy). "Oh! The dick!"

"Don't worry..." Slurp! "I got to..." Slurp! "Unnnh! Taste this pussy first!"

"Ummmmm! That feels so good. Hell! Lick that pussy! Slurp! Unnh!! (Daniel places both hands on Wendy's ass and forces her pussy onto his extended tongue). "Unnnh! Damn! Unnnh!!! Da...unnnh!!!

Da– Unnnh!!! Damn, baby! Unnh!" (Daniel pulls his head back). (Wendy breathing hard). "Shit! Niggah! What the fuck was that!"

"Oh! I told you I miss this pussy!" (Daniel stands up, flips Wendy around, and guides her to place her elbows on the desk).

"Awwwwwe yeah. That's what I'm talking about."

"Look at that fat ass pussy! Shit nice and wet now!" (Daniel places one hand on Wendy's hip and the other in the small of her back. He moves up closer to ass). "Oh yeah! That's my shit there. Go ahead, baby. Put your face on my desk."

"Ummmm!"

"Bring your arms back and hold those ass cheeks apart. That's right. Sssssss...ohhhhhh... Look at my pussy."

(In a voice distorted by her jaw being pinned to the desk). "Co...me on. Now...Hi...it that Shitttttttttttt!!!" (Daniel slides his dick in and out rapidly). "Unh!"

Plop!

"Unh!"

Plop!

"Unh!" (Daniel goes faster. Wendy begins to almost hold her breath since she can't even moan between thrusts). Plop! Plop! Plop! Plop! Plop! Plop! Plop!

"Oh mutha-fucka! Hit that shit! Ummmm! Unnnnnh!"

"Oh Wendy! I'm about to cum!"

Plop! Plop!

"I am about to..."

(Wendy lifts one of her hands up to stop Daniel mid stream while placing the other hand on the desk) (Whispering). "Shhh!"

(In a quiet voice). "Oh, baby! I don't think I can hold it."

"Shhh! Did you hear that? Someone came through the door."

(Grace is approaching Daniel's door. Jerry heard her come through the door and runs out of his office to notify Grace about the conference call).

"Hey, Grace." (Daniel hears his wife's name and starts to cum. Wendy stands up in reaction to hearing her new boss' name. Daniel places a hand over his mouth and tries to catch the cum from his dick).

(Quietly muffled) "Arrrrrrrrrrrrrrrrrrrrrrrgh! Oh God! That's my wife out there."

(Wendy puts both of her hands to her mouth in shock) (Very quiet). "What! Grace is your wife!"

"Yes…" (Daniel and Wendy stand motionless with clothing undone to see what Grace is going to do as she talks with Jerry outside of Daniel's door).

"Oh, hi, Jerry."

"Hi Grace. As you can probably see, your husband is on a conference call."

"Yeah, I see." (Grace is carrying two large binders that she almost drop trying to knock on Daniel's door).

"Whoa, Whoa! Let me give you a hand with that."

(Daniel and Wendy look at each other shaking their heads. Daniel is trying to figure out how he didn't know that Wendy worked for Grace. They speak just audible enough to determine what they are saying by reading each other's lips). "You're in the bagging department. How is Grace your boss?"

She's my new boss! I've been on loan to her department for the last few weeks."

"Damn, that's it. I always keep up with the organization charts to avoid a situation like this!"

(Jerry continues to notify Grace of the conference call). "He left specific instructions not to be disturbed."

"Ok, that's no problem. I will just wait over here on the couch until he is done."

"Ok, suit yourself. I just put these binders right here."

"Thanks so much, Jerry."

(Wendy's eyes get big as she looks around the room in panic. She puts one hand on her forehead while speaking audible enough for lip reading). "Oh…God! We're fucked. Fucked, fucked, fucked."

(Grabbing Wendy's arm). "Calm down, baby. It's going to be ok."

"What! Are you crazy? We are so fired! Oh my God! I just became a supervisor…"

"Shhhh! She's across the room. Fix your clothes." (Wendy straightens her bra and begins buttoning her shirt. She slowly pulls up her pants and begins stuffing her shirt in her pants. Daniel wets a napkin with bottle of water he was drinking earlier to wipe cum off his dick. Wendy is still panicking about the situation).

"We're fired. Damn, damn! We are so fired!"

(Daniel puts his hand up to his head and tries to come up with a way to get Grace from in front of his door). "Got it!" (He decides to put a page out for Grace to come to the front office).

(Low whispering). I'm going to have her paged to the front office. We just need her to leave so you can get back across the plant." (Daniel walks slowly over to the phone to avoid tripping on his pants. He dials zero for the plant operator).

"Plant operator? How may I assist you?"

(In a low voice). "Please page Grace Ellerbee to the front office."

"Could you repeat that, sir?"

(Slightly higher voice). "Page Grace Ellerbee to the front office."

"Ok, thank you, sir. Will that be all?"

"Yes."

"Thank you, sir. Goodbye."

(Daniel slowly lowers the phone back to its base. He then begins to carefully fix his clothes).

"Paging Grace Ellerbee to the front office. Paging Grace Ellerbee to the front office."

(Grace hears the page and walks down to Jerry's office) "Jerry?"

"Yes, Grace?"

"Tell my husband I came by and to call me as soon as he is done with his conference call."

"No problem, Grace."

"Thanks Jerry."

"See you."

"Bye, Grace." (Grace rushes toward the front office leaving the binders behind.)

(Daniel and Wendy wait for the door outside the office to close and listen for Grace descending the steps). "Ok. Ok. Wait about a minute. Just in case she turns around." (Daniel hands Wendy a small inspection mirror to make sure she has her hair together. They both look over each other to ensure everything looks normal. They wait for about a minute. Daniel peers from behind the conference call sign and sees that no one is in the area).

(In a rushing voice) "Ok, baby! Go out the second entrance to the department."

"Ok."

"Hurry!" (Daniel swings open the door and Wendy rushes around to the second entrance and leaves. Daniel removes the conference call sign and begins to fan his office).

(Oh my goodness. This office smells like dick and pussy. Where is that air freshener?)

"Spray!" "Spray!"

(Daniel coughs from the fumes) "Cough! Cough!"

"Whew! That shit is strong."

(Jerry hears Daniel coughing. He shouts out the message Grace left with him). "Daniel!"

"Cough! Cough!"

"Yes?"

"Your wife came by. Said call her soon as you are done."

"Thanks, Jerry!"

"No sweat!"

(As Wendy approaches the steps that lead by the Cafeteria, she sees Grace walking down the stairs heading back to Daniel's office. Wendy waves at Grace hoping that she will wave and keep going. Grace stops Wendy in the middle of the stairs). "Hi, Wendy."

"Hi, Grace. I see you didn't get stuck in the bone yard."

(Nervously) "Oh...Oh...No!"

"That's good."

"Actually, where are you headed?"

"Oh, I left some binders by my husband's office."

(Damn! This shit was too damn close. I ain't never doing this shit again. Never, ever! And don't forget, I work for his wife! His fucking wife!).

"He works in engineering and his department is right through the doors," (pointing over Wendy's shoulder) "and up the stairs." I'm just headed back to get the binders. Hopefully, he's off his conference call by now. I came by earlier to talk with...Wendy?" (Wendy is still thinking about how close and awkward the situation is). "Wendy?" (Wendy tunes in).

"Oh...Yes."

"Yes what, Wendy?"

"Ummm..."

"Ok, you didn't hear anything I said."

"I'm sorry."

"Anyway, look forward to you coming aboard."

(Wow!...Wow! This is going to be something). "I'm looking forward to it as well."

"Great! Well, I will let you go. Let me go get these binders so I can get up to the front office. See you later."

"Bye, Grace." (Wendy quickly texts Daniel to let him know his wife is coming)

"Buzz!" "Buzz!" (Daniel reads Wendy's message) "Baby, hurry. Leave office. Wife coming back).

"Oh shit!" (Daniel pops up from his desk. Turning the light off and closing the door as he leaves. As soon as he starts to trot down the stairs, he sees Grace coming up the stairs. He slows down to a walk). "Hey, baby. I was coming up front to see you. Jerry told me you were over here."

"Yeah. I came over to talk to you about a report I have due next week to the plant manager."

"Oh...ok."

"Well, let's go to the cafeteria then and discuss it."

(Daniel grabs Grace on the shoulder and starts to turn her toward the cafeteria).

"Ok, but wait. I need to get..." (Grace notices Daniels collar is not sitting correctly. She reaches up to straighten it). "Let me straighten this collar."

(Daniel swallows hard).

"Ok, that's better."

"Oh thanks, baby."

"Yeah. No problem." (Grace looks at Daniel with uncertainty). "Hmmmyou must have been really focused on your conference call."

(Twitching his neck and placing one finger inside his collar). "Ummmm...well, it was a little nerve racking."

"Onh Honh. To say the least."

"Let's go, baby."

"One second. I left two binders on the couch upstairs."

"Want me to get'em?"

"No, no. Just wait here."

"I'll be right back."

"Ok, baby."

Chapter 13

Two For The Price of One

"Hey, man! Come here quick!"
(Wyatt briefly turns around from making copies). "What is it now, Manny?"

(Manny waves frantically for Wyatt to check out this female on their office floor). "Get off that copier, man! Quick! Before you miss her!"

(Wyatt steps outside the copy room near Manny. Manny puts his hand on Wyatt's shoulder and points in the direction of the female) "Mmm, mmm, ummh! Who in the hell is that with all those hips and ass!"

"You mean the girl standing near the water cooler?"

"Yeah dude! Isn't that obvious!"

"Ha, ha, ha! I'm just playing man. I know who you're talking about. That's just Vonda from accounting on the 7th floor."

"That's just Vonda?"

"Ha, ha, ha. Yes, I know." (Wyatt goes back to the copier followed by Manny as Vonda walks from their view towards the elevators). "She's nice isn't she?"

"Is she nice??? Is she nice???" (Looking at Wyatt as if he was crazy) "... man, I know you are not asking me that question! You had to see..."

"Yeah, I mean... She's..."

"Damn! I should've known! You done hit that shit ain't you?"

(Wyatt has a big smile on his face). "Well..."

"You lucky mutha fucka! I knew that shit! There is no way you would react like that if you haven't seen her before. I know your ass!"

"Ha! Ha! I thought you knew man."

"You thought I knew!...Yeah right! Can't blame you though, I would keep that one under wraps to."

"He, he. It's not like that, man." (Whispering to Manny). "She's married dude."

"What?" (Covering his mouth). "She married?"

"Yep."

"Damn bruh. What the fuck is up with her husband?"

"You know? That's a damn good question. From what she tells me, he's a workaholic and he doesn't spend enough time with her, not even for just simple shit."

"So, let me get this straight. His wife is sexy as hell, has good job, just wants simple affection..."

"Exactly! Even beyond all that. She does... I don't think you ready, dawg."

"She does what? What, niggah!"

"She does it all! When I say all, I mean *all!*"

"Damn you lucky! That could only mean one thing. Please don't tell me she's down with chicks too?"

"Bingo! You're smarter than I thought you were. Ha, ha, ha!"

"Awe hell naw!" (Looking at Wyatt with envy). "Fuck you! Damn, how the hell you luck up on that?"

"It just worked out that way, man. Both of our situations are similar, so it just worked out. You know how conservative my wife is...but anyway, that is just a thought. She used to be in a relationship with a chick a little while back for a couple of years, but has been off that for a bit."

"Yeah, still sounds nice regardless. Meaning, there is always a chance."

"Yeah I guess so. But believe me, she's more than enough to handle."

"Um hum...I bet she is."

"He, he, he." (Wyatt looks up at the clock after gathering his papers off the copier). "Oh shit!" (Walking backwards quickly towards his office). "Got to scoot, my man. Meeting in 10 minutes across the street."

"All right, big pimpin. Ha, ha, ha! I will catch up with you later." (Manny turns and heads back to his office).

"Whatever, hater! Ha, ha, ha!" (Manny keeps walking and doesn't turn around to Wyatt's comments, so that he doesn't give Wyatt the satisfaction).

(Damn, this meeting is boring as hell! Don't none of this shit have anything to with my work. Glad it's almost over).

(Big yawn) "Urrrrrrghhhh..." (Wyatt quickly covers his mouth to conceal his yawn). (Shit. I wasn't trying to be that loud).

"Ok, folks, that's all I have. Next week, we'll meet in our building back across the street. Don't forget to bring updates on your respective project budgets."

(Good! I'm getting the hell out of here. That's the best news I have heard all morning. That gives me a good reason to go by and see Vonda).

(Wyatt leaves the conference room and heads back across the street).

"Hey, let me get that for you." (Wyatt trots into an associate to hold the door open for her). "I see you got your hands full."

"Oh thank you so much!" (The associate recognizes Wyatt as she passes through the door). "Wyatt?"

"Um, yes?"

"Patrice? From marketing?"

"Oh damn. Patrice! I didn't recognize you. Did you..."

"Yes, I cut my hair much lower than I used to have it."

"Oh my goodness! I'm sorry. I can see you now. The hair threw me off." (Wyatt presses the up button for the elevator).

"He, he. It's fine. It's really good to see you."

"It's good to see you too. It's been a while."

"Yes it has."

"Ding!" (Wyatt blocks the elevator door from closing. Patrice walks in the elevator). "So what floor you going to?"

"Nine. I'm all ready late for another meeting."

(Wyatt presses floor 7 and 9). "Lucky you." (Sarcastically). "I just got out of an exciting meeting."

"He, he, he! I bet."

"I know for real. Ha, ha, ha!"

"Ding!"

"Ok, here is my stop. See you later, Patrice."

"See you, Wyatt. Let's do lunch soon."

"Sounds good. Later." (Patrice nods her head as the elevator door closes. Wyatt goes down the hall to Vonda's office).

(Hmm...Patrice knows she can get it too. Her fine little short ass! Love those sexy lips. Unh! I can just see my...ok, now wake the fuck up! That shit will never happen. I know she been fucking the VP of marketing. Has to be about a year now...oh well, who am I to talk... He, he, he).

"Hi, Wyatt." (Wyatt approaches Vonda's administrator's desk).

"Hey, Judy. Is..."

"Yes, she's in."

"He, he, he! Why does it have to be like that?"

"Be like what? Oh you came to see me?"

"Well no, but I came to check on my project budget."

"Yeah, Wyatt. Ha, ha. You can stop now. How many budgets do you have?"

"I know, but..."

"Say no more. Go ahead in. She's in there."

"Thank you, Judy. And next time, I'm making a special trip just to see you!"

(Sarcastically). "Whoopee! Look, I'm holding my breath."

"He, he, he! Judy, you are too funny." (Wyatt walks into Vonda's office).

"Hey, Vonda! How are you doing today?"

"Very well, thank you. Just wonderful."

"That's good to hear."

"Come on in and have a seat." (Wyatt takes a seat at the small meeting table in Vonda's office).

(Vonda walks over and takes a seat near Wyatt at the table). "Before I get started, I have just one question."

"What is that?"

"Where in the hell did you find Judy?"

(Laughing loudly) "Ha, ha, ha!" (Whispering) "You are so crazy. She came over when we reorganized. She's something, but I wouldn't replace her for nothing."

"Yeah, I can see that. But she's a mess. He, he, he."

"Yeah, I know. She's itching to ask me about you. But, that's none of her damn business."

"Ha, ha, ha. That's what I figured...anyway, I actually have a legitimate purpose for visiting. Imagine that!"

"Let me guess. You need a statement of project funds left in your budget?"

"Damn your good. He, he."

"Well, Wyatt, you have perfect timing; I just finished reconciling your budget."

"Oh great!"

"Would you like me to review it with you?"

"Oh sure, that would be very helpful. We got asked for our remaining budgets in the meeting this morning."

(Vonda pulls out Wyatt's budget). "Hey, before we get started, could you close the door for me?"

(Wyatt jumps up anticipating Vonda to get real close and personal in her office). "Yes, ma'am!" (Wyatt peaks out the door and closes it slowly. He turns around to face Vonda while leaning against the door). "So, what's up, baby?"

"He, he. Wyatt, get your mind out of the gutter."

"What do you mean? I am talking about the..."

"Yeah right. Actually, I wanted to discuss something else with you. We got plenty of time to go over your budget."

(Wyatt moves back over to the table and sits down next to Vonda. He scoots his chair closer with a look of concern on his face). "All right, baby. Go ahead."

"Well, it's a little personal...shit...ain't like you don't know all my business anyway..."

"Baby, you know, I am here to help you on whatever it is. So, baby, what's on your mind."

"Well you know my husband has been in and out of the hospital for stomach pains."

"Um hum..."

"Well, yesterday his pains were much more severe and he had to be rushed to the hospital. They finally determined that he needs to have his gall bladder removed. Normally, it wouldn't be so serious, but he has had several other surgeries from his past career as a motor cross rider."

"Oh ok, yeah that does sound serious! How are you holding up?"

"I am hanging in there."

"I know he drives you nuts sometimes as you have told me repeatedly, but I wouldn't wish that on anyone."

"Yeah, thank you. So I'm trying to deal with it in addition to the fact that it's month-end! So, I'm just a little stressed right now."

"Believe me, Vonda, I understand completely. Is there anything I can do for you, baby?"

(Vonda starts to be drawn in by Wyatt's voice). "Hey watch it. You know what that does to me when you say that and look into my eyes?" (Vonda starts rub Wyatt's arm lightly). "And don't forget, we're at work." (Vonda catches herself). "See, I told you..."

"Hey, hey. I'm sorry. But, I didn't do anything. He, he."

"Yeah, I know. But it is just something about your eyes..."

"Well...I remember you saying that before. Well, thank you. I'll try and cover my eyes while I talk."

"Ha, ha, ha! Whatever."

"No seriously, as your doctor, I recommend you get some rest and relaxation after you leave work. Leave your laptop and turn off your 'crackberry.'"

"Ha ha!" (laughter). "Ok, Doctor Love! He, he, he. I really appreciate you, Wyatt. You always know how to lighten things up and make me feel better. Wish I could say that for my husband."

"Well, you know that's why I am here for you."

"There you go again..."

"What, what?"

"That voice and those eyes." (Licking her lips and looking down at Wyatt's dick through his pants). "Keep on and you know what's going down."

"Sorry, sorry...I think. He, he, he."

"Actually, doctor, I have taken the initiative."

"What! No way. Oh, you trying to act like you know me."

"Well...yes, I believe I do. So, I reserved a hotel room downtown next to the hospital. His surgery is in the morning and this will keep me from having to fight traffic home and be already down near the hospital."

"Well, well. Shut my mouth. That's really good to hear. I must say, I have taught you very well."

"Yes you have, you have been such a great supporter in my life. You have done so much for me and you really don't have a clue how much."

"Wow! I'm really flattered. Thank you, baby..."

"Baby, I should be thanking you." (Vonda reaches over and squeezes Wyatt's wrist).

(Vonda's touch has started Wyatt thinking about spending time with Vonda to really comfort her). "Hmmm, so since you are going to be downtown in a...umm uh... I mean in a hotel all alone..."

"Umm uh, what?"

"I thinking maybe" (trying to look serious about coming to see her) "tonight or early morning, I could stop by for moral support?"

"Moral support! Yeah right, you ain't trickin' nobody. You just want to tap this ass!"

"Oh no! I mean...yes! But this is strictly for medical reasons."

"Ha, ha, ha!"

"Seriously! He, he, he. I know for sure it's supported by the American Medical Association!"

"He, he, he. Ok, I believe I've heard that before. My last prescription," (Vonda reminisces about her and Wyatt's last rendezvous), "my goodness! I almost OD'd!"

"He, he, he. Well, you did say almost."

"Yes, I did." (Vonda contemplates Wyatt's offer). "Well...that is very tempting, Lord knows I need it, but I all ready have my girlfriend stopping by to keep me company."

"Ok then. As long as you're fine, that's good with me. I just wanted to make sure you would be ok."

"You sure you're ok with it?"

"Oh yeah, baby. You know I look forward to any time I can spend with you. But I know you have a lot on your mind. You know what's best for you."

"Thanks again, Wyatt." (Vonda leans into Wyatt and gives him a quick peck on the cheek).

Kiss!

(Slightly aroused). "Humph...ok, ok. Count to 10."

"He, he, he. You're so crazy."

"Can't help it, baby, can't help it." (Wyatt turns his head to the side and back at Vonda) (That's not like Vonda to pass it up like that...Shelia. Um hum). "Hmmm, just curious."

"Yeah, baby?"

"Sooooo, which of you girlfriend's is coming by to keep you company?"

"Oh, just Shelia. Why you ask?"

"Just Shelia!" (Raring back slightly in his chair). "Just Shelia!" (Shaking his head up and down signifying yes) "I knew it! I knew it, I knew it! He, he, he. You won't be getting much rest tonight."

"It's not like that, Wyatt."

"That is your ex-girlfriend right?"

"Yes, but it has been a long time since we were together like that. We don't get down like that anymore."

"Hmmmm..."

"Oh wow! Do I sense some insecurity? He, he, he."

"Naw, naw, baby...I just know you. And plus, women in relationships like that are just like..."

"No, we aren't like men."

"He, he, he. Well, I'm just saying. I mean, the opportunity is there."

"Yeah, but I have moved past that."

"Ok, baby, ok. Really, I'm cool with it. Actually, I think it will be good for you."

"What do you mean by that?"

"I mean...it would be good to relieve some stress and satisfy that itch for a woman's touch..."

(Vonda looks at Wyatt with a surprised look). "Satisfy that itch?"

"Yes, the itch. I've noticed it here and there over the time we've been together."

"Oh really, so you think you know me huh?"

"Well...I think I know quite a bit."

"That you do. That you do."

"And don't get me wrong, I know you loves da dick, but you do like the touch of a woman from time to time."

"Humph. But it's been a long time since we were together like that. And frankly, I'm not in that frame of mind at this time."

"Well, true. That is very understandable."

"On the other hand, I know sh'll be trying to fuck me, so maybe I should call my other girlfriend."

"Hey...well...unh!" (Wyatt pictures Vonda and Shelia making out).

(Shaking the thoughts from his head). "Ok, that's up to you. I am ok either way."

"Unh what?"

"Oh nothing...I mean the thought of two women together, turns me the hell on. But beyond that, I believe she will respect how you feel if you let her know the situation. So go ahead and keep your plans. "

"Thanks, honey, you always know how to talk me through things."

"Well, just let me know if there is anything else I can do."

"Ok, baby. You've done enough as always. Just you listening is more than enough."

(Wyatt stands up). "Ok, Vonda, have a good rest of the day and I will check on you tomorrow to see how the surgery went. Don't worry, everything will go just fine."

(Vonda stands up and gives Wyatt a hug). "Thanks, Wyatt."

"Mmmmm. Damn, baby, you feel so good." (Wyatt gives Vonda a kiss on the cheek).

Kiss!

"Mmm. Alright then. I'm gonna head back up stairs."

"Alright, baby. See you later." (Wyatt leaves and heads back to his office).

(Wyatt has been responding to emails for the last two hours after leaving Vonda's office. He prepares to leave the office after sending out one last email for the day. (Typing) "Carl, I will meet you in conference room C on floor 21 tomorrow afternoon at 1:00 p.m. I usually got to the gym early in the morning so I will not be available to meet at the earlier time. I look forward to discussing the Xylan project in more detail." Ok. Send. That's done! Let me shut this...)

(Manny barges into Wyatt's Office). "Hey, Wyatt!"

(Slightly startled). "Compu...Oh!...What's up, Manny?"

"Ha, ha, ha! What you scared of, man?"

"I... I...was just about..."

"To jump out your pants! Yeah right. You must have been in some deep thought."

"Naw, naw. I was about to shut down my computer."

"Um hum...anyway, I came by here earlier. Where were you?"

"Oh, I had the meeting across the street."

"Yeah, I know, but I didn't think it would last that long."

"Well...uh...they kept going over the..."

(Turning around and pretending to walk out of Wyatt's office). "I should have known!"

"What?"

"You went to see Vonda, didn't you?"

"Well, I..."

"Didn't you?"

"Ok, ok, you got me."

"Ha, ha, ha! I knew that shit! I knew it!"

"I just had to man. I thought about that ass all meeting." (Wyatt stands up and begins to straighten a stack of papers and looks over at Manny). "Well, can you blame me?"

"Hmmm...you do have a point there. The girl is fine."

"He, he, he. See, that's what I'm talking about, playa."

"Right, right...so did you get anything done when you went down there?"

"Oh yeah, I went down to check on my budget."

"Check on your budget?...Negro please!"

"No seriously!"

"Whatever, look at you trying to get up on it at work!"

"Naw, dawg, nothing like that. Actually, she's going through some things right now."

"Like what?"

"Damn you nosey!"

"He, he, he. Shoot man! Inquiring minds want to know."

"Yeah, yeah. Yo ass still nosey! Anyway, her husband is having, I think gallbladder surgery tomorrow. On top of that, she's swamped with work here."

"Oh my bad, dude. I know she must be torn from everything going on."

"No prob, dawg. She should be fine. She got a hotel downtown near the hospital to get some rest and prevent from driving all the way from their home."

"Hmmm...sounds like you got a long night ahead. I know you're going to stop by later for a little..." (Clearing his throat) "Um... Um... Moral support?"

"Actually, not at all. She's having her girlfriend come by later to keep her company." (Responding quickly) "And before you ask, yes it is the one she used to be involved with from a while back."

"What?? Oh you know what's going down tonight!"

"Ummm...nothing! Well, she says that she's not really up for that."

"Hmm...yeah right!"

"No seriously, man."

"Ok, whatever you say, bruh-man. Whatever you say."

"Yeah, I believe her. She's always taking every opportunity for us to hook up."

"Oh, I know. You better believe her."

"Yeah, I think she really needs her rest."

"Cool. You know your girl."

"Well, Manny, I'm out of here." (Wyatt walks around the desk and follows Manny out of his office. He flicks the light as he walks out).

"Yeah, me too. Wait up a second, I'll walk out with you. Let me go get a form off the printer right quick." (Manny scurries off to the copy room).

"All right then, see you at the elevators."

(Wyatt turns up his radio as he backs out of his driveway headed for the gym)

(Radio DJ) *"Welcome to the WEJJ, your old-school radio station, where we are giving away $5,000 to the tenth caller that can answer the question of the day! Here it is? How much wood could a Wood-Chuck, Chuck, if a Wood-Chuck could chuck wood? Now back to the music."*

"What! What kind of question is that? He, he, he. Nobody will ever get that."

(Music from radio) *"... I will give it to you, just the way you like it..."*

"Oh that's my jam!" (Humph, maybe I should call in... Nah...I'm never the tenth caller...) "Hey watch it man, use a signal next time!!! Jack-ass!" (Man, these fools need to learn to drive!)

"I don't care about your other girls, just be good to me..."

"I love me some S.O.S band..."

(Wyatt sees several cars stopped ahead). "Damn it! What now? East North Street is closed! Shit! I'll have to take Carver Street. This is just not my fuckin' day! Come on, go past. I'm trying to get over dick head! Thank you. Thank you." [ding-doh-ding!] "Hmm? A text message this early in the morning!" (Must be a wrong number or something) "Oh snap! It's from Vonda." (I know the surgery is today, I hope nothing is wrong).

(Reading text message) "Good morning honey! We are both here waiting on you! 10th floor, Room 1002!! Poinsett Hotel."

(Wyatt's   car   swerves   slightly)   "Oh   my   God! I...umm!...Damn!...what the...fuck it, it's on!" (Guess I will be skipping the gym this morning).

(Wyatt pulls up to the front of the Poinsett Hotel). "Morning Sir, welcome to the Poinsett Hotel."

"Good morning!"

"Are you checking in?"

"No..." (Wyatt looks back and for the between the valet attendant and the hotel front entrance). "Uh... just visiting. I have an early breakfast meeting with a client."

"Ok then, here is your ticket. Since you are going to eat at our restaurant, please get it validated before returning to pick up your car."

"Ok, thank you very much, I appreciate the tip."

"Enjoy, sir."

(I'm planning on it! Oh my God, if he only knew! If he only knew!)

(Wyatt walks into the hotel lobby trying to look as inconspicuous as possible). "Good morning."

"Hello, sir, welcome to the Poinsett."

"Th...Thank you." (Ok, ok, where are the elevators? Shit, I hope I don't look nervous? Whew...cause I am about to fuckin' explode! There they are).

(Wyatt steps into the elevator and searches the elevator panel for the 10th floor as the doors close. Circling his index finger around the buttons to find floor 10). "Ok, ok...hmmm... There it is. 10." (Wyatt looks up at the elevator lights counting each floor). "Oh man, I am shaking like Shake and Bake! Whew! Ok, Ok. Snap out of it son. You represent the South Click. South Cack-a-lack!" (You always wanted the chance to be with two women, well here is your chance). "Time to pay the piper!" (All right, so what to do first...) "Damn! Can't go out like a succah!" (Ok, remember your training...) "What the hell am I talking about? Just be yourself man." (The rules, the rules. Let her bring you in and feel your way around slowly. Ok, 1, 2, 3, breathe!).

(Takes deep breath). "Whew!" (Ok, show time. Room 1002).

"Knock!" "Knock!"

(Ok, I hope Vonda comes to the door first).

"Hey, Wyatt, glad you could make it! I know it was last minute."

(Last minute! Fuck that! Thank you! Act cool). "No problem Von—da." (I'm about to explode!) I mean…I just wanted to make…"

"Don't even go there, niggah! Yo' ass just loves this pussy!"

"Oh my dear, Vonda, I am appalled. He, he, he."

"And the chance for two pussies!"

"Well…" (Putting one hand under his chin). "Hmmm…"

"Come on in fool."

(Wyatt walks in and shuts the door. He whispers to Vonda). "Where is your girl?"

"Oh she's in the back room lying down."

(Looking around the room). "Man, this is a nice room. This shit looks like an apartment!"

"Well you know how the hubby likes to spoil his princess."

"Ha, ha, ha! Princess? With your high-class tastes!"

"Shhh! Keep it down."

"Oh, oh. Sorry about that."

"It's cool. She's still a little sleepy from staying up late talking."

(Yeah, right. Talking my ass). "Oh ok."

"So get comfortable, baby and come on back and join us in bed."

"All right, baby, be right back then." (Oh my goodness! I can't believe this is actually happening. Let me pinch myself.) "Ouch!" (Guess I'm awake).

(Wyatt removes all his clothes and places them on the couch). "Well, time to man-up…"

(From the back bedroom) "Did you say something baby?"

"No, no. I was just singing." (Rubbing his hands in anticipation) "Let's do this shit."

"Hey, baby, come on and get in the bed."

(Wyatt walks back to the bedroom and kisses Vonda before getting in the bed).

Kiss!

"Mmmm…that was good baby. I'm so glad you could make it, baby."

"He, he, he." (Whispering) "I know you knew better than that. There was no way I was not going to come!"

"Ha, ha ha! You're too funny. Muah!"

(Whispering) "Really, baby, I don't care if nothing happens, I am just happy to be here! Hercules, Hercules!!!"

"Ok, Mr. Clump. You too stupid!"

(Vonda's friend yawns lightly). "Ummmmm..."

(Vonda nudges her girlfriend). "Get up, girl! Meet my friend Wyatt."

(Turning on her back while propping up on her elbows).

(In a sleepy voice) "Ummm...hi, Wyatt, Umm..."

"Wyatt, meet Marie."

"Hi, Marie. Very nice to meet you." (Unh! Damn, look at the nice little perky round ass peeking out from under the sheet. Damn, that shit is nice!)

"Girl, I'm so sleepy."

"You should be, keeping me up so late this morning."

"He, he, he. You guys must have had some real serious stuff to talk about."

(Vonda and Marie laugh) "Ha! Ha! Ha!"

"Oh y'all got jokes!"

"Naw, just a little inside joke, baby."

"Onh honh!"

"Well, I'm going to let you guys chat. I am going to try and catch a nap." (Marie turns onto her side with Vonda directly behind her. Wyatt moves up close behind Vonda placing his arm over them both).

(Whispering) "Thank you God." (Can't believe this shit).

(Vonda turns her head back toward Wyatt and whispers).

"We stayed up half the night. She was trying to fuck me so bad." (She turns her head back briefly to Marie to make sure she's asleep). "We kissed and rubbed each other a little while, but nothing more than that."

(Whispering) "Um hum...I knew you guys were doing a little more than talking. Not that it matters. Actually, I would like to see you guys do the damn thing."

"You are such a whore! Freaky ass!"

(Sleepy voice) "Ummm...I guess I'm not going to be taking a nap."

"Ha ha ha! Sorry about that, girl. Let me make it all better." (Vonda moves Wyatt's arm and turns back to Marie and start to kiss her on the neck from behind while massaging her breasts).

Kiss!

"Ummm! Ummm! Shit bitch! (Deeply inhaling) "Ssssss...don't stop! That feels good!" (Vonda moves one of her hands down to massage Marie's clit). "Unnnh! Oh, baby! That's what I need."

(Damn! This is really some hot shit!)

"Oh shit, Vonda! I love the way you touch me!"

"Oh you do?"

"Whose pussy is it!"

"Yours, Vonda..." (Vonda pushes her finger deep into Marie's pussy). "Unnnnnh!! Yours baby! Yours!"

(This shit is crazy! I can't believe this shit!)

(Vonda takes her hand out of Marie's pussy and grabs Wyatt's hand. She guides his hand on top of Marie's pussy).

"Wooo!" (Damn, this pussy feels good. It's so fucking wet!)

(Vonda turns and whispers to Wyatt). "Don't push anything. Let her bring you in."

"Ok, baby."

(Marie grabs Wyatt's index finger and gently pushes it in and out of her pussy). "Oh yes! Unnh! Oooh, this feels so good!"

(Oh my God, I am about to fucking explode! I know Vonda feels my dick throbbing...I still can't believe this shit!)

(Marie turns over and embraces Vonda while kissing her wildly in the mouth) "Mmmmm..."

Kiss!

(Damn, I got to see this).

(Marie and Vonda continue kissing and feeling each other up. Marie ends up on her back as Marie climbs on top to ride Vonda as if Vonda had a dick). "Fuck me, bitch! Fuck me!"

(Vonda grabs the sides of Marie's waist and thrust upward as if she was fucking her). "So you wanna...unh...be...unh...fucked!...unh!"

"Oooh! Oooh! Oooh! Oh Vonda! Unh! Unh!"

(Damn! What the fuck! Unnh! I'm just happy to be here!)

(Vonda suddenly stops in the middle of grinding with Marie. She gently pushes Marie away). "I'm sorry." (Shaking her head) "I got to stop. I feel..."

"It's all right, baby. I know you got a lot on your mind."

(Placing her hand on Vonda's head). "Vonda, it's ok. It really is."

"I guess I'm feeling just a little guilty knowing Roger is getting ready to have major surgery."

"Baby? Really, we understand. If you want me to leave, I will."

"No, no...I'm good, I'm good. I don't know why I do that sometimes. That niggah probably ain't even thinking about me."

"Well, we all know that is just you, baby. And it's ok. Be you."

"Thanks honey."

"Ow!" (Marie reaches up to grab her back)

"What's wrong girl?"

"Ooh, ooh! My back has been paining me ever since I got off last night. Girl, I got to find me another job!"

"Yeah right, you know you not leaving that job."

"Well, I am just sayin'..."

"Yeah, I hear that. But just a few minutes ago, your ass was riding on top, talking about fuck me, fuck me...Your back wasn't hurtin' then."

"Yeah, true. But we all know how sex just erases pain. I mean, it's crazy."

(Marie lies on her stomach with her entire naked body out. Wyatt reaches over and begins to massage her back).

"How does that feel?"

"Mmmh...Mmmh...Oooooh! Oh yesss! Damn! That feels good."

"Glad you like it. I can really feel the tension. Let me come over and knock that out for you."

"Thank you. I could really use..."

"Oh, you an expert now huh?"

"He, he, he. Come on, Vonda. You know it ain't like that."

"Well, I'm just saying."

(Wyatt comes to his knees). "Excuse me, baby, let me slide right past you."

(Vonda looks at Wyatt with a "don't get out of hand" look). "Oh no, problem, honey."

"Oh one thing?" (Vonda grabs Wyatt's dick as it passes her mouth).

Slurp!

"Mmm!"

"Ooh, damn baby, that feels...hey why did you stop?"

"Uh, aren't you supposed to be giving a massage?"

"Right, right...you are so dirty."

"I know! Ha, ha, ha! You just remember whose dick that is?"

"Girl, you know I wouldn't..."

"Yeah, I know yo ass!"

(Vonda and Marie laugh together) "Ha, ha, ha!"

(Wyatt straddles Marie on his knees).

(Ummm...damn! That little ass looks good).

"Ummm...Vonda, thank you for letting me borrow your man for a minute."

"You just keep that in mind, my man! My man!"

"Ha ha ha! Whatever, girl."

(Damn! My baby got good taste. Look at that smooth juicy brown ass! Mmm, mmm, unnh! Look at that phat pussy peeking back at me. Ummh!)

(Wyatt lowers his body down upon Marie's ass, letting his dick lie between her ass cheeks). "Um hum...you good, Marie?"

"Oh, I'm fine."

(Damn this little ass feels good...focus, niggah, focus!)

(Wyatt looks over at Vonda). "Hey, baby, throw me that bottle of lotion."

"All right now. Don't get beside yourself."

"Baby! You know me, I don't do things half-ass."

"Yeah, but just watch it."

(Wyatt squirts a few drops of lotion into his hand. He rubs his hands together to slightly warm the lotion. He begins spreading the lotion over Marie's back) "Ummmm...um hum."

"Oh...you like that, huh?"

"Oh yes, that feels really good."

(Wyatt squirts more lotion into his hands. He lotions Marie's ass and the sides of her breast while putting lotion on her back). "Yeah...that should get the tension out."

"Unnnh! Oh my God! Unnh! Damn, girl! Your man's hands are fucking magical."

"Believe me, I know."

(Wyatt takes the lotion bottle up high above Marie's ass. He squeezes out small droplets one by one from the center of her neck to the crack of her ass). "Oh my God! That shit gives me goose bumps! Whew!"

(Wyatt takes his forearm and begins to smooth out the lotion droplets on Marie's back.)

"Ohhhhhhhhh fuck! What the hell is that! Unnnnnnnnnh! Damn, I have never felt shit like that. Ooh. Ooh. Ooh...this shit is so good...fuck! I feel like I'm about to cum!"

"All right, bitch! Watch yourself. Don't be enjoying that shit so damn much! Wyatt, you never gave me a massage like that!"

"Awe...come on now, Vonda, you know I have. He, he, he."

"Yeah, but...I'm just saying. Don't make that bitch feel too good. Girl, you better enjoy it, but don't enjoy it that much!"

"Ummmm...ok. Ummm... Ok Von... Unnh!"

(Shit, all this moaning is killing my ass. My dick is hard as a steel rod and throbbing like hell. Look at Vonda over there rubbing that phat pussy). "Do that shit, baby!"

"Fuck this. I am over here hot as hell! Let's get this shit going."

(Vonda comes over and starts to suck Marie's pussy from behind).

Slurp!

"Ummmmh! Oh my God!"

Slurp!

"Damn, bitch! Eat that puuuuu–ssy! Umm!"

(Vonda reaches around Wyatt to grab his dick while sucking Marie pussy). "Damn, baby! Your shit is hard as a brick!"

"Ummm...Um hum." (Vonda gently strokes Wyatt's dick). "Oh shit! That feels good, baby."

(Vonda comes up behind Wyatt's back and whispers in his ear) "Ummm...baby? You want some of that pussy don't you, baby?"

"I don't..."

"It's okay baby. Slide back off her ass a little, baby." (Vonda moves around to Wyatt's front) "Lift up a little bit, baby."

"Ok, baby. Ohhhhh! Damn! What the fuck are you doing?" (Vonda uses the side of her mouth to guide the head of Wyatt's dick into Marie's pussy) "Unnh! Damn, baby! Damn! What the fuck!"

(Vonda grabs the back of Wyatt's ass forcing him to move in and out of Marie's pussy) "Unnnnh! Damn! Ummm! Fuck! This dick is... Unh!"

"Get that pussy, niggah! Fuck it!"

"Oh my God, Vonda! Shit! I ain't never..." (I didn't know my baby could get this freaky! Damn!). "I can't believe...I think I'm about to..."

"Oh hell no! You not cumming yet!"

"Oh damn, baby! Shit!" (Pleading to Vonda) "That's torture baby!"

"Oh damn! Put the dick back in! Girl, come on..."

"Girl come on! Girl, come on! Please, you aren't going to leave me out!"

"Baby?" (Wyatt looks at Vonda). "Let me show how to get this ho really turned on!"

"Watch me fuck the hell out this bitch!"

(Vonda lies on her back and tells Marie to climb on top of her in the 69 position).

Slurp!

"Umm! Eat my pussy bitch!"

(Marie stiffens her tongue and jams it into Vonda's pussy). "Unnnnh! Yeah! Unnnh! Yeah, bitch!"

(Vonda starts to suck Marie's clit harder) "Ummmmmm! What the...ummmm! Damn! Ummmm!" (Marie has to stop eating Vonda's pussy as Vonda begins to suck Marie's pussy wildly). "Unh! Ummmm! Unh! Ummmm! Suck that...umm! Pussy!"

(This is some wild shit! Fuck, these ho's is freaky as hell!) "Eat the hell out of that pussy, baby! Eat that shit!"

"Oh God! Unh! Oh God! Unh! Unh! Unh! Unnnnnnnnnnnnh!" (Marie jumps off Vonda as she cums). "Fuuuuuuuuuuucckkkk! Damn, Girl! Shit! That was so damn good!" (Breathing hard) "Whew! You must have eaten my insides out! Damn!"

(Vonda lies on her back fingering herself as Marie recovers) "Ummm...ummm...that feels good." (Looking at Marie) "I told you I was going to fuck the hell out of you."

"Oh you did? Well...let me show you what I can do." (Marie gets between Vonda's legs with her face down at Vonda's pussy. Marie is on her knees with her ass facing up at the edge of the bed).

Slurp!

"Mmmmmm..."

Slurp!

"Damn bitch, you got some sweet as pussy!"

"Ummm! Yes! Ummm! Yes! Eat your pussy, girl! Ummmm!"

(Wyatt goes around to the edge of the bed where Marie's ass is sticking out. He rubs her pussy to use in lubricating his dick). "Ummm...girl, you got a phat little pussy looking back at me." (He puts only the head of his dick in and out of her pussy). "Ooooh that feels good." (I better not go all the way unless she says something...he, he, he. I couldn't last but a few strokes anyway). "Unh...damn...unh..."

(Marie sticks two fingers into Vonda's pussy while pulling strongly on Vonda's clit with her mouth). (Mumbled) "Mmmmmm mmmmm mmmmmm...give me that cum, baby! Come on now!"

"Unh!"

Slurp! Unh! Unh! Oh Marie!"

(Vonda's body tightens up as she cums and squirts on Marie).

"Unnnnnnnnnnnnnnnnnnnnnnnnnnnnnnnnh! Woo! Woo! Unnnnnnnnnnh!" (Breathing hard) "Oh shit! Oh God!" (Vonda's arms flop down by her side. Marie sits up on the bed and gently massages Vonda's breast). "Damn girl. You must have learned some new shit."

"He, he, he."

(Vonda sits up and starts to softly kiss Marie).

(Wyatt stands at the edge of the bed). "Damn, girls! That was just...I mean, that was just beautiful."

(Vonda and Marie laugh) "Ha, ha, ha!" (Vonda and Marie both turn towards Wyatt giving him a sneaky look). "Mmmmmm..."

"What? What you girls up to? Why you looking at me like that?"

(As if on cue, Vonda and Marie move towards Wyatt at the edge of the bed). "Oh my God! This can't be happening!" (Vonda grabs Wyatt's dick and starts to suck it. Marie waits patiently to taste his dick as well).

Slurp! "Damn this dick tastes good!"

"Come, girl, share!" (Vonda passes off Wyatt's dick to Marie like passing a baton).

Slurrrrrp!

"Ummm..."

(What the fuck! This only happens in pornos!) "Oh goodness! Ummm... Ohhhhhh Shit....oh, girl, suck that dick! Unnnhh!"

"Pass that shit back, bitch!"

Slurp! (Rapid sucking)

"Unh!" Slurp! Slurp! Slurp! Slurp! Slurp!

"Oh my God! This is incredible! Ummm! Ummm!" (Keep it together man). "Unnnh! Damn, Vonda! I...unnnh! I have never..."

(Marie grabs the back of Wyatt's ass). "Ummm...let me have some more, girl."

(Vonda starts sucking the side of Wyatt's dick while motioning Marie to suck the other side).

Slurp!

"Umm!"

Slurp!

"What the fuck! You're gonna make me cum! Unnnh! Unnh! Oh damn! I don't know...unh! If I...unh! Can hold it! Unh! Unh!" (Breathing hard) "Unnh!"

(Vonda pushes Marie off the dick and takes all of Wyatt's dick in her mouth. She places on hand on each ass cheek and jams Wyatt's dick to the back of her throat). (Mumbled) "Umm, umm, umm, umm, umm..."

"Suck that dick, girl! Make that shit pop!" (Maria is rubbing Vonda's pussy and breasts). "Make that ship pop!"

"Oh shit, baby! Unh! Oh shit! Unh! Oh shit! I can't..."

"Don't you do it! Don't you cum! Don't you..."

"Umm! I'm tryin...I'm trying not toooo...! Oh fuck! Oh shit! I'm about to cum, baby! Here it comes! Ohhhhhhh Shi..." (Wyatt goes silent as his body freezes from cumming so hard).

(Vonda chokes slightly from the force of the cum at the back of her throat). "Arrrrrggh..." (talking with a mouth full of cum). "Mmmmm...take some, girl."

(Marie grabs Wyatt's dick and sucks out the rest of the cum). "Mmmm..." Slurp! "Mmmm...so tasty!"

"Oh God! I'm about to fall the fuck out." (Wyatt plops down on the bed). "Whew! Shit!"

"Damn that was good. Give me some of that cum, bitch." (Vonda turns to Marie and kisses her to share more of Wyatt's cum).

Kiss! "Mmmmmmmmm...yes! That's some good shit!"

"Damn! (Wyatt can't believe what he just saw). "I'm in love! You some nasty, freaky ass bitches!" (Wyatt shakes his head in disbelief). "Damn! Just Damn!"

(Vonda and Marie laugh). "Ha, ha, ha! I told yo ass baby, I had some shit for ya!"

"Well, baby, you and Marie are the fucking bomb! I think I'm going to cry! I never knew it, but now I know what it means to become a man!"

(Vonda and Marie laugh hysterically) "Ha, ha, ha! Ha, ha, ha!"

"Damn! That was a hell of a work out! Shit, I can't even imagine getting any work done today."

"Like you do work anyway! He, he, he."

"What? I do work. I have all these meetings and reports..."

"Seems like the type of job I need. Trade jobs with me and you will find out about work."

"Hmmm...well, putting it that way. I guess...I'm going to take a shower."

"Ha, ha, ha! Wait up, baby. I'll join you."

Chapter 14

Second to One

"So are you ready to take the big plunge?"

"I...I think so. I'm just a little nervous, Ben! (Crystal takes a sip of her coffee).

(What does she mean, she thinks so!). "Look here, Crystal, you've been dating Rick for almost three years including your engagement. You guys belong together. Mrs. Boyd to be!"

"You're right, you're right." (Staring off into space). (But what you don't know Ben is that I still have feelings for you. Ooooh...the times we spent on business trips...oh shit! The way he had me on that computer desk...Fuck!...Ok, ok, girl, you are getting married Saturday).

"Crystal?...Crystal?..."

"Oh...yeah, Ben..."

"So get ready to marry this man on Saturday."

"Ok, Ben. You always know how to make me feel better."

"No problem, baby girl, you know I got your back."

"Thanks Ben."

"So where are you going for the honeymoon?"

"Ding!" "Ding!" (Crystal's meeting reminder) "Oh shit! Hold that thought, Ben, I got to run to my department meeting."

"Ok, Crystal, we'll catch up later. If not, see you at the wedding."

"Oh, for sure. I'll be there." (Crystal rushes off to her meeting).

(Crystal arrives at the meeting 10 minutes late). "Hi everybody. I apologize for being late."

"Oh, no problem, Crystal. Actually you have perfect timing."

(Crystal sits down at the last seat open on the far end of the table). "Ok. What do you need?"

"Well, you mentioned in our last meeting that the juice filling unit is due in 12 weeks after placing an order. Is there any way to move this date up?"

(Shit!...I can't stop thinking about Ben....Damn!). "Crystal?...Crystal?..."

"Oh...yes?"

"I was trying to confirm the timeline for the filling unit."

"Oh...yes, sorry...12 weeks is pretty much carved in stone."

"Hmmm... ok then, we'll have to make sure we don't slip on anything to make the launch date. Tight schedules as always...It is, what it is! Well, if there are no more..."

"Oh... oh! One thing for the group!"

"Yes, Crystal?"

"Just a reminder to everyone, I am getting married this weekend!"

"Oh wow, that's right. Congratulations, Crystal!!!"

"Yes, congrats, Crystal! I'm sure you will have a long and fruitful marriage."

"Thank you all so much! I really mean that from the bottom of my heart. I hope to see all of you there. And...oh yeah, I will be on my honeymoon all next week. So don't even think about contacting me."

(Meeting attendees laugh). "Ha, ha, ha!"

"Ok, just one thing, Crystal?" (A long sigh) "Hmmm..."

"Yesssss, Lonnie!"

"I just wanted you to know that it's not too late to back out!"

(Meeting attendees laugh). "Ha, ha, ha!"

"Awe, Lonnie, you are too crazy. I am..."

"Naw girl, you know I am just kidding. I wish you all the best!"

"Why thank you! Much appreciated. Again, thank you all. Hope to see you Saturday."

"Ok team, well if there is no other business, this meeting is adjourned." (Meeting attendees depart the conference room. Crystal heads back to her desk).

(Man...Lonnie may have a good point. The way I've been thinking about Ben, I might consider his proposal...Arrrrgh!!! Stop it, girl. Rick is good for you and has been with you through thick and thin. He is a good man. Right. Focus on Saturday).

"Hi, Crystal. Congratulations! I heard about you getting married this weekend."

"Thanks, Edna. Yep, I can't wait." (I think).

"That's great, Crystal! I know you're excited."

"Yes. I've been looking forward to it since last May." (Why am I lying? I am so confused).

"Well, congrats again. I will see you when you get back from your honeymoon."

"Ok, Edna. Thanks. See you." (Crystal continues to her desk).

"Bye, Crystal."

(Crystal finally makes it back to her desk). "Whew! When is this day going to be over? Seems like I've been here for two days." (Crystal plops down in her desk chair). "I can't wait to get out of here." (Crystal notices a sticky note in the lower right corner of her computer screen). "Hmmm? I wonder who left this sticky note on my computer screen? Oh wow! It's a note from Ben."

(Reading note) "Crystal, I have a day trip this Friday so I won't be able to wish you well before Saturday. If you have time, stop by Vastie's Café off Ellerbee Street for a quick drink. Benzo."

"Oh shit! He used the nickname I used to call him. I hope he's not going to make me even more confused! Well, he did say just for a drink and to wish me well. Can't be any harm in that, right? Ok, let me call Rick to let him know that I will be just a few minutes late."

(Phone ringing for Rick)

(Rick picks up phone) "Hello, baby."

"Hey, sweety."

"So how did things go today?"

"They went pretty well actually. The day is feeling long though." (Don't let him know I am having doubts). "But that may be because I'm so ready for Saturday to get here."

"Oh really?"

"Yep. I told everybody how excited I am to spend the rest of my life with my wonderful husband-to-be!"

"Oh, baby, you did that? I feel so blessed to have you in my life. I am excited as well!

Saturday can't get here fast enough. It's been three months since we made our sex pact to wait until our honey moon. It'll be like our first time! Oh my God Girl! I am going to tear that..."

"Ok, Be—en (Hope he didn't catch that). "Uh, Rick, don't get me all worked up."

"Ok, baby, you're right, I...I... just lost my mind for a minute."

"No problem..."

"I mean, it will be like our first time together. That is going to be..."

"Ok, ok, enough on that. Don't get me all worked up."

"Right, right! Sorry about that, baby."

"It's all good, Rick...Oh, I called to let you know that I will be home a little later than usual. One of my coworkers invited me to have a drink after work to celebrate and wish us well in our marriage."

"Oh that is really nice of her."

"Um...Uh..." (Better not tell him it's not a female).

"Enjoy yourself, sweet pea. I'll see you later when you get home."

"Okay, baby, see you then. Smooches!" (Crystal hangs up the phone).

(Man! That was close. I really need to get myself together. I thought it would be easy to get married, but I don't know why I'm having thoughts about Ben! Is this normal? Arrggggh! Get it together girl!)

(Big sigh) "Whew!" (Let's wrap things up. I hope that Ben will be able to clear things up for me. He's real good at that).

(Crystal finishes her work and decides to leave for the day to meet Ben at Vastie's Café).

(Crystal arrives at valet parking in front of the restaurant). "How's it going, ma'am?"

(Looking up at the attendant). "Not too bad, not too bad."

"Well that's good to hear."

"Thank you."

"Welcome to Vastie's Cafe! That'll be $5.00 for valet parking, ma'am."

(Flirtatiously) "Wow, you mean you aren't going to let me park for free?"

"I surely wish I could." (Looking Crystal up and down). "You do look real very nice today, ma'am."

"Why thank you!"

"I know someone like you must all ready have a husband."

"Excuse me? Are you trying to pick me up?"

"Oh no, ma'am, I just think you look great today."

"Well, ok then, just checking. Anyway, you are half-way right. I am jumping the broom this Saturday."

"Oh, good, congratulations! Good for you and too bad for me."

"Ha, ha, ha!"

"Well, you are all set ma'am. Here is your valet ticket. Just hand it to the attendant to your right as you walk out."

"Great!"

"Ok, enjoy your dinner."

"I most certainly will."

(Crystal enters the restaurant and stops at the hostess station). "Good evening, ma'am. How many will be dining with us tonight?"

"Actually two, but I'm meeting a colleague here."

"Oh yes, are you Ms. Crystal Ellis?"

"Yes, that it is I."

"Perfect, your colleague described you right to a "T" almost as if he was your husband."

(Whoa! This is really getting scary! Here I'm about to be married Saturday and I keep thinking about Ben and complete strangers are thinking about him as well or at least as my husband. Damn! Am I doing the right thing? Fucking crazy shit!). "Oh...really. You really think...never mind."

"Ok, right this way, Ms. Ellis."

(Ben is sitting down in a nice cozy corner of the restaurant. He raises his head and greets Crystal smiling as she walks to the table). "Oooooh! Ooh! Those pearly white teeth against all that that smooth chocolate. Ummmh...ummmh!"

(Ben moves out of the booth as Crystal approaches. He stands and waits for her to enter the booth).

(Look at that 6 foot 4 inch...Broad shoulders and toned biceps....damn! My pussy is getting so moist! I am going to pass the fuck out!)

"Hello, Crystal!" (Ben open's his arm's to give Crystal a big hug). "Helloooo... Crystal!"

(Day dreaming) "Oh...sh...sorry, daydreaming again...Hey Benzo!" (Ben squeezes Crystal tight against his chest). (Damn! This shit feels good! I know this feeling from somewhere. Um hum...after-sex. Ummmh).

(Hostess interrupts Crystal and Ben's embrace). "Ms. Ellis?... Ms. Ellis..."

"Oh, umh... yes, yes!"

"Your server will be right with you."

"Oh I'm sorry, Thank you very much." (Ben kisses Crystal on the cheek and releases his hug).

Kiss!

"Well, have a seat, Crystal. So glad you could make it."

"Yes, I am glad I did too." (Crystal sits down followed by Ben sitting next to her). (Oh damn, I can feel those rock hard thighs....ummm...shit! This was a bad idea...but good...but bad...Fuck it! I don't know!)

"You know I couldn't let my baby girl go out in to the big world of marriage without wishing her well."

"Awwe, Ben, you're so sweet."

"Well, you know me, I've always cared for you, Crystal. I never stopped even when we used to hang out."

"Wow, I didn't know you felt quite that way."

"Yep, you know how it goes. When folks go separate ways, they tend to try not an express their emotions."

"True, true."

"But enough of that, what about this wedding? Tell me all about it."

"Hmm, ok, well you know what the colors are..."

"Oh, let me guess, crimson and crème."

"Ha, ha, ha! Yes, you know I love my sorority!"

"Yes, that we do know. That we do know."

(Excited) "Oh, and the reception will have a live band and a bride and groom ice sculpture."

"What! You got to be kidding me."

"Why...why...you think that it's too much?"

"Oh no, I forgot who I'm talking to Ms. High Society from Yorkshire"

"Ha, ha, ha!"

"Awe Ben. Stop it! You know I'm not like that..."

"Yeah, yeah...ok, I was just kidding. You know I am very happy for you."

"Thank you so much, it means a great deal to have your support."

"Not even a question baby, not even a question."

(Umm...stop calling me, baby. Damn!)

"So, Ms. Ellis, where are you planning to go for the honeymoon?"

"Well, that is a very good question. I wish I knew the answer."

"What! Oh...Rick decided to surprise you?"

"Nope... He doesn't even know either."

"You got to be joking."

"Not at all. Very serious."

"Wow!"

"Rick's father just told us to pack warm for 7 days and that was it."

"Hmm. Very interesting. Actually, that does make it very exciting."

"Yes, it does. But you best believe, I didn't like the idea at first."

"Yes, I know you didn't."

"I know how you like to coordinate with everything. Down to the letter!"

"Ha, ha, ha! Stop it! Ben. He, he, he!" (Crystal places her hands on Ben's thighs). (Ooooh...oh damn, that feels good).

(What the hell she go and do that for? Keep on girl...) "Well it's true. I know your ass, girl."

"True, true."

"Anyway, I know you guys will have a great time."

"Thank you, Ben."

"No problem baby girl."

"Wow, girl! I can't believe..."

(Interrupted by waiter). "Good evening, what can I start you guys off with to drink?"

"Well I..."

"Bring a dirty martini for the lady and a Long-Island Iced tea for me. Thank you."

"Coming right up."

(Crystal looks at Ben in surprise) "Oh!!! So you just going to order for me, huh? You act like you know me, hmmm..."

"Well, let's say I know a little bit about you. I think you know what I mean."

"Ha, ha, ha! And..."

"Tell me that you weren't going to order a dirty martini."

"He, he, he. Uh... Ok, I was but..."

"Nuff said. I thought so! He, he, he."

(Damn! This was a bad idea. Even Rick doesn't know that's my favorite drink. Damn! Here we go Crystal...you thinking too much. Should I be...Stop it!) "So, now that you have told me...you were about to say something when the waiter came over."

"Oh yeah, I was just going to say, I can't believe my best girl is finally getting married. I am so happy for you and Rick, but I..." (Don't say it bruh). "Nevermind."

"No, no! What were you about to say?"

"Nah, it's not important..."

"No tell me please, please!" (Grabbing Ben's arm tightly).

"Ok, this is a little hard, but...umm, but I have thought about whether you and I should be tying the knot versus you and Rick. Ok, there you go, I said it!"

(Damn! I'm shocked. Shit, I asked for it!) "Really?"

"Yes. But I knew..."

(Placing her hands to Ben's lips). "Shhh! Shhh! Don't say it. I have a confession. To be honest with you, I have kinda been thinking the same thing."

"Whoa! Whoa! Oh my God!"

"Yeah, I guess it could be cold feet."

"Do you think?"

"Yeah, yeah, I think you are right."

"Let's drop this. You and Rick are made for each other."

"I guess you are right." (They both sit up straight and slide apart).

"Here are your drinks."

(In unison) "Thank you."

"Are you guys ok?"

"Yeah, yeah, we are fine."

"Ok then, just let me know if you need anything."

(Damn! The waiter is on to us. Maybe I should talk to Rick and call this thing off. I mean...I keep thinking about Ben and he is thinking about me. But what about Rick? He is a good man. And I...)

"Crystal?"

(...really couldn't ask for...)

"Crystal!"

"Oh, um. Sorry, Ben."

"No problem, but you have to stop all that daydreaming, girl."

"I know, I know. I'm sorry."

"So what were you thinking about?"

"Umm...nothing."

"Yeah right! I bet you were thinking about nothing."

"No, no. Seriously!"

"Ok Crystal, whatever!"

"All right, all right Ben, I was going to tell you more about the wedding."

(Give me a break Crystal! I will let you think that I am Mr. "Nutty Buddy," Mr. Simple). "Oh you were? Oh ok. Well go ahead then...I guess you have decided to go through with it then."

(I hope he buys this). "Oh yeah, and I just wanted to remind you that the wedding is at..."

(Ben interrupts) "I know, I know 3 o'clock!"

"Oh my goodness, you remembered!"

"Yes, I got it, babe." (This really sucks. I can't believe my girl is getting married). "I wouldn't miss it for the world. I know in the past that I've been a little raggedy keeping up with dates and times."

"Yes indeed, with your raggedy ass! Ha, ha, ha!"

"Whatever girl. You didn't have to agree! Dang! Oh..."

"It's all good, Benzo. You know that I'm playin. I really appreciate that you are going to be there. For some reason, I don't think I could go through with it without you there. I...I..."

(Ben interrupts) "So let me be clear. You can't be serious! Why would me not being there keep you from getting married?."

"Ben, I...I don't really know."

"Maybe it's just cold feet."

"Yeah, that must be it."

"You know Rick is right for you. You guys are great together."

(Long sigh) "Hmmm...I guess you are right. What am I thinking?"

"What! You guess? Baby there is no guessing, this is a decision for the long haul. At least that is what most people expect."

"Damn it, Ben! You're always right."

(In unison) "Well, I'm not trying to be right. I..."

(They both laugh) "Ha, ha, ha!"

"See, Ben! There it goes again. We know each other too well!"

"You got that right. He, he, he. Well, on that note, I would like to propose a toast to my best girl on her upcoming marriage."

"Oooh!...ooh!..." (Excitedly) "Let me get my drink!"

(Ben picks up his drink) "Crystal...this is really hard for me, but here it goes. My feelings are mixed, but I am overwhelmingly happy for my girl. Sooo!...Damn this is hard." (Ben's eyes are slightly tearing while Crystal wipes one tear from her eyes). "I hope and..." (Shaky) "and...I pray that Crystal and Rick will have a long, happy and wonderful marriage.

(They both raise and tap their glasses and take a drink). (In a soft, quiet voice). "Thanks so much Benzo. I really appreciate that."

(Big sigh) "Whew! You're welcome. baby girl."

"Thank you, thank you, thank you!" (Crystal wipes her face and smiles) (Taking a deep breath) "Ok. Now a toast to you."

"Awwee, baby, you don't have to do that."

(There goes that baby thing again) "No, no, I do. Ok, pick your drink up again. Let's interlock arms like we used to back in the day."

"Are you serious?"

"Yes, I am. Come on."

"Ok girl, just like you, can't hold your liquor."

"He, he, he. No, I am just fine."

"All right then. Go ahead." (They both pick up their glasses and interlock their arms forcing them closer).

(Oh damn girl! You are full of bright ideas! Ummh...this mother fucker smells so damn good! My pussy is tingling).

"Crystal? Crystal?"

(In a dreamy voice) "Yes..."

"The toast, baby."

"Oh yeah, ok." (Crystal takes a deep breath). "Ben, you have been my strongest supporter and closest friend. I make a toast to our friendship. I want it to last forever. You know that you will always have a place in my heart. "

"Oh damn, baby girl, I feel..." (Crystal forces both glasses down to the table and begins to passionately kiss Ben on the mouth).

"Mmmmm..."

(They both abruptly push away in shock and try to avoid eye contact) "Oh my God! Oh my God! I am so sorry, Ben! I just don't know what got into me." (Ben is staring back at Crystal in silence with mixed feelings). "I am so embarrassed! I am so scared! I just..."

"Baby! Baby! It's ok. No harm done, baby, no harm done. It's ok to be scared, this is a really big step." (Ben puts his arms around Crystal and pulls her to his chest. He continues to console her while stroking her hair).

(Sulking) "I just don't know, Ben."

(Continuing to sooth Crystal) "Baby...baby...it really is ok. That stays between us. To be totally honest, I'm glad it happened. To feel the passion from your tender lips just one last time was just great. We can't change our past and its ok going forward to remain good friends."

(In a high and slightly crying voice) "But I'm getting married in two days! I am so freakin' confused!"

"Again, baby, it's ok, everything will work out fine."

"Ok, Ben, I'm so glad you are here for me."

"Always, baby."

"You really know how to calm me down. Thank you so much."

"You're welcome, baby."

(Grabbing both of Crystal's shoulders and looking into her eyes). "You feel better?"

"Yes, I do."

"Ok, let me get the check and let's get out here before, I change my mind."

"What!"

"Ha, ha, ha! Gotcha, babe!...Waiter?"

(The waiter comes over to their table) "Are you guys ready to order?"

"Oh no, we would like the check please."

"Not even dessert?"

"No thank you."

"No problem, I will be right back sir."

(After paying the check, they both stand up and give one last embrace before leaving). "Ok baby, I will see you on Saturday."

"You better be there."

"You know I am there."

"Thanks for everything Ben."

"You're welcome, baby...so, where did you park?"

"In Valet."

"Ok, I will walk you to the attendant." (Ben holds the door as Crystal walks out of the café. Crystal hands the attendant her Valet ticket). "Ok, girl. Remember, it will all work out."

(I sure the hell hope so). "Thanks again. Be safe, Ben. Have a good night."

"Night."

(Crystal arrives home after meeting with Ben) . "Beep!" "Beep!" "Beep!" (Crystal presses the alarm code 7, 7, 7, 9, "Off". She closes the door and resets the alarm).

(A big sigh) "Man oh man! This has been some night." (Looking through the mail on the counter and feeling a little beat). "Bank statement...Tax bill...Triad Health...Forget this! I'll go through this tomorrow." (She turns off the light and begins to walk up stairs to the bedroom.)

(Rick slightly wakes to Crystal coming in). (Groggy) "Hey baby, everything ok."

(Crystal perks up so that Rick will not notice how much went on during her evening). "Hey, my love! Everything is just fine. I had a great time chatting with co-workers during my well wish."

"Good, that is great to hear." (Crystal wants to cut the conversation off before Rick wants more detail).

"So how..."

"You get some sleep, baby, we got a lot of things to get done tomorrow for the wedding. I am so excited." (Getting undressed and heading for the bathroom). "Get some rest, babe. I'm going to hit the shower."

"All right, baby, I will see you in the morning then." (Crystal turns around and rushes back to the bed and gives Rick a quick kiss on the forehead). "Mmmm...Muah!"

"Good night, my sweet man."

"Night."

(Crystal turns on the shower and gets in. Rick listens to Crystal humming in the shower). (Well, she does sound happier now that she's in the shower. I was a little worried at first since she took longer than normal to get upstairs. I can only imagine that sexy body in the shower. Unnh! Calm down boy, it's been a while since you had some or even tasted it for that matter. But that's changing in one day and hmm...9 hours. I just hope I can hold on for more than one minute!) "Shit! Take your ass to sleep." (Now you got little man all in a frenzy. Damn, I need to take another shower! A real cold shower!)

(Rick drifts off to sleep).

(Crystal finishes her shower and joins Rick in the bed.)

(In a soft voice) "Baby...baby...are you asleep?" (Rick doesn't move.)

(In a quiet voice) "Good night."

(Crystal tosses and turns for hours. She looks over at the alarm clock) "2:02 a.m.!" (She quiets herself).

(My goodness, I can't sleep a wink! I'm trying to block it all out of my mind, but I keep thinking about me and Ben at the restaurant. Please Jesus, keep me near the cross! Give me a sign! Let me know what to do. Am I doing the right thing with Rick? Should I let Rick know how I am feeling? I am just so confused. Ok, ok, let me compare them. What am I saying! I can't believe I'm feeling this way less than 2 days from my wedding! I'm suppose to be happy, jumping for joy...at least I think I'm suppose to be feeling that way. Arrrrrgh! I do know that both of them are good men. They both will do anything for me. But it's something about Ben that makes me just ...ummmmmmm! Explode inside. Damn, just thinking about him has got me wet again! Oh my God, the way we kissed in the Café and how he put me on his chest. Damn, I wish he would have flipped my ass on that table and pounded this pussy into oblivion! Oh shit, I can feel him now!)

(Crystal puts her finger on her clit under the cover)

(Moaning quietly) "Ummmm...ummmm...ooooh...ummm..." (She slides her finger into her pussy). "Ohhhh...ummm..." (That's right Ben, slide that dick up in there. That's it baby. You know what I need!) "Ummm...ummmm...ummm! Ummm!" (Crystal slightly wakes Rick).

(In a sleepy voice) "Baby...are you ok?"

(Crystal realizes she was getting loud and quickly resolves the situation.) "Oh yes, baby, I'm fine. I was dreaming about us on our honeymoon. Thinking about how great it is going to be when..."

"Don't even get me started, girl. I am going back to sleep!"

"Night, baby." (Rick lifts up and kisses Crystal and turns over to go back to sleep.)

"Night my dear, I'm taking my ass to sleep as well." (Crystal finally drifts off to sleep).

"Crystal? Crystal?" (Rick lightly pushes Crystal on the shoulder while sitting on the edge of the bed) "Wake up, baby, wake up."

(In a groggy voice) "Morning, baby. What's going on?"

"I need you to get up and come downstairs for breakfast."

"Hmm...what time is it? Its 9:00 AM. What, I slept that long? I usually get up at 6:00 like clockwork."

"Yep, I know babe. I think you were just really tired. But we got to get up and going to get things ready for the rehearsal dinner. And you know your girl Zelma is meeting you at 1:00 p.m. to go over everything for the wedding tomorrow."

(Crystal flips around in the bed to face Rick) "Thanks, baby. Here is some juicy morning breath. Muah! There you go, for better or for worse."

"Baby, you know I will take your breath any time of day, morning, noon or night!"

"Oh you will? Well you better hope you don't turn into a frog later."

"He, he, he. That's a good one, babe. That is too funny."

"Well, if that is what it takes to spend the rest of my life with you, then pucker up!"

"Ha, ha, ha! Ok, babe, let me get up and brush my teeth and I will be right down."

"All right, baby, hurry up. I don't want the food to get too cold."

"Ok sweety, I'm moving." (Rick heads back downstairs)

(That is such a wonderful man. Got up and cooked breakfast for his lady. I am really lucky).

(Crystal brushes her teeth and washes her face quickly and goes downstairs for breakfast).

"Hey, babe. Have a seat." (Crystal sits down at the breakfast table).

"What would you like to drink?"

"Oh, baby, I can get it."

"You will do no such thing!"

"What will you like to drink? It's my time to wait on my wife. Uh...wife-to-be."

"Oh you said it right."

"He, he, he."

"Awee...that is so sweet. My husband. Thank you, baby. Give me some of the Ruby Red grapefruit juice."

"Excellent choice. Coming right up. I got your food in the warmer." (Rick serves Crystal her food and drink. They both begin eating).

"Damn baby, you put your foot up on these pancakes! They are absolutely perfect. They are even better than the Pancake House restaurant."

"Thanks, honey, just making sure you have your energy to get things done today."

"He, he, he. Uh huh...you might have done the opposite baby. I might take my ass too sleep after eating this slamming breakfast."

"He, he, he. Oh no, Zelma is not going to kill me. You are going even if I have to take you myself."

"What! I thought you were letting me do whatever I want."

"Yes, I am, but not on that one. Nope, nope, nope!"

"Ha, ha, ha!" (They both finish eating breakfast).

"Excuse me, baby, I'm going to get myself together so I can meet Zelma."

"No problem, baby. I will get the kitchen cleaned up and get ready myself. I'm meeting with Jamal and the rest of the groomsmen at the tuxedo shop. See you at rehearsal. Not too long baby. And it's forever!"

"Oh wow, I can't believe that is finally going to happen. Yes, it's here, baby. After rehearsal then it's at the altar."

"Oh, that's right, you and the fellas are staying at Regency for tonight."

"Yep, you know that's where they're having the bachelor party."

"Oh yeah, the bachelor party hmmm!"

"No, no, baby, it's not like you think. I know they will be setting up the scrabble game and the dominoes table. That's about it."

"Yeah right!"

"Ha, ha, ha!"

"Well, I think that is how it's going to go."

"Please! How many strippers are you having?"

"Oh no! I am appalled my woman thinks I need to look at strippers. Oh dear. Why would I want to look at a phat, juicy round ass shaking in my face? Who would want that!"

"Ha, ha, ha!"

"Ok, honey, I'm going to get ready so I won't be late meeting Zelma. See you later, sweety."

(Crystal goes to take a shower while Rick goes to the sink to wash the dishes and clean up the kitchen).

(That's what I like about Rick. We make each other laugh and we have great conversation.) "Ahhh, this water feels good!" (Thanks for breakfast baby. Now, I remember why I want to marry you). (Crystal finishes her shower and gets dressed to go meet Zelma. Rick heads off to the meet Jamal).

(Rick and Jamal arrive at the church the afternoon of the wedding) "Dude! It's 1:00 p.m.! It's about time you and Jamal get here! We were about to get worried."

"It's no sweat playa, no sweat. There is no way I am going to miss this day. The most important day of my life! Are you kidding me?"

"Yeah, I know that man, but you are cutting it close. Zelma wants us to take some of the wedding party pictures at 1:30 p.m. The wedding is at 3:00 p.m.!"

"Ok, Henry, really it's cool. Thanks for looking out though. I really appreciate it."

"No problem, dude. So the big question is, are you ready to do this man?"

"Am I ready? I am so ready, man, you wouldn't believe it! First off, I am marrying the woman of my dreams! I can't tell you how much I love her and I am looking so forward to spending the rest of my life with her."

"Wow, man, you definitely got to turn in your playa card."

"Ha, ha, ha!"

"Oh, I am more than willing."

"Shit, I wish I had a woman that I wanted to marry that bad!"

(In unison) "Yeah right, niggah!"

"You ain't never getting married, Sedrick. Never!"

"Ha, ha, ha!"

"But...but..."

"Please!"

"He, he, he."

"I guess you guys are right, but I want to."

"So then, what else is pushing you to get married?"

"Well, this one is kind of personal, but since you'll are my boys I am going to share it with you. Crystal and I wanted something to start off our marriage with that we feel will make it stronger and last forever."

"Hmmm... Ok, go on!"

"Well, we decided to make a pact a few months back to not have sex until we got married!"

"What the fuck! Few months! Negro please! I can't go a week let along a few days."

"Wait, wait! It's worth it if you believe you are with the right person and the sacrifice, and yes it has been a sacrifice. But we know that it will make our commitment to each other stronger for the long haul."

"Ok, dude. That sounds great, but I don't think I can do that. That is just too long for me!"

"Well, it's not for everyone, but it has meant so much to me. Just think about it, it will be like our first time when we get on the honeymoon!"

"True, true...true that."

"And most of all, it will be like my first time. Ummm... Unh! I can't wait!"

"All right dawg...down boy...down!"

"Ha, ha, ha!"

(Zelma walks in) "Okay guys, let's go and take pictures. Chop! Chop! We don't have much time, let's get these pictures out the way. We have more to do after the wedding. Ok fellas, mount up." (Zelma leads the guys to the courtyard for pictures).

"Ok, you guys are done. Go back inside so I can bring out the bride and the bridal party. Rick, stay in the dining hall until I come get you guys."

"No problem, Zelma."

"Good. You know you aren't supposes to see the bride before the wedding?"

"Yes, I got it Z."

"Thanks, move along."

"Ha, ha, ha!"

"Man, that Zelma be running shit!"

"Yep, she ain't no joke." (The guys go back to the dining hall).

(Zelma finishes the picture with the bride and begins to put the final touches on Crystal). "Ok, Crystal, we have approximately 45 minutes before you walk down that aisle. I'm going to wait about 15 minutes prior to let your hair out and do your make up. Are you ready? Is there anything else you need?" (Crystal is starring off into space). "Crystal?...Crystal?"

"Umm...yes!"

"Are you ok?"

"Yes, I feel...no, I'm not ok! I'm so nervous and confused!" (Damn it! I'm thinking about Ben again) "I just don't know what to do."

"What! You pick a fine time to be confused, girl. I can understand nervous, but confused. What is it!"

(I can't tell her about Ben, she will act a fool up in here. Come on girl, think. Think!) I'm ok now, girl. I reminded myself of how much Rick means to me and how great a husband he is going to be. I really love him. I really am good now." (I'm and so scared and confused.)

"Are you sure?"

"Yes, positive!"

"Bing!" "Bong!"

"Oh, that's my cell phone. Could you hand it to me?"

"Where is it?"

"Over there in my purse."

"Ok, I'll get it."

"Here."

"Thanks."

(Reading message) "Hey Crys, In church. Told you I wld B here! Good luck! - Benzo" (Oh damn, its Ben. I have to talk to Ben before I go through with this. He knows how to get me focused. Let me get her out of here.) "Ha ha. Iris is so funny. She text me telling me that it's not too late. Her and the girls have a getaway car out back.

"Ha, ha, ha! That girl is a fool."

"Yes, she is."

(Crystal replys to Ben's text message) "Thx Ben. Pls come to pastors qtrs. Back of church. Now!"

"Oh, one more thing, Zelma."

"Yeah, girl?"

"Could you go get me a bottle of water from the dining hall?"

"Ok, no problem."

"Oh...and check on Rick while you are there. I hope he's doing ok"

"Will do. I will be right back."

"Ok, thanks. (Zelma leaves for the dining hall and bumps into Ben coming around the corner in the hall way)

"Whoops! Sorry about that."

"That's ok."

"Hey, how you doing?"

"I'm blessed and highly favored."

"That's great. Have a good day."

"You do the same." (Ben continues on to the pastor's quarters.)

"Knock!" "Knock!" (Crystal flings the door open, pulls Ben inside and locks the door.) "Whoa!...whoa!"

(Frantically) "I'm sorry Ben, I... I...am just so nervous and still scared. I need you to get me focused. You got to help me! I just don't know!"

(Ben puts one finger up to Crystals mouth and grabs the middle of her back with his other hand and pulls her close) "Shhh! Shhh!! It's ok, baby, it's ok. I know it exactly what you need. Just relax...just relax."

(In a relaxed voice) "Okay Ben, I trust you...I trust you."

(Ben puts his hands on the side of Crystals face.) "You have been on the edge, baby. Let your daddy take care of you."

"Ok, baby, I know you can. That's why I need you here."

(Ben begins to lightly kiss Crystal) "Mmmm..."

Kiss!

"Oh Ben, ummmm...mmm"

(Ben reaches down to pull Crystal's wedding dress up. He in reaches into her panties and slides a finger into her pussy) "Ummm! Ohhhh...Ummmm!" Kiss! "Mmm... Unnnh!"

(In a dreamy voice) "Oh Benzo...Oh my God! That feels so good."

"You feel that, baby..."

"Oh hell yes...ummm! Unnhh!!! Oh you hitting my spot!! Oh damn!! Ummm! That's what, daddy want. Ummm!"

"Grab my dick, girl. Grab it! Ooooh yeah. I missed that touch, baby."

"Oh, Ben...ummm! Unnh!!! I got to feel you! Unnhhh! Please let me feel it! Ummm!!!"

"Unzip my pants, baby." (Ben takes his fingers out of Crystals pussy) "Take that dick out. Yes! That's it."

"Oh shit! I got to suck on first!"

"Go ahead baby, suck daddy's dick." (Crystal squats down and puts Ben's dick into her mouth).

Slurp!

"Unnh! That's right Crys, suck it baby! Ummm! You know this is always going to be your dick! Suck it! Oh shit, girl!" Slurp! "Slow it down...slow it down. Shit feels too good! Damn baby...whew!" (Breathing hard) "Whew baby! Stand up..."

"Ok, daddy. Turn around. Bend over and put your hands on that desk."

"Oh shit baby, put that dick in this pussy! Fuck me, niggah! Fuck me!"

"Oh you want this dick huh!"

"Yes, daddy, yes daddy!" (Ben flips Crystal's wedding dress over her head and pulls her panties off).

"Oh shit, baby! I can't stand it."

(Crystal forgets that she's about to be married in anticipation of feeling Ben's dick. She urges him to hurry up as she peers at the clock through the lace in her dress). "Hurry, baby!"

"Ok, baby! Just admiring the view!"

"Oh, I gotta feel that dick!" (Ben loosens his belt and pushes his boxers with his pants to the floor. He puts the bottom of his shirt in his mouth and pushes his suit jacket to the side with one hand and places one hand in the center of Crystal's plump ass).

(In a muffled voice). "Unnnh...unnh, baby. That pussy is so phat looking back at me." (Ben takes his fingers and spread Crystal's ass cheeks to open her pussy up and thrusts his dick in). (Stroking rapidly) "Unh! Unh! Unh! Unh! Unh! Unh!"

(Deep slow thrusts) Ummmm!...Ummm!!! You feel that baby! You feel it!"

"Oh shit yeah! Fuck it, baby! Unnhh!!! Oh, niggah! You...unh! Are so right... unnnh! Give me what I need!! Oh yes, baby!" (Very slow and deep thrusts) "Ummmmmmmmm!!!"

"Oh Crystal...this pussy is so damn good! Ummmmmmmmm!!!"

"Oh, Benzo...ummmmmmm! You hitting my spot!! I'm about to cummmmmmmm! Ummmm!!"

"Me too baby...Ummm...ummmmmmmm!!! Oh shit! Take it all, baby! Take it! Take it! Ohhhhhhhhhhhh!!! Ummmmmmmmmm!" (Ben and Crystal cum at the same time).

(Trying to catch her breath) "Oh...Benzo...oh my God!" (Relieved) "Whew, girl..."

"Oh shit, oh shit! Don't move. Ohhhhhhhhhh...unnnnnnnhhh! Damn that was good! After shocks are a bitch! Damn!"

"Do you feel better, baby?"

"Do I? Oh my God! I feel fantastic."

"Hold on...let me pull out slowly. I got my handkerchief. Don't want to get any on the dress."

"Ha, ha, ha!"

"Oh please don't!"

(Ben wipes most of the cum out of Crystal's pussy).

"Ok, as clean as I can get it."

"Wait, Ben. Let me clean you up." (Crystal sucks the rest of the cum out of Ben's dick).

"Oooh! Oooh! Oooh! Unnh! Damn, that shit is sensitive."

"Mmmm...tasty!"

"Girl, you off the chain. Here, let me pull your panties back up."

"Thanks, you're so helpful."

"He, he, he."

Kiss!

"Mmmm..."

"So, baby, you can do this right?"

"Oh yes, baby. Yes. I guess I needed that last shot to get me focused. It's like my mind is really clear now. No one would ever understand this, but I guess they will never find out."

"Yes, they will never find out."

"To the grave baby, to the grave!"

"Well, baby, I'm glad I could help."

"Oh, I bet you are! Ha, ha, ha!" (Straightening her dress and getting herself together). "Ok, ok...you better hurry up and get out of here. Zelma will be back shortly."

"Oh ok, that must be who I bumped into in the hallway."

"Yes, I timed it perfectly." (Crystal gives Ben a quick kiss and rushes him out of the room).

Kiss!

"Go., go now! Before she gets back. Thanks, baby."

"Ok, I'm out." (Crystal pulls herself together and sprays and fans perfume throughout the room. One minute after Ben left, Zelma returns).

"Hey, girl. Here is your water."

"Oh thank you, Zelma."

"Hmmm...what got into you?"

(More than you think) "Awe, nothing. I'm just excited about getting married. I took the time while you were gone to reflect on my life ahead. I am seriously focused now."

"Now that's what I am talking about. Oh, and Rick is doing fine. He is so excited about marrying you. That's all he talked about while I was over there. Girl, you got a good man."

"I know...I know." (Zelma puts the finishing touches on Crystal's hair and make-up)

"It's that time girl. Stand up. Come over here by the mirror." (Zelma stands behind Crystal as they both look in the mirror). "Everything looks right?

"Perfect, Zelma, perfect!"

"All right, here comes the bride."

(Yep, you got that right! Here cums the bride. All dressed with white cum in her pussy) "Ok, girl. I'm ready."

"Ok. Let me make sure the coast is clear." (Zelma looks out in to the hall to make sure Rick is not anywhere around).

(Oh shit! I can feel Ben's cum dripping in to my panties. Thank God I wore some today. Un! That would be a mess. He, he, he. First thing after the wedding...douche, shower, kegel exercises and a little estringent. Pussy will be good as new! Rick is expecting virgin pussy. Ha, ha!) "He, he, he."

"What are you laughing at?"

"Oh nothing. Little inside joke."

"Um hum. Girl, let's go."